CONTENTS

Targeting English Homework
Year 5

ISBN: 978 1 925726 62 6

Published by Pascal Press
PO Box 250
Glebe NSW 2037
www.pascalpress.com.au
contact@pascalpress.com.au

Author: Susan Wilson
Publisher: Lynn Dickinson
Editor: Marie Theodore
Cover Designer: Janice Bowles
Typesetter: Stacey Grainger
Images & Illustrations: Dreamstime (unless otherwise indicated)

Acknowledgements
Thank you to the publishers, authors and illustrators who generously granted permission for their work to be reproduced in this book.

Introduction

Targeting English Homework aims to build and reinforce English skills. This book supports the ACARA V9 Australian Curriculum for Year 5 and helps children to revise and consolidate what has been taught in the classroom. ACARA codes are shown on each unit, and a chart explaining their content descriptions is on pages v and vi. The inside front and back covers show the topics in each unit.

The structure of this book

This book has 32 carefully graded double-page units which are divided into three sections:

- ★ Reading and Comprehension – includes a wide variety of literary and cross-curriculum texts
- ★ Grammar and Punctuation
- ★ Phonic & Word Knowledge.

Each unit also includes a Comprehension Reflections segment for children to rate their comprehension experience. This encourages critical thinking.

Comprehension Reflections

Look at the top of the opposite page. This text is an I__________ text – N__________.

Write one thing you learned or found interesting:

____

Write one question you have or something you want to find more information about:

____

____

Rating

Assessment

Term Reviews follow Units 1–8, 9–16, 17–24 and 25–32 to test work covered during the term and allow parents and carers to monitor their child's progress. Children are encouraged to mark each unit as it is completed and to colour in the traffic lights at the end of each segment. These results are then transferred to the Marking Grid. Parents and carers can see at a glance if their child is excelling or struggling!

- **Green** = Excellent — 2 or fewer questions incorrect
- **Orange** = Passing — 50% or more questions answered correctly
- **Red** = Struggling — fewer than 50% correct and needs help

SCORE /18 0-6 8-14 16-18 *Score 2 points for each correct answer!*

How to Use This Book

The activities in this book are specifically designed to be used at home with minimal resources and support. Helpful explanations of key concepts and skills are provided throughout the book to help understand the tasks. Useful examples of how to do the activities are provided.

Regular practice of key concepts and skills will support the work your child does in school and will enable you to monitor their progress throughout the year. It is recommended that children complete 8 units per school term (one a week) and then the Term Review. Every unit has a Traffic Light scoreboard at the end of each section.

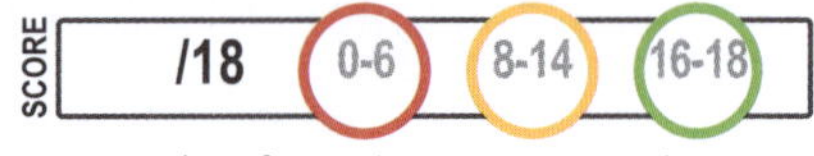

Score 2 points for each correct answer!

You or your child should mark each completed unit and then colour the traffic light that corresponds to the number of correct questions. This process will enable you to see at a glance how your child is progressing and to identify weak spots. The results should be recorded at the end of each term on the Marking Grid on page 1. The Term Review results are important for tracking progress and identifying any improvements in performance. If you find that certain questions are repeatedly causing difficulties and errors, then there is a good reason to discuss this with your child's teacher and arrange for extra instruction in that problem area.

My Reading List

The Reading List on page 146 provides a handy log for your child to record and rate the books they have read each week. It can be photocopied and shared with their teacher or kept as a record. If your child is an avid reader, then photocopy an extra copy before they start to fill it out.

Answers

The answer section on pages 147–162 can be removed, stapled together and kept somewhere safe. Use it to check answers when your child has completed each unit. Encourage your child to colour in the Traffic Light boxes when the answers have been calculated.

TARGETING ENGLISH HOMEWORK YEAR 5 © PASCAL PRESS ISBN 978 1 925726 62 6

Australian Curriculum Correlations Year 5 English		Reading & Comprehension	Grammar & Punctuation	Phonic & Word Knowledge
CODE	CODE DESCRIPTION	UNITS	UNITS	UNITS
LANGUAGE				
AC9E5LA01	Understand that language is selected for social contexts and that it helps to signal social roles and relationships	9	4, 9	
AC9E5LA02	Understand how to move beyond making bare assertions by taking account of differing ideas or opinions and authoritative sources	13	4	
AC9E5LA03	Describe how spoken, written and multimodal texts use language features and are typically organised into characteristic stages and phases, depending on purposes in texts	13, 17, 30	4, 9, 15, 30	
AC9E5LA04	understand how texts can be made cohesive by using the starting point of a sentence or paragraph to give prominence to the message and to guide the reader through the text		3, 28, 29	
AC9E5LA05	Understand that the structure of a complex sentence includes a main clause and at least one dependent clause, and understand how writers can use this structure for effect	8	3, 8, 11, 13, 14, 24, 26, 28, 30	
AC9E5LA06	Understand how noun groups can be expanded in a variety of ways to provide a fuller description of a person, place, thing or idea	3	1, 2, 10, 16, 27, 31, 32	
AC9E5LA08	Understand how vocabulary is used to express greater precision of meaning, including through the use of specialist and technical terms, and explore the history of words		2, 7, 12, 13, 14, 15, 16, 23, 31	3, 29
AC9E5LA09	Use commas to indicate prepositional phrases, and apostrophes where there is multiple possession		5, 17, 21, 25, 26, 27, 28	
LITERATURE				
AC9E5LE02	Present an opinion on a literary text using specific terms about literary devices, text structures and language features, and reflect on the viewpoints of others	1, 30		
AC9E5LE03	Recognise that the point of view in a literary text influences how readers interpret and respond to events and characters	1, 4, 10, 25, 26, 30, 31	10	
AC9E5LE04	examine the effects of imagery, including simile, metaphor and personification, and sound devices in narratives, poetry and songs	1, 3, 17, 20, 22	1, 20, 22	
AC9E5LE05	Create and edit literary texts, experimenting with figurative language, storylines, characters and settings from texts students have experienced	22	22	
LITERACY				
AC9E5LY01	Describe the ways in which a text reflects the time and place in which it was created	31		
AC9E5LY03	Explain characteristic features used in imaginative, informative and persuasive texts to meet the purpose of the text		9, 10, 13	
AC9E5LY04	Navigate and read texts for specific purposes, monitoring meaning using strategies such as skimming, scanning and confirming	All units		
AC9E5LY05	Use comprehension strategies such as visualising, predicting, connecting, summarising, monitoring and questioning to build literal and inferred meaning to evaluate information and ideas	All units		
AC9E5LY06	Plan, create, edit and publish written and multimodal texts whose purposes may be imaginative, informative and persuasive, developing ideas using visual features, text structure appropriate to the topic and purpose, text connectives, expanded noun groups, specialist and technical vocabulary, and punctuation including dialogue punctuation		2, 6, 14, 18, 19, 23, 27, 31	
AC9E5LY08	Use phonic, morphemic and vocabulary knowledge to read and spell words that share common letter patterns but have different pronunciations			1, 7, 25, 26, 27, 28, 29
AC9E5LY09	Build and spell new words from knowledge of known words, base words, prefixes and suffixes, word origins, letter patterns and spelling generalisations			All units
AC9E5LY10	Explore less common plurals, and understand how a suffix changes the meaning or grammatical form of a word			4, 5, 8, 9, 18, 25

Australian Curriculum Correlations Year 5 English		Reading & Comprehension	Grammar & Punctuation	Phonic & Word Knowledge
CODE	CODE DESCRIPTION	UNITS	UNITS	UNITS
CROSS CURRICULAR COMPREHENSION TEXTS				
SCIENCE				
AC9S5U01	Examine how particular structural features and behaviours of living things enable their survival in specific habitats	17, 18, 19		
AC9S5U02	Describe how weathering, erosion, transportation and deposition cause slow or rapid change to Earth's surface	29		
AC9S5U03	Identify sources of light, recognise that light travels in a straight path and describe how shadows are formed, and light can be reflected and refracted	2, 5		
AC9S5U04	Explain observable properties of solids, liquids and gases by modelling the motion and arrangement of particles	12, 14		
HISTORY				
AC9HS5K01	The economic, political and social causes of the establishment of British colonies in Australia after 1800	23, 24		
AC9HS5K02	The impact of the development of British colonies in Australia on the lives of First Nations Australians, the colonists and convicts, and on the natural environment	25, 26		
AC9HS5K03	The role of a significant individual or group, including First Nations Australians and those who migrated to Australia, in the development of events in an Australian colony	25, 27		
GEOGRAPHY				
AC9HS5K04	The influence of people, including First Nations Australians and people in other countries, on the characteristics of a place	20, 21, 28		
AC9HS5K05	The management of Australian environments, including managing severe weather events such as bushfires, floods, droughts or cyclones, and their consequences	21		
CIVICS & CITIZENSHIP				
AC9HS5K06	The key values and features of Australia's democracy, including elections, and the roles and responsibilities of elected representatives	4, 7		
AC9HS5K07	How citizens (members of communities) with shared beliefs and values work together to achieve a civic goal	7		
ECONOMICS & BUSINESS				
AC9HS5K08	Types of resources, including natural, human and capital, and how they satisfy needs and wants	9, 11, 15		
HEALTH & PHYSICAL EDUCATION				
AC9HP6P01	Explain how identities can be influenced by people and places, and how we can create positive self-identities	32		
AC9HP6P03	Investigate how the portrayal of societal roles and responsibilities can be influenced by gender stereotypes	31		
AC9HP6P10	Analyse how behaviours influence the health, safety, relationships and wellbeing of individuals and communities	10		

TARGETING ENGLISH HOMEWORK YEAR 5 © PASCAL PRESS ISBN 978 1 925726 62 6

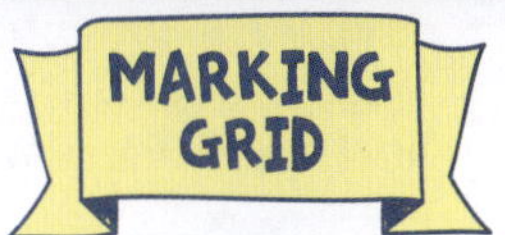

UNIT	Reading & Comprehension	Grammar & Punctuation	Phonic & Word Knowledge
1			
2			
3			
4			
5			
6			
7			
8			
TERM 1 REVIEW			
9			
10			
11			
12			
13			
14			
15			
16			
TERM 2 REVIEW			
17			
18			
19			
20			
21			
22			
23			
24			
TERM 3 REVIEW			
25			
26			
27			
28			
29			
30			
31			
32			
TERM 4 REVIEW			

Green = **Excellent** — 2 or fewer questions incorrect
Orange = **Passing** — 50% or more questions answered correctly
Red = **Struggling** — fewer than 50% correct and needs help

Transfer your results from each unit to the grid above. Colour the traffic lights red, orange or green.

  ISBN 978 1 925726 62 6

AC9E5LY04, AC9E5LY05, AC9E5LE02, AC9E5LE03, AC9E5LE04

Imaginative text – Narrative

Dracula

On that night, I could not believe my eyes. It had been exactly seven years since I had last seen him. Seven years ago, I moved to a seaside town in England called Whitby, where I had hoped to escape his evil presence and start a new and happier life. Little did I know that my past would catch up with me.

He swept silently into the cafe, as quiet as death. A chilled silence fell onto those who observed him, for there was something foreboding about his presence that created an unease and fear among the onlookers. Some gasped in surprise while others physically leaned away from him, causing their bodies to look as if they were caught in a giant gust of wind.

He was a tall, old man clad completely in black from head to toe without a speck of colour anywhere. His strong face was long and thin with a prominent, aquiline nose which had the appearance of being curved or slightly bent. Long, pointed ears framed his powerful face and created the feeling that he was not entirely human, a feeling that sat in the minds of those who observed him.

His eyes were the cold, inhuman eyes of a predator, always watching, seeking his next victim. They scanned the room like search lights, lingering momentarily on each person sitting in the café, holding them captive, unable to move. I inched further to the corner of the café. His cruel mouth was framed by unusually ruddy lips for a man of his age, dark red and plump and firm. However, it was the strange white teeth that protruded over the lips that unnerved me.

When I looked up again, he was looking straight at me. My heart jumped into my throat and choked me with its pounding. The man did not move. Not one muscle of his face moved. Only his eyes bore into me. I didn't move either; I didn't even breathe.

TARGETING ENGLISH HOMEWORK YEAR 5 © PASCAL PRESS ISBN 978 1 925726 62 6

Reading & Comprehension

TERM 1

Write the answer or shade the bubble next to the correct answer.

The answers to these questions are in the text.

1. What town was the narrator living in at the time?

___

2. Why did the onlookers look like they were caught in a **giant gust of wind**?

___

3. What feature of the man's face created the feeling that he was not entirely human?

___

4. What shape was the man's nose if it was **aquiline**?

___

Think about these questions and search for the answers in the text.

5. How did **people react** to the visitor who walked in? Name two reactions or things that they did.
Example: There was a chilled silence.

___

___

6. How did the **narrator react** to the visitor who walked in? Name two reactions or things that they did.
Example: could not believe his eyes

___

___

7. Only the title tells you the visitor is Dracula, a fantasy character that is an evil vampire. Name **two clues** in the text that help you to infer he is Dracula.
Example: clad in black, not a speck of colour

___

___

8. A simile is an interesting way of describing something by comparing it to something else, using 'like' or 'as'. Write one **simile** from the text.
Example: He swept silently into the cafe as quiet as death.

___

___

Use inferencing skills to answer these questions. The answers are not in the text. Think about what you know and what the author says.

9. Find **foreboding** in the second paragraph. The sentences around it give you an idea of its meaning. Which word has a similar meaning?

○ threatening ○ funny ○ unhappy

10. Why did the narrator **inch further** into the corner of the café?

___

___

Use your experience and opinions to answer this question. The answer is not in the text.

11. When have you felt fear that would make your heart pound in your chest? Write two sentences to describe the situation.

___

___

___

Comprehension Reflections

Look at the top of the opposite page. This text is an I__________ text – N__________.

Write one thing you learned or found interesting:

___

Write one question you have or something you want to find more information about:

___

___

Rating 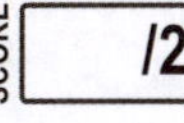  

Score 2 points for each correct answer!

SCORE /22 

Grammar & Punctuation

AC9E5LA06, AC9E5LE04

TERM 1

Description – Noun groups

Description is important in writing. Noun groups provide a fuller description of the nouns. Remember, nouns are words that name a person, place or thing. The words can be added before or after the noun.

Examples from Dracula:

Words coming before the noun	Noun	Words coming after the noun
His strong	face	long and thin
unusually ruddy	lips	dark red and plump and firm

Add your own words before and/or after the noun to describe Dracula.

Words coming before the noun	Noun	Words coming after the noun
①	hands	
②	skin	
③	teeth	
④	breath	

Underline the words that describe the bold nouns.

⑤ A chilled **silence** fell onto those who observed him.

⑥ He had a prominent, aquiline **nose.**

⑦ I wanted a new and happier **life.**

⑧ He had long, pointed **ears** that framed his face.

Description – Similes

A simile is a way of describing something by comparing it to something else using 'like' or 'as'. You compare two different things to create the meaning you want.

Example: As quiet as an elephant or as quiet as a mouse? If you want to be quiet, you choose the mouse. If you want to be noisy, you choose the elephant.

Complete the sentences with comparisons using 'like'.

You are describing ...	Simile (Be creative!)
⑨ a really good swimmer	She swam like
⑩ a struggling swimmer	She swam like
⑪ a terrible singer	He sang like
⑫ a dazzling smile	His teeth were like
⑬ rain clouds	The clouds were like

Score 2 points for each correct answer! SCORE /26   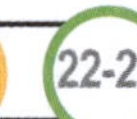

TARGETING ENGLISH HOMEWORK YEAR 5 © PASCAL PRESS ISBN 978 1 925726 62 6

Phonic & Word Knowledge

AC9E5LY09, AC9E5LY08

Morphology – Latin base 'capt'

'Capt' is a Latin base word meaning taken or seized.

Example: In the story, *Dracula*, the people in the café are held **capt**ive by his eyes.

Build words using the base word capt.

Example: capt	+	-ive	→	captive
① capt	+		→	
② capt	+		→	

Morphology – Greek base 'path'

'Path' is a Greek base word meaning emotion or feeling and it can also mean disease.

Example: Dracula did not show any sym**path**y or feeling to the people in the café. In fact, they were potential victims.

Choose the correct word to complete each sentence. You may need a dictionary to help you.

em**path**y	**path**ology	a**path**etic

③ The student was very ____________ when it came to completing his homework before dinnertime.

④ The doctor showed great ____________ to her patients when they were ill.

⑤ The patient was waiting for the ____________ report about the wound inflicted on her by Dracula.

Spelling generalisations

Do you know the spelling generalisation when adding suffixes to –y words? In *Dracula*, the word happier is used. The base word is happy, and the suffix added to the end of the word is –er. The 'y' is replaced with 'i'.

Example: happ**y** + **er** = happ**ier**

Complete these 'y' words with the suffix, following the generalisation.

⑥ carry + –ed = ____________

⑦ busy + –ness = ____________

⑧ beauty + –full = ____________

⑨ study + –ous = ____________

Complete these words where the letter before the 'y' is a vowel.

⑩ play + –ed = ____________

⑪ buy + –er = ____________

Complete these words that do not follow the generalisation.

⑫ lay + –ed = ____________

⑬ shy + –ness = ____________

⑭ say + –ed = ____________

⑮ mislay + –ed = ____________

Homophones

Homophones are words that sound alike but mean different things.

Example: I had hoped to escape his evil **presence** and start a new and happier life.

My grandparents brought me lots of **presents** from their holiday in Europe.

Circle the correct homophone in these sentences.

⑯ On my birthday, I hope to receive many birthday (presents / presence).

⑰ I became scared when told my (presents / presence) was needed at the principal's office.

⑱ My (presents / presence) in the school play made my family very proud.

Score 2 points for each correct answer!

SCORE /36   

Reading & Comprehension

AC9E5LY04, AC9E5LY05, AC9S5U03

Informative text – Report

The Invisibility Cloak

A tall, muscular stranger walked towards me, covered from neck to toe with clothes and shoes. He wore a wide-brimmed hat and a thick, long-sleeved coat and gloves. His face was hidden entirely by wide, white bandages that covered his scalp, face and ears. Only blue-tinted sunglasses sat where his eyes would be.

Why is this person bandaged so heavily? The stranger happens to be the Invisible Man, a character in a book by H. G. Wells, written nearly 130 years ago. It tells the story of a scientist who discovered he could become invisible using a mixture of special chemicals.

J.K. Rowling in the *Harry Potter* series also wrote about being invisible. In her stories, the characters became invisible with the aid of an invisibility cloak. Being invisible captures our imagination, but is it really possible?

What would you do with an invisibility cloak? Would it be a wonderful toy to play with or is it a dangerous idea? While true invisibility cloaks are still a topic of scientific research and development and have not yet been invented, there have been notable advancements that scientists have made.

Invisibility technology relies on controlling light waves. Normally, when light hits an object, it is either absorbed or reflected, making the object visible. An invisibility cloak would need to bend light from all directions around the object so that it appears invisible from any angle.

To change the direction of light, light waves are either reflected or refracted.

Researchers have started to develop ways to bend and redirect light to make objects seem invisible. You may not be able to make things seem invisible, but you can bend light. It is all about how light waves behave.

What do we know about light?

- Light travels in waves and moves in a straight line.
- When light hits a mirror, it is reflected back in a straight line. When the mirror is put at an angle, the direction of light changes.
- When light travels through other materials, such as water, it is slowed down.
- When light speeds up or slows down, it changes direction. This is called refraction.
- If you've ever put a straw into a glass of clear water, you notice that the water in the glass appears to bend the straw where it enters the water. The water doesn't bend the straw, but it does bend the rays of light reflecting off the straw. This is refraction.
- If light is reflected or refracted, it changes direction.

Invisibility relies on changing the direction of light waves. Scientists are testing materials that would bend light waves around objects so that they seem to be invisible. That means, scientists are using their knowledge of refraction and reflection.

Perhaps, in the future, you will be storing your invisibility cloak for those times you do not want to be seen. But for now, it is still a subject for fantasy stories.

TARGETING ENGLISH HOMEWORK YEAR 5 © PASCAL PRESS ISBN 978 1 925726 62 6

Reading & Comprehension

Write the answer or shade the bubble next to the correct answer.

The answers are in the text.

1. **Scientists have perfected an invisibility cloak.**
   - ◯ True
   - ◯ False

2. **What happens to light when it hits a mirror?**

   It is ____________________ back.

3. **What makes an object visible?**

   Light is either ________________ or ________________, making the object visible.

4. **What are two ways to change the direction of light? (Shade only one bubble.)**
   - ◯ rest and relaxation
   - ◯ retention and rendering
   - ◯ refraction and reflection

5. **Water can bend a pencil or straw.**
   - ◯ True
   - ◯ False

Think about these questions and search for the answers in the text.

6. **What does invisibility technology rely on? (Shade two bubbles.)**
   - ◯ controlling light waves
   - ◯ changing the direction of light waves
   - ◯ putting objects in water
   - ◯ using pencils

7. **Refraction is the bending of light waves. How can you bend light waves?**
   - ◯ speeding up or slowing down light waves
   - ◯ putting waves of light through water
   - ◯ both of the above

Use inferencing skills to answer these questions. The answers to these questions are not in the text. Think about what you know and what the author says.

8. **If refraction is the bending of light waves, what does refract mean?**
   - ◯ fraction
   - ◯ a small part
   - ◯ change course

9. **Why would the Invisible Man need to wear glasses over his bandages even if he had good eyesight? Write one reason.**

   ____

   ____

   ____

   ____

Use your experience and opinions to answer this question. The answer is not in the text.

10. **Why might invisibility be a bad idea? Write two reasons.**

    ____

    ____

    ____

    ____

Comprehension Reflections

Look at the top of the opposite page. This text is an I__________ text – R__________.

Write one thing you learned or found interesting:

____

Write one question you have or something you want to find more information about:

____

____

Rating   

Score 2 points for each correct answer!

SCORE | /20 | 0-8 | 10-14 | 16-20

Grammar & Punctuation

AC9E5LA06, AC9E5LA08, AC9E5LY06

Verb tenses

Verbs are action words that can tell us what a person is doing or can describe the way a person is feeling. When you are writing, you use verbs to show if the events have already happened, are happening now or will happen in the future. These are called verb tenses.

H.G. Wells, the author of *The Invisible Man*, wrote stories that dealt with the past, the present time of his day and what he thought the future may look like.

Simple tenses

Circle what tense for each sentence. The verbs are in bold to help you decide.

1. The invisible man **wears** glasses over his eyes.
   past / present / future
2. The invisible man **wore** glasses over his eyes.
   past / present / future
3. The invisible man **will wear** glasses over his eyes.
   past / present / future

Perfect tenses with have, has, had

Circle what tense you think each sentence portrays. The verbs are in bold to help you decide.

4. Scientists **had worked** on perfecting an invisibility cloak for many years.
   past / present / future
5. Recently, scientists **have worked** on the invisibility cloak.
   past / present / future
6. By the time I am an adult, scientists **will have worked** on perfecting the invisibility cloak.
   past / present / future

Progressive tenses with was, am, will

Circle what tense you think each sentence portrays. The verbs are in bold to help you decide.

7. I **will be covered** in bandages when I become invisible.
   past / present / future
8. Yesterday, I **was covered** in bandages due to an accident.
   past / present / future
9. Most days I **am covered** in bandages because I am very clumsy.
   past / present / future

Irregular verbs

Many verbs just add –ed or –d to show past tense. These are called regular verbs.

Examples: pack pack**ed** arrive arriv**ed**

Irregular verbs do not follow that pattern. They do not end in –ed or –d.

Examples: come **came** think **thought**

Complete the table with the past tense of verbs.

	Present tense verb	Past tense verb	Regular or irregular?
	make	made	irregular, change spelling
	walk	walked	regular, add –ed
10	try		regular
11	invent		regular
12	give		irregular
13	keep		irregular
14	know		irregular
15	leave		irregular
16	have		irregular
17	see		irregular
18	do		irregular

Score 2 points for each correct answer! SCORE /36   

TARGETING ENGLISH HOMEWORK YEAR 5 © PASCAL PRESS ISBN 978 1 925726 62 6

Phonic & Word Knowledge

AC9E5LY09

Spelling generalisations

The text demonstrates the many different spelling generalisations that determine how words are spelt. When adding a suffix to the end of a word or prefix to the beginning of a word, you change its meaning. You also have to think how to spell these new words.

	Generalisations (Vowels are a, e, i, o, u. The other letters are consonants.)
a	Words ending in 'e', drop the 'e' if the suffix starts with a vowel. *Example:* care + ing = car**ing**
b	Words ending in 'e', keep the 'e' if the suffix begins with a consonant. *Example:* close + ly = clos**ely**
c	Change a final 'y' to 'i' before adding a suffix. *Example:* silly + er = sill**ier**
d	Words ending in a vowel and 'y', add the suffix –ed or –ing without making any other change. *Example:* del**ay** + ed = delay**ed** del**ay** + ing = delay**ing**
e	Drop one 'l' in full when adding as a suffix to a word. *Example:* care + full = carefu**l**

Words ending in 'tion'

In the text, there are several words that end in –tion which have a 'shun' sound.

If a root word ends in 't', then add –ion on the end. *Example:* reflect + ion = reflec**tion**

If a root word ends in 'te', then remove the 'e' and add –ion on the end.

Example: hesita**te** + ion = hesita**tion**

Complete the missing –tion words.

13. invent + ion = ______________________
14. direct + ion = ______________________
15. refract + ion = ______________________
16. complete + ion = ______________________

Use the four words above to complete these sentences.

17. An invisibility cloak would be a great ______________ for a toy company.
18. I know scientists are working on it, but it is nowhere near ______________.
19. Reflection and ______________ change the ______________ of light waves.

Complete the missing parts of the table, marked with an *. Look in the text for the words. Then match the word to the spelling generalisation (a to e in the table above).

	Base word		Suffix		New word	Which generalisation? a, b, c, d or e?
	Example: wonder	+	–full	=	wonderful	e
1	*	+	–ing	=	making	*
2	entire	+	*	=	entirely	*
3	advance	+	–ment	=	*	*
4	*	+	*	=	development	No generalisation needed
5	note	+	–able	=	*	*
6	change	+	–ing	=	*	*
7	rely	+	–s	=	*	*
8	imagine	+	–ation	=	*	*
9	*	+	*	=	heavily	*
10	*	+	*	=	using	*
11	play	+	–ing	=	*	*
12	*	+	*	=	stories	*

Score 2 points for each correct answer! SCORE /38    

Informative text – Explanation

Fantasy

Fantasy is a type of fiction. Fantasy stories are not true and could never be true, but they open the door to your imagination with different worlds and characters. Fantasy stories have beings, places and events that could never occur in real life. The characters, such as witches or elves, can have magical powers, or characters can have abilities, such as talking animals or talking toys.

The plot or storyline of a fantasy often features an imaginary world where the characters make difficult decisions. The plot can contain magic or a hero's journey or quest and a battle between good and evil.

To create fantasy, authors use a lot of description to help the reader picture the scene in their head. For example, what do you see in your mind when you read this?

The warrior was immensely tall and tanned. His jet-black hair hung below the polished helmet that hugged his skull. He stood at the door with his long, blue cloak reaching down to the straw on the floor. Those in the room saw that his strong arms were circled with ring after ring of gold. They saw deep tattoo marks across his forehead and cheeks. This is a good man, thought those who did not know him. Those who did, thought evil had entered the room.

The author extends the noun groups with adjectives, which are words to describe a person, place or thing, so that you, as the reader, can form a picture in your head.

In fantasy, authors also extend verb groups, which describe an action or what has occurred. Verbs are doing words. For example, instead of, 'she walked away', how did she walk? 'She walked quickly' or 'she marched' or 'she sprinted'. 'Marched' and 'sprinted' tell us that she's likely to be in a hurry. If we continue with the description of the warrior and describe what is happening using verb groups, does it help you picture the scene in your head?

He strode confidently into the centre of the room and stood with folded arms. He looked around the room and, as he did so, his hair brushed the back of his cloak. He smiled a soft, dangerous smile, showing his white teeth.

The author describes how the warrior entered the room with one word – strode – a powerful way to describe a powerful man. 'He stood with folded arms' is more powerful than saying 'he stood inside the room'.

The setting in a fantasy genre can be an imaginative place, an outdoor setting like the woods or somewhere more familiar like a school. A fantasy story may take place in other worlds or at different times through history or even in the future.

Fantasy is where our imagination can run wild. Have fun reading and creating your own!

TARGETING ENGLISH HOMEWORK YEAR 5 © PASCAL PRESS ISBN 978 1 925726 62 6

Reading & Comprehension

Write the answer or shade the bubble next to the correct answer.

The answers to these questions are in the text.

1. **Fantasy stories are not true.**
   - ◯ True
   - ◯ False

2. **Another name for a storyline is**

   ______________________________________.

Think about these questions and search for the answers in the text.

Circle the words that make the noun group that provides a greater description of the bold nouns. A noun group is a group of words that comes before or after the noun.

Example: The **warrior** was (immensely tall and tanned.)

3. His jet-black **hair** hung below the polished **helmet**.
4. He stood at the door in his long, blue **cloak**.
5. He smiled a soft, dangerous **smile**.

Circle the words that help provide more information to the bold verbs.

6. He **strode** confidently. (Strode how?)
7. He **looked** around the room. (Looked where?)
8. His long, blue cloak **reached** down to the straw on the floor. (Reached where?)

Use inferencing skills to answer these questions. The answers are not in the text. Think about what you know and what the author says.

9. **Find strode in the second paragraph. The sentences around it give you an idea of its meaning. Which word has a similar meaning?**
   - ◯ crawled
   - ◯ marched
   - ◯ wandered

Choose the best words to suit the warrior's character. The bold verbs are coupled with adverbs that describe how the action occurred.

10. ◯ **bowed** respectfully
    ◯ **skipped** joyfully
    ◯ **whispered** nervously
    ◯ **stared** silently

11. ◯ **hopped** merrily
    ◯ **laughed** menacingly
    ◯ **sang** sweetly
    ◯ **spoke** excitedly

12. **When could this story have taken place: in the past, now or the future? Name two clues that are in the text.**

The time the story could be set in ...	Clues in the description ...

Comprehension Reflections

Look at the top of the opposite page. This text is an I__________ text – E__________.

Write one thing you learned or found interesting:

____

Write one question you have or something you want to find more information about:

____

____

Rating   

Score 2 points for each correct answer!

SCORE /24   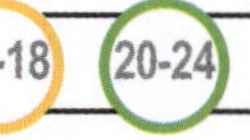

Grammar & Punctuation

AC9E5LA04, AC9E5LA05

TERM 1

Sentence beginnings – Jigsaw

It can be boring reading sentences that all begin the same way. Instead of always starting with 'the', you can jigsaw the sentence and start with a different part of the sentence.

Example: The warrior stood outside the school while waiting for the parents to leave.

While waiting for the parents to leave, the warrior stood outside the school.

Jigsaw the sentence by writing the underlined group of words at the beginning of each sentence.

1. The powerful warrior appeared as the students sat quietly in the classroom.
   ____
   ______________________________,
   the powerful warrior appeared.
2. The warrior strode around the room while his blue cloak trailed the floor.
   ______________________________,
   the warrior strode around the room.
3. The warrior's inhuman eyes continued scanning the room until the doomed student stood up.
   ______________________________,
   the warrior's inhuman eyes continued scanning the room.

Rewrite the sentences by starting with the second part of the sentence.

4. The student gave a little gasp as a deep-throated laugh escaped from the warrior.
   As ______________________________
   ______________________________,
   the ______________________________
   ______________________________.
5. The strong arms remained folded while the gold rings glinted in the fluorescent light.
   While ______________________________
   ______________________________,
   the ______________________________
   ______________________________.
6. The student continued to shake in fear until the teacher intervened.
   Until ______________________________
   ______________________________,
   the ______________________________
   ______________________________.

Sentence beginnings – 'ing' verbs

Another way to start a sentence is with an 'ing' verb. Put the verb at the beginning of the sentence and add the suffix –ing.

Example: The student **burst** into tears and rushed out of the room.

Bursting into tears, the student rushed out of the room.

Start the sentences with the verb in bold. Add the suffix –ing onto the end of the verb.

7. The teacher **picked** up her umbrella and approached the warrior.
   P____________________ umbrella, the teacher approached the warrior.
8. The warrior **lent** towards the teacher smiling a soft, dangerous smile.
   L____________________ teacher, the warrior smiled a soft, dangerous smile.
9. The teacher **lifted** the umbrella and struck the warrior across his folded arms.
   L____________________
   umbrella, the teacher struck the warrior across his folded arms.
10. The teacher **saw** anger in the warrior's face and called for backup.
    S____________________
    face, the teacher____________________.
11. The warrior **picked** up the student and stomped towards the door.
    P____________________ student, the warrior____________________.
12. The teacher **blocked** the warrior's path of escape and demanded the return of the student.
    B____________________ escape, the teacher____________________.

Score 2 points for each correct answer!

SCORE /24    

0-10 12-18 20-24

TARGETING ENGLISH HOMEWORK YEAR 5 © PASCAL PRESS ISBN 978 1 925726 62 6

AC9E5LY09, AC9E5LA08

Descriptive words

Writers of fantasy stories need to form pictures in the reader's head using only descriptive words. The people in fantasy stories can be villains or heroes, determined by the words used to describe their appearance and character.

The words below describe heroes and villains. Circle the odd one out.

Example: hulking massive (slender) bulky

① neat	dishevelled	untidy	rumpled
② deformed	straight	twisted	hunched
③ sinister	repulsive	fascinating	forbidding
④ ungainly	clumsy	awkward	graceful
⑤ agitated	ruffled	perturbed	composed

Synonyms

Synonyms are words which mean the same as another word. If you write that someone looks 'scared' in your story, you could choose a stronger word with a similar meaning.

Examples: Synonyms of scared: frightened, alarmed, startled, unnerved, horrified, appalled.
The student looked **alarmed**.

Instead of overusing simple words such as 'big', you can use better words.

Example: Synonyms of big: sizable, prodigious, large.
She had a **sizable** nose.

⑥ – ㉚ **Increasing your knowledge of synonyms will help you choose better words to create effects in your writing. The words in the list are synonyms of amazed, sneak, powerful and dangerous. Write all the synonyms in the appropriate box.**

aghast	vigorous	slink	robust
risky	skulk	astonished	steal
flabbergasted	threatening	bewildered	
perilous	lurk	awed	thunderstruck
formidable	treacherous	brawny	
prowl	forceful	creep	dynamic
precarious	potent	hazardous	

Amazed	Sneak

Powerful	Dangerous

Score 2 points for each correct answer! SCORE /60  0-26  28-54 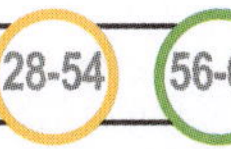 56-60

Reading & Comprehension

AC9E5LY04, AC9E5LY05, AC9E5LE03, AC9HS5K06

Persuasive text – Argument

To my Elected Member of Parliament

Dear Ms Wilson,

I am writing to you on behalf of all Year Five students across Australia. At school, we have been learning about our system of democracy in Australia, and I wish to exercise or use one of the important values in our system of government, that is, freedom of speech.

I wish to express my idea that I could be elected to Parliament to represent all the primary-aged children who would like some say in our education system, especially around homework policies. I'm sure every school student has an opinion around homework. Before you laugh off my suggestion, I will tell you how smart Year Five students are and how much we know about our system of government.

We know that Australia is a democracy. The word comes from ancient Greek words meaning people's rule. A democratic country has a system of government where the people have the power to be part of the decision-making process. However, a non-democratic country has a system of government where people have little or no power.

Australia is a representative democracy, which means that we don't all attend Parliament but vote for the people we want to represent us. This is what happens at elections. That's like the Year Five students voting for me to speak on their behalf. There is one sticking point, however. It seems that voting is only for Australian citizens over the age of 18.

I'm sure we can change that rule and allow Year Five students to stand for election and to vote. After all, Australia was one of the first places in the world to allow women to vote. In 1902, women in Australia over the age of 21 could vote in national elections and stand for election in the Australian Parliament. Unfortunately, First Nations men and women only gained the right to vote in national elections in 1962.

Year Five students know that Australian democracy depends on everyone following the behaviours or values that we expect. These include freedom, which also means freedom of speech or expressing your ideas freely, as I am doing here. Other values or behaviours include obeying the laws and treating people fairly, equally and with respect.

Therefore Ms Wilson, let's be one of the first countries in the world to let Year Five students stand for election to Parliament and vote. I would love to pass many rules about homework and perhaps about extending the summer holidays. I look forward to hearing your reply.

Sincerely yours,

P. Wilson (Thanks Mum)

TARGETING ENGLISH HOMEWORK YEAR 5 © PASCAL PRESS ISBN 978 1 925726 62 6

Reading & Comprehension

Write your answers on the lines provided.

The answers to these questions are in the text.

① What does **democracy** mean?

② What language does it come from?

③ Australia was one of the first places in the world to allow women to vote. When did this occur?

④ Unfortunately, First Nations men and women only gained the right to vote in national elections in ________.

⑤ What is a **representative democracy**?

Think about these questions and search for the answers in the text.

⑥ Australian democracy depends on everyone following the behaviours or values that we expect. Name five of these values.

⑦ What is the difference between a **democratic** and **non-democratic** system of government?

⑧ P. Wilson wants to stand for election to Parliament. What is stopping her?

⑨ What rules would P. Wilson like to take to Parliament to discuss?

Use inferencing skills to answer these questions. The answers are not in the text. Think about what you know and what the author says.

⑩ Why would the author of the letter put **(Thanks Mum)** at the end?

⑪ P. Wilson talks about freedom of speech and says she is practising it in the letter. What does **freedom of speech** mean?

Use your experience and opinions to answer this question. The answer is not in the text.

⑫ If you were elected to Parliament and had the power to change the homework policy in your school, what would you realistically change it to? Explain why you want this change. Remember, you have the responsibility of doing the 'right thing' for your citizens, the Year Five students.

Comprehension Reflections

Look at the top of the opposite page. This text is a P__________ text – A__________.

Write one thing you learned or found interesting:

Write one question you have or something you want to find more information about:

Rating   

Score 2 points for each correct answer!

SCORE /24   

AC9E5LA01, AC9E5LA02, AC9E5LA03

Modality

The letter is a persuasive text, trying to persuade Ms Wilson to allow a Year Five child to be elected to Parliament. To write a persuasive text such as an argument, you need to use persuasive devices. One device is modality.

Modality refers to the language used to express how definite we are about something. Low modality language is uncertain, while high modality is strong and to the point. It all depends on what verbs you choose. These verbs are called modal verbs.

Strong modality – certain
will / won't
must / must not
have to / can't
should / shouldn't
may / may not
could / might / might not
Weak modality – uncertain

Underline the **modal verbs** in the following sentences.

1. I wish to express my idea that I could be elected to Parliament.
2. All primary-aged children should have a say about how much homework they get.
3. Year Five students must share their opinions with their school.
4. Parents might not agree with extending summer holidays.

Write these sentences with a **stronger modal verb**. Choose a verb from the box, but do not use the same verb twice.

5. I **may** clean up my room.

____

____

6. I **might** do my homework.

____

____

7. I **could** help with the dishes.

____

____

8. I **may not** go to sleep.

____

____

9. I **might not** eat all my vegetables.

____

____

Choosing the right modality depends on who you are talking or writing to. Circle the best modal verb for each circumstance.

10. The principal to you: You have stuck stickers all over my car about how Year Fives are invisible. We (could / must) discuss how you go about campaigning for your idea.
11. The principal to you: You (will / may) not like the consequences if you do not come to my office after school to discuss this matter.
12. You to the principal: I (might / will) come to your office after school to discuss my behaviour.
13. Your friend to you: You (have to / should) come with me after school to play that new game. I only have it for one day. Don't let me down!

14. You to your friend: There is a problem, I (have to / might) see the principal after school.
15. What would you do? I (might / would / could / may / may not) turn up at the principal's office after school.

Score 2 points for each correct answer! SCORE /30 0-12 14-24 26-30

TARGETING ENGLISH HOMEWORK YEAR 5 © PASCAL PRESS ISBN 978 1 925726 62 6

Phonic & Word Knowledge

AC9E5LY09, AC9E5LY10

TERM 1

Democracy – Root word and suffix

The word democracy comes from the Greek word 'demokratia', meaning rule by the people. The root word 'demo' comes from the Greek word 'demos' meaning people, so words with the root 'demo' refer to people or to population.
In English, democracy has the suffix 'cracy' which means rule.

The words below contain the suffix 'cracy'. Match each word to its meaning. You may need to use a dictionary.

(1) aristocracy	A form of government in which scientists and technical experts are in control
(2) democracy	A political system governed by wealthy people
(3) plutocracy	A group of people who have titles, such as Lord and Lady
(4) technocracy	Government of the people, by the people

The words below contain the root word 'demo'. Match each word to its meaning. You may need to use a dictionary.

(5) democrat	Someone against the idea of democracy
(6) demography	The fear of crowds or masses of people
(7) demophobia	One who supports rule by the people
(8) antidemocratic	The study of populations, births, deaths, etc

The paragraph below is missing eight words. Use the 'demo' and 'cracy' words in the previous questions to fill the gaps.

Parliament was in session and P. Wilson, the Year Five representative, stood up to speak.

"Ladies and gentlemen and fellow Year Fives, thank goodness we are in a (9) ______________ so that you have a government of the people."

Just at that minute, a scientist, who wanted a government ruled by scientists, called a (10) ______________, stood up to speak. She was determined to be heard. Unfortunately for her, Lady Susan, who is an (11) ______________, pushed her out of the way while twirling her pearl necklace. Lady Susan loved studying numbers and populations. She studied (12) ______________. Unfortunately, Lady Susan was against democracy, so she was (13) ______________. No sooner had she started to speak, when $100 notes floated across the room. They were from the billionaire mining boss, S. Digg, who wanted to form his own government ruled only by wealthy people. This form of government is called a (14) ______________. Thankfully, he had a fear of crowds, called (15) ______________, and had to quickly leave Parliament. P. Wilson once again stood to speak. She was a (16) ______________ because she supported rule by the people, even if she was only in Year Five.

Score 2 points for each correct answer! SCORE /32

Informative text – Explanation

Somewhere Over the Rainbow

A rainbow fills the sky, and someone tells you that there is a pot of gold at the end where it touches the earth. Unfortunately, this is an old folktale so don't start chasing rainbows. Science tells us that rainbows do not have an end since they are full circles reflected from raindrops. Rainbows also seem to move further away from us as we move towards them, making any treasure impossible to find.

Most rainbows form when the sun's rays strike raindrops falling from faraway rain clouds. Water can slow down light waves, so when light enters a raindrop, it slows down and bends. This is refraction.

White light is composed of all the different colours (red, orange, yellow, green, blue, indigo, violet) that the human eye can see. This kind of light is known as visible light because we're able to see it with just our eyes alone. Light travels in waves, and because the different colours have different wavelengths, they bend differently. Therefore, in a rainbow, white light is split into the different colours you see spanning across the sky. The white light scatters into all seven different colours. This scattering is what we call refraction.

Okay, white light is made up of different colours, so how do I see a lemon as yellow? When light hits an object, the object reflects some of that light and absorbs the rest of it. Some objects reflect a certain wavelength of light, and that's why you see a certain colour. For example, a lemon reflects mainly yellow light, and a strawberry reflects mainly red light. Reflection is part of why we see colours in objects.

But what about black and white? Objects that absorb all wavelengths of light appear black, and objects that reflect all wavelengths appear white. That works perfectly with light, but what about mixing paint? You know that when you mix all the colours of paint together, you get a muddy, brown colour. When paints are mixed, more and more wavelengths of light are absorbed and not reflected back to our eyes. Since we don't see as many wavelengths of light reflected, the mixed paint appears darker in colour.

But wait, there is more! There are other colours that our eyes can't see; they are infrared and ultraviolet. Your remote control uses infrared, but you cannot see the stream of light towards your TV screen, and medical and dental treatments use ultraviolet.

Next time you see a rainbow, be sure to tell the adult you are with that it is to do with the bending of light, called refraction – also, that white light is made of many colours mixed together. Oh, and don't bother looking for that pot of gold because you will never find it. Or will you?

TARGETING ENGLISH HOMEWORK YEAR 5 © PASCAL PRESS ISBN 978 1 925726 62 6

Reading & Comprehension

TERM 1

Write the answer or shade the bubble next to the correct answer.

The answers to these questions are in the text.

1. When light enters a raindrop, it slows down and bends. What is this process called?

____

2. Name the colours that make up white light.

____

____

3. Why is this white light called visible light?

____

____

Think about these questions and search for the answers in the text.

4. Reflection of light waves is why we see colours in objects. So how do we see lemons as yellow?

- ◯ White light is reflected from the lemon to you.
- ◯ No light is reflected from the lemon to you.
- ◯ Only the yellow wavelength of light is reflected from the lemon to you.

5. Why do we see an object as black in colour?

- ◯ The light casts a shadow.
- ◯ All wavelengths of light are absorbed and not reflected back to you.
- ◯ All wavelengths of light are reflected back to you.

6. What two colour wavelengths can't we see?

____

____

7. When paints are mixed, why does the paint appear darker?

- ◯ We don't see as many wavelengths of light reflected.
- ◯ The light waves are bent away from our eyes.
- ◯ It is not stirred enough. Once stirred, the colours join to form white paint.

Use inferencing skills to answer this question. The answer is not in the text. Think about what you know and what the author says.

8. You are painting a project for school. You have many colours, but you don't have brown or black paint. You need brown paint, so how could you make it? Explain your thinking.

____

____

Use your experience and opinions to answer this question. The answer is not in the text.

9. If a rainbow is a circle and we only see half, where could the other half be? Write one sentence to explain.

____

____

Comprehension Reflections

Look at the top of the opposite page. This text is an I__________ text – E__________.

Write one thing you learned or found interesting:

____

Write one question you have or something you want to find more information about:

____

____

Rating   

Score 2 points for each correct answer!

SCORE 

Grammar & Punctuation

AC9E5LA09

Apostrophes for omissions – Contractions

A contraction is a word made by shortening and combining two words. Words in the text such as that's (that is) and don't (do not), are contractions. You use contractions in both speaking and in writing. The apostrophe shows where letters have been omitted or left out. **You do not** use apostrophes when you add an 's' to a word to show it is plural or more than one.

Example: Correct: **It's** better to eat peeled **bananas**.

Incorrect: ~~**Its**~~ better to eat peeled ~~**banana's**~~.

Underline the correct sentence in each question.

1. I like to look for rainbows.
   I like to look for rainbow's.
2. The dog chased its tail.
   The dog chased it's tail.
3. Your going to be very happy.
   You're going to be very happy.
4. Don't eat it, that's theirs.
   Don't eat it, that's their's.

Add apostrophes to the following sentences. There are nine.

5 – 13

Its terrible when its raining and you have to stay inside. However, you can always hunt for gold after it rains because theres often a rainbow. If youre lucky, you can find a pot of gold at the end of it. Dont be disappointed if you do not find gold. You cant always find it the first time, but Im sure that if you keep looking, one day youll find gold. Thats a promise!

Apostrophes for possession

An apostrophe can be used to show possession, which means that something is owned.

Example: The **sun's** rays are bent by raindrops. (The rays of light belong to the sun).

You add an apostrophe and an 's' to the end of 'sun' to show possession or ownership. Remember, you do not add an apostrophe if you add an 's' to make something plural, which means more than one.

Circle the correct word in the sentences below.

I went to the cupboard to find some (14) (biscuits, biscuit's), but unfortunately, they were only the (15) (dogs, dog's) biscuits. I was hungry so I ate them anyway. My (16) (bodys, body's) reaction surprised me. I dropped to the floor and started to chew my (17) (brothers, brother's) shoe. My (18) (toes, toe's) grew furrier and I wanted to go for a walk.

Apostrophes and plural nouns

If a noun is plural and ends in 's', you only add an apostrophe at the end to show possession.

Examples: The biscuits belong to several **dogs**. They are the **dogs'** biscuits.

The books belong to the **students**. They are the **students'** books.

Finish these sentences with apostrophes on the plural nouns.

19. The cars belong to the **teachers**. They are the ________________ cars.
20. The room belongs to the Year **Fives**. It is the Year ________________ room.
21. The ball belonged to a group of **boys**. It was the ________________ ball.

22 – 27

Now put all you know about contractions together as we continue the story of the biscuits. There are six apostrophes to add.

We only have one dog, and I ate its biscuits. I suppose I shouldve felt guilty, but I didnt. After eating the biscuits, my toes became hairy, and I chewed my brothers shoe. Then my nose started to grow, and my tongues surface became wet and rough. To my delight, the familys two cats entered the room and started hissing at me. Both cats eyes looked at me with alarm, and I looked at them with a smile. This was going to be fun.

Score 2 points for each correct answer! SCORE /54

AC9E5LY09, AC9E5LY10

Word building – Compound words

A compound word combines two simpler words to form one longer word. This compound word has a whole new meaning from the two words that are used to create it.

Example: rain + bow = rainbow

Match the words to form compound words that are found in the text. Write the compound words in the correct spaces below.

wave	there	rain	some	folk
rain	fore	drops	lore	lengths
	bow	one		

To form a (1) ____________ you need the sun's rays to strike (2) ____________. This causes the light to bend, and we can see different coloured (3) ____________ of light. Some stories in (4) ____________ say you can find gold at the end of a rainbow. (5) ____________ told me this is not true; (6) ____________, it is impossible to find the end of a rainbow or, in fact, any gold.

Root word 'vis'

Root words are the core of a word. You can add prefixes and suffixes to change meaning or form longer words, such as 'visible' from the text.

root word from Latin means 'to see' — suffix means 'to be able'

Example: vis + ible = visible (means 'to be able to be seen')

The root word vis can include different spellings such as 'vise', 'vide' and 'vid'.

Choose the correct suffix from the bottom of the following table to create a word that is defined in the last column.

	Prefix	Root	Suffix	Definition
	Example: in–	vis	–ible	Not able to be **seen**
7	tele–	vis		Device where pictures are **seen** from far away
8		vis		To go to **see** someone
9	pro–	vide		A person who **sees** that you have the things you need
10	re–	vis		To **see** something again
11		vis		Relating to **seeing** or sight
12		vis		A person who is **seeing** someone
13		vid		Moving pictures **seen** on a screen
14	e–	vid		Items thoroughly or fully **seen** in a court case
	Suffix: –ion –it (–ible) –itor –ence –eo –er (one 'e' is dropped) –ion –ual			

Latin prefix 'ultra'

Prefixes are added to the beginning of a root word.

Example: ultra + violet = **ultra**violet

The Latin prefix 'ultra' means beyond or extreme, so ultraviolet is beyond the violet wavelength.

Complete the following sentences with the ultra– words below.

ultrafast	ultrafine
ultramicroscope	ultracold

(15) The scientists were looking at something too small to be seen with ordinary equipment, so they needed an ____________.

(16) Some vaccines or medications must be stored at extremely low or ____________ temperatures.

(17) Strong and ____________ football and netball players push their bodies to the limit.

(18) My grandmother makes pasta out of ____________ sheets of semolina dough.

Score 2 points for each correct answer! SCORE /36  0-16  18-30  32-36 

AC9E5LY04, AC9E5LY05

Imaginative text – Narrative

Who's the Boss?

I remember it as if it were yesterday. One minute I was free to do what I wished, and the next, I was cruelly snatched away and imprisoned behind metal bars. We are more than capable of speaking their language and communicating with them; however, they do not believe we can. If only they knew.

I must be careful not to speak back to them or show understanding, as any sign of intelligence would mean my death. They would haul me away kicking and screaming just to examine my brain. In fact, I purposely fail the tests they give me and try to run in different directions each time. I believe they like to use us in tests because our bodily structure and genetics are like theirs, but we are more intelligent.

They don't realise that we control the results of all the testing. We can all easily find our way through mazes; we just pretend sometimes not to be able to find the cheese at the end. That way, we don't show our intelligence.

We live very close to them in large cities, under their homes, but they don't know we are there. We listen to them and laugh at them. They don't know that we actually control the world. They think they are testing us, but we're just playing with them. We are usually very good at not getting caught, except that time I was caught raiding the dairy cabinet. There's something about cheese I cannot ignore.

I love watching TV with them, especially the shows about animals and vets although we are not often featured on these shows. As a group, we are very fast, nimble and agile. However, as I'm in captivity, I am forced to run in circles all day as a form of exercise in some sort of contraption. It's rather boring, but I admit that it can become addictive.

******

"Okay, Chris, we need to test this mouse again on its ability to run through the maze. Hopefully it can find the cheese this time."

"I'm really surprised at their memory, or lack of. Sometimes they find the cheese easily, and the next time they forget where it is. You don't think they are playing with us, do you?"

"Really, Chris! Mice intelligent enough to trick us? Don't be silly. Next, you'll be telling me they can talk."

TARGETING ENGLISH HOMEWORK YEAR 5 © PASCAL PRESS ISBN 978 1 925726 62 6

Reading & Comprehension

TERM 1

Write the answer or shade the bubble next to the correct answer.

The answers to these questions are in the text.

① How does the narrator **purposely fail** the tests?

____

____

② What is something the narrator **cannot** ignore?

- ◯ cheese
- ◯ TV
- ◯ tests

Think about this question and search for the answer in the text.

③ What type of tests does the narrator have to perform?

- ◯ maths test
- ◯ running through a maze
- ◯ English test

Use inferencing skills to answer these questions. The answers are not in the text. Think about what you know and what the author says.

④ The narrator of the story ends up in a cage. What creature is the narrator?

____

⑤ **We live very close to them in large cities.** What type of creatures are **them**?

◯ cats ◯ humans ◯ mice

⑥ What job would Chris have?

- ◯ farmer
- ◯ pet store owner
- ◯ scientist

⑦ **I am forced to run in circles all day as a form of exercise.** After reading the whole story and realising what creature the narrator is, what could this device in the cage be?

- ◯ a school oval
- ◯ an exercise wheel
- ◯ a racetrack

⑧ Find **haul** in the second paragraph. The sentences around it give you an idea of its meaning. Which word has a similar meaning?

◯ invite ◯ scare ◯ drag

⑨ What would it mean if this fantasy story was true? (Choose any that apply.)

- ◯ Mice can talk.
- ◯ Mice really control the world.
- ◯ Mice control the results of all the testing they are used for.

Use your experience and opinions to answer this question. The answer is not in the text.

⑩ Think of a maze you have walked into or completed as a puzzle. What makes mazes so difficult to complete?

____

____

____

____

Comprehension Reflections

Look at the top of the opposite page. This text is an I__________ text – N__________.

Write one thing you learned or found interesting:

____

Write one question you have or something you want to find more information about:

____

____

Rating

Score 2 points for each correct answer!

SCORE /20 0-8 10-14 16-20

Grammar & Punctuation

AC9E5LY06

Direct speech – Quotation marks

The text has spoken words that are called direct speech. The direct speech is marked by quotation marks "__". The quotation marks only go around the spoken words.

Example: "I like cheese," said the mouse.

Place quotation marks around the direct speech in the following sentences.

1. I love cheese too. I could eat it all day, said her friend.
2. Surely not all day, said the mouse.
3. All day. Just you wait and see, said her friend.
4. The mouse said, Be careful or you'll explode.

Saying verbs

People in real life speak in a variety of ways, ranging from quiet, sleepy or bored to excited, furious or hysterical. It depends on their personality and the situations they are in. To show how something was said, we can use saying verbs other than 'said' to make our writing more descriptive.

Examples: whispered, shouted, pleaded, screamed

Replace said in the conversation below with better saying verbs. Circle one saying verb in each list.

5. "I like cheese," **said** the mouse.
   (wailed screamed pleaded remarked)
6. "I love cheese too. I could eat it all day," her friend **said**.
   (boasted sang gargled cackled)
7. "Surely not all day," **said** the mouse.
   (commanded begged exclaimed muttered)
8. "All day! Just you wait and see!" her friend **said**.
   (whispered hummed snapped begged)
9. The mouse **said**, "Be careful or you'll explode!"
   (warned demanded gulped croaked)

Punctuation

In direct speech the first spoken word starts with a capital letter.

Example: I said, "Come to dinner. We have cheese."

The punctuation marks at the end of the quote go inside the quotation marks. They tell us how the words were spoken.

Examples: I exclaimed, "We have cheese!"

I questioned, "We have cheese?"

Circle the best punctuation mark for the end of the direct speech. Look at the saying verbs to help you decide.

Example: "I want cheese_" the mouse demanded.
((!) . ?)

10. Her friend queried, "At this time of night_"
    (! . ?)
11. "Why not _" snapped the mouse.
    (! . ?)
12. "Well," her friend yelled, "this time it will be you that explodes_" (! . ?)
13. "Oh, I hope not_" the mouse replied.
    (! . ?)

Commas

In direct speech, if there is no other punctuation mark, a comma is used to separate what is said and who said it.

Examples: The mouse said, "I want cheese."

"I want cheese," the mouse said.

Complete these sentences by adding a comma to each.

14. "I dream of cheese " stated the mouse.
    The mouse stated "I dream of cheese."
15. "Me too " agreed her friend.
    Her friend agreed "Me too."

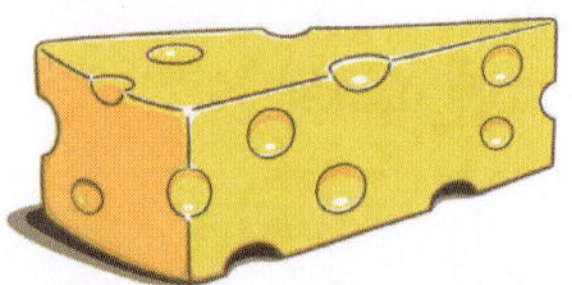

Score 2 points for each correct answer!

TARGETING ENGLISH HOMEWORK YEAR 5 © PASCAL PRESS ISBN 978 1 925726 62 6

Word building – Prefixes and suffixes

The words in the table have been divided into their parts. Put them back together and write them in the 'New word' column. Find them in the text to check your spelling. In the last column, circle the antonym (opposite meaning) of the word.

English is based on Latin and Greek words. We take a base word and add a prefix to the front and suffix to the end of a word to create a new word with a different meaning.

prefix ↓ base word ↓

Examples: un + happy = **un**happy
happy + ness = happi**ness**

↑ base word ↑ suffix

	Prefix	Root word	Suffix	Suffix	New word	Antonym
	Example:	cruel	–ly		cruelly	harshly (kindly)
1		snatch	–ed			seized repelled
2	im–	prison	–ed			released caged
3		care	–full			wary foolish
4		purpose	–ly			knowingly unintentionally
5		body	–ly			physically mentally
6		easy	–ly			laboriously comfortably
7		hope	–full	–ly		surely doubtfully
8	ad–	mit				confess deny

Word building with 'ad' and 'mit'

The prefix 'ad' is from Latin, meaning toward or to. The base word 'mit' comes from Latin, meaning to send. Admit is a form of acceptance used when you are agreeing that something is true, especially when you may not want it to be true.

Example: I **admit** that I could have completed my homework on time, but I didn't want to.

Place the 'ad' prefix words in the correct spaces to complete the sentences in the following column. You may need to use a dictionary.

advert advise adverse adopt admit

When I ate the cheese, I had an (9) __________ reaction. I broke out in a rash and felt very itchy. I must (10) __________, I do eat too much cheese, so I may have to take up or (11) __________ a different eating plan. The doctor did (12) __________ me to eat more fruit instead. However, every time I see an (13) __________ about cheese on the TV I instantly find myself in the fridge, eating cheese.

Circle the correct 'mit' root word to complete each sentence.

(14) The doctor said she would __________ me only one slice of cheese a day.
(admit, permit, commit)

(15) I agreed, so I had to __________ my eating plan to her every day.
(omit, permit, submit)

(16) I eat one slice of cheese a day, although I __________ how big the slice is.
(omit, permit, submit)

Score 2 points for each correct answer! SCORE /32

AC9E5LY04, AC9E5LY05, AC9HS5K07, AC9HS5K06

Informative text – Procedure

Year Fives RULE!!!! Achieving a Civic Goal

Dear Diary (DD), Day 1 – The teacher has given us homework about being active citizens in our Australian democracy. I think she said Year Five students were like citizens or members of a community at school. In a healthy democracy, citizens can have a say on matters that are important to them. So, I have to come up with an idea or goal that's important to me and that will benefit the group. Hanging out with my friends is important to me, but I don't think that is a goal. Or is it?

DD, Day 2 – I've got it! The first step is **deciding on a problem**: the Year Five students are feeling a bit lost. We are not the oldest or youngest students in the school but somewhere in the middle. We have lost our identity; we are invisible. My fellow citizens, or Year Five classmates, share this belief. Together, we could achieve the goal of gaining some importance in the school and being visible once again. But how?

DD, Day 3 – I listened in class, and now I know what to do. The second step is to **make a decision**. I will decide how to make Year Fives visible in the school. I have some ideas. We could:

1. shave our heads
2. have a common room just for Year Fives to use at lunchtimes
3. wear our school T-shirts backwards.

I have decided on number 2. I'll find an old room for us to use. I don't really want to shave my head, and I don't think we'll look cool with the back-to-front T-shirt idea.

DD, Day 4 – My next step is to **research**. I need to find a room or space we can use in the school. I might interview the principal for spaces we could use. I could look at plans of the school to see if any room has been forgotten. Hey DD, I have a room in mind, but it's being used for storing sports gear. I'll have to come up with another place to store the gear. I think each classroom could store something that their class would like. I'll take all the pumped-up balls into my classroom.

DD, Day 5 – The teacher said the next step is to **activate and take action**. My classmates and I need to plan how to get the message across to all groups in the school community. We'll talk to our teacher and the principal. As a class, we could make flyers explaining the idea of a special Year Five room and give them to students, parents and staff. I'll ask my fellow Year Fives to stand up at lunchtime and make speeches explaining the idea.

Only after everyone is informed do we take the last step. As a group of citizens in the school, we'll ask the students and staff to **vote** on the proposal. That's 5 steps in all that we must go through to achieve the goal as a group.

DD, Day 6 – I have realised that homework can be fun after all. I have also realised that I can make a difference and have a voice. Maybe that's because I live in a democracy and go to a school that lets me practise being in a democracy.

Reading & Comprehension

Write the answer or shade the bubble next to the correct answer.

The answers to these questions are in the text.

① **What happens in a healthy democracy?**

Citizens can ______________________________

______________________________________.

② **Who are the citizens in this text?**

- ◯ Year Five students
- ◯ parents
- ◯ all Australians

③ **The first step in achieving a goal for a group of citizens is working out the problem. What is the problem?**

- ◯ Year Five students have homework.
- ◯ Year Five students feel invisible in their school.
- ◯ Year Five students have to make speeches.

④ **The author of the diary made a decision on how to solve the problem. How did they decide to solve the problem?**

____

____

⑤ **One of the steps involves research. What did the author of the diary have to research?**

____

⑥ **Another step involves taking action. Name three ways the Year Fives plan to get their message across to the school community.**

____

____

____

Think about this question and search for the answer in the text.

⑦ **There are five steps mentioned in the diary in achieving a goal for a group of citizens. Write the steps below.**

____

____

____

____

____

Use inferencing skills to answer this question. The answer is not in the text. Think about what you know and what the author says.

⑧ **Why do you think the author of the diary wanted the pumped-up balls in their classroom?**

____

____

____

Use your experience and opinions to answer this question. The answer is not in the text.

⑨ **You can also be an active citizen in your school or community. What problem could you see a group of you working to solve in your community or school?**

____

____

____

Comprehension Reflections

Look at the top of the opposite page. This text is an I__________ text – P__________.

Write one thing you learned or found interesting:

____

Write one question you have or something you want to find more information about:

____

____

Rating   

Score 2 points for each correct answer! SCORE **/18**   

Grammar & Punctuation

Speeches – Opening line

In the text, the author asks the students to create speeches to deliver at lunchtimes. Correct grammar and pronunciation are essential in public speaking.

The start of a speech is where you grab the audience's attention. The best start creates an opening line that states your intention or asks a question and possibly shares a startling statistic or fact. You can even start with a quote.

1. **Choose which start would be the best to grab the audience's attention.**

   a Hello, my name is Chris, and I want to talk to you about my ideas.

   b Have you ever felt invisible and would like people to notice you?

   c Hi, my first point is that we should have a separate room for lunch.

Introduction

Once you have the audience's attention, you need to introduce yourself and your topic. Tell them who you are and why you are making the speech.

2. **Choose which sentence you would use next.**

   a I am a Year Five student. I live on Fort Street, and I have two dogs and three cats.

   b We want a special room at lunchtime.

   c As a Year Five student, I want Year Fives to feel special by having their own lunchroom.

AC9E5LA08

Passive voice

Once you have introduced the topic, you then need to make your points. When persuading an audience in written or spoken text, you can use passive voice. This is another persuasive device.

In a sentence, you ask: Who or what is the subject? What is the sentence about?

Then you ask: Is the subject doing the action (active voice)? Or is the subject having the action done to them (passive voice)?

Example: Active voice – <u>Year Fives</u> **want** a separate room for lunch.

This sentence is active because the subject, Year Fives, is doing the action. Year Fives **want** a separate room, so they are doing the action of 'wanting'.

Example: Passive voice – A separate room for lunch **is wanted** by <u>Year Fives</u>. This sentence is passive because now the subject is 'a separate room for lunch' and the room is not doing the action of 'wanting'.

Circle if these sentences are active or passive. The verb is in bold and the subject underlined.

Example: <u>Sarah</u> **was drawing** a picture.
(active) passive

3. <u>Fred</u> **drew** a picture of a mouse.
   active passive
4. <u>The window</u> **was broken** by Sally.
   active passive
5. <u>George</u> **broke** the TV.
   active passive
6. <u>A picture of a mouse</u> **was drawn** by Fred.
   active passive

Write these active sentences as passive sentences. The sentences have been started for you.

7. Active: <u>Year Fives</u> **took** action.
   Passive: Action ______________________________
   ______________________________.
8. Active: <u>Year Fives</u> **created** flyers.
   Passive: Flyers ______________________________
   ______________________________.
9. Active: <u>Year Fives</u> **presented** speeches.
   Passive: Speeches ______________________________
   ______________________________.

Score 2 points for each correct answer! SCORE /18   

TARGETING ENGLISH HOMEWORK YEAR 5 © PASCAL PRESS ISBN 978 1 925726 62 6

Phonic & Word Knowledge

AC9E5LY08, AC9E5LY09

Pronouncing words correctly

The text called on Year Five students to make speeches. Correct pronunciation is essential in public speaking. How do you make sure you pronounce the words you read correctly?

Some strategies to help you are:

- sound out the letters of the word
- listen to and imitate others
- check you have your tongue in the right position
- break the word into syllables
- check you are not mixing up similar sounds.

Circle how you say the words in the first two columns. Then tick the last column once you have practised the correct pronunciation.

Did you say?	What you should say	Practise: Tick when done	
could of	could have	1	
should of	should have	2	
probly	prob-ab-ly	3	
pitcher	pic-ture	4	
anyways	anyway	5	

Circle the correct pronunciation in column A or B.

	Word	Pronunciation A	Pronunciation B
6	library	lie-berry	lie-brair-ee
7	chemist	kem-ist	chem-ist
8	February	feb-you-air-ee	feb-ree
9	subtle	sub-tel	suh-tl
10	jewellery	joo-uhl-ree	joo-ree
11	Wednesday	wenz-day	wed-nez-day
12	stomach	stum-ick	sto-match

Difficult words

It is difficult to know how to say some words. They can have the same word parts but are pronounced differently.

Examples: thorough, thought, tough, through, although

13 **Read the whole paragraph three times correctly with NO MISTAKES. When completed, tick the box, or ask an adult to listen to you and then tick the box.**

Repeated correctly three times with no mistakes. Tick when complete. ☐

All through the night, I thought I heard a squeaking noise. After a thorough search, nothing was found, although scattered cheese crumbs littered the floor. I looked through the fridge and thought I had found tiny footprints through the butter although a thorough search through the fridge found no other signs. Could it be mice? It would be tough for them, I thought, to open the fridge door.

Homophones

14 – 19 **Circle the correct homophones in these sentences. Homophones have the same sound but different meanings.**

I cannot (bare, bear) to be without music. I (buy, by, bye) the latest songs online and listen to them at (knight, night) in bed. I have (two, too, to) many to name. I also have records, but I wait until there is a (sail, sale) before I (buy, by, bye) them.

Score 2 points for each correct answer!

TERM 1

Informative text – Explanation

Jokes and Complex Sentences

The comedian asked, "Why did the chicken cross the road?" The audience waited expectantly for the punchline, except for the librarian who decided that this was a good time to talk about complex sentences.

The librarian explained that a complex sentence joins ideas together. This type of sentence has two different types of clauses joined by subordinating conjunctions or joining words, for example, 'as', 'after', 'when', 'because', 'if' and relative pronouns such as who, that, which and whose.

A clause, the librarian explained, is a part of a sentence that has a verb and a subject (the thing you are talking about). In a complex sentence, there is a main (also called 'independent') clause that makes sense on its own and at least one dependent (also called 'subordinate') clause that adds information but doesn't make sense on its own. Writers use complex sentences for greater effect in their writing.

By this time, the comedian and the chicken were looking confused, so the librarian then gave examples of complex sentences. In these examples, brackets ( ) have been used to show the dependent clause because it does not make sense on its own. The conjunction or relative pronoun is in bold.

- The chicken said it would cross the road (**if** the comedian paid a fee).
- The chicken crossed the road (**because** the comedian paid it to do so).
- (**After** it crossed the road), the chicken looked expectantly at the comedian for its payment.
- (**While** the chicken crossed the road), the comedian signed a deal with the neighbourhood chicken shop.
- The chicken knew (**that** the comedian was up to no good).

By this time, the chicken was feeling nervous. The librarian continued to explain that you can even have a dependent clause in the middle of the sentence and gave the following examples using the relative pronoun 'who' to link the clauses.

- The comedian, (**who** licked his lips while looking at the chicken), invited the chicken into the chicken shop.
- The shop owner, (**who** was sharpening her knives), smiled hungrily at the chicken.

It was at this time that the chicken refused to cross the road which the librarian took as another opportunity to give examples of complex sentences.

- The chicken did not cross the road (**because** it did not want to be on the menu of the local chicken shop).
- (**When** the chicken refused to cross the road), a magician offered the chicken a job as her rabbit had disappeared.
- The chicken accepted the offer (**if** the magician agreed not to eat it).

It was at this point that the comedian decided to tell jokes about ducks instead.

TARGETING ENGLISH HOMEWORK YEAR 5 © PASCAL PRESS ISBN 978 1 925726 62 6

Reading & Comprehension

TERM 1

Write the answer or shade the bubble next to the correct answer.

The answers to these questions are in the text.

1. **What are conjunctions?**

___

___

2. **The librarian gave an example of five subordinating conjunctions. List three.**

___

___

___

3. **Name two types of clauses.**

___

___

4. **Which type of clause is in brackets in the examples given in the text?**

___

5. **The chicken crossed the road because the comedian paid it to do so. Find this sentence in the text and answer the next three questions.**

The main clause is ___
___.

The dependent clause is ___
___.

The conjunction to join them together is
___.

Think about these questions and search for the answers in the text.

6. **Does a conjunction that joins two clauses have to be in the middle of a sentence?**
   - ◯ Yes
   - ◯ No

7. **Why was the chicken feeling nervous?**
   - ◯ The magician lost the rabbit.
   - ◯ It did not understand complex sentences.
   - ◯ The comedian was doing a deal with the chicken shop.

Use inferencing skills to answer this question. The answer is not in the text. Think about what you know and what the author says.

8. **Find expectantly which is used twice in the text. The sentences around it give you an idea of its meaning. Which word has a similar meaning?**
   - ◯ daily
   - ◯ eagerly
   - ◯ fearfully

Use your experience and opinions to answer this question. The answer is not in the text.

9. **Write your own answers to these jokes.**

Why did the chicken cross the road?

___

___

Why did the duck cross the road?

___

___

Comprehension Reflections

Look at the top of the opposite page. This text is an I__________ text – E__________.

Write one thing you learned or found interesting:

___

Write one question you have or something you want to find more information about:

___

___

Rating   

Score 2 points for each correct answer! 

SCORE	/18	 0-6	 8-14	 16-18

Grammar & Punctuation

AC9E5LA05

TERM 1

Complex sentences

Complex sentences have at least one main clause and one dependent clause. The main clause makes sense on its own while the dependent clause does not.

main clause

Example: The chicken would cross the road **if** the comedian paid a fee.

conjunction — dependent clause

Circle the main clause in these sentences. Both clauses are in brackets.

Example: (After it joined the magician), ((the chicken was paid in worms).)

1. (The chicken became angry with the magician) (because it expected money).
2. (The chicken would only work for the magician) (if it was paid in cash).
3. (When the magician paid cash), (the chicken agreed to help with magic tricks).

Choose the best subordinating conjunction or relative pronoun to fit each sentence: if, because, when, after, who, that. Only use them once.

Example: The comedian agreed to pay the duck **if** it crossed the road.

4. ____________ the duck crossed the road, the comedian signed a deal with a neighbouring pet shop.
5. This is a duck ____________ knows it can't trust people.
6. The duck and chicken became good friends ____________ they could trust each other.
7. ____________ the comedian found out, he decided to quit show business.
8. The librarian, ____________ started the whole explanation, felt disappointed that they never heard the end of the joke.

Join these clauses together with the conjunction or relative pronoun in brackets. You may need to add, leave out or change words when you write the new sentence.

Example: I do magic tricks. I call myself a magician. **(when)**
When I do magic tricks, I call myself a magician.

9. Magicians use rabbits. They are easy to handle and can fit into a hat. **(because)**

____

10. The duck crossed the road. It saw the comedian and the pet shop owner together. **(after)**

____

11. The chicken and the duck came to a decision. The comedian and magician were not to be trusted. **(that)**

____

Tricky commas

If a complex sentence begins with a dependent clause, a comma is used to separate the two clauses.

Example: If you have found the page, please begin reading.

dependent clause — comma

If a complex sentence begins with a main clause, no comma is used between the clauses.

Example: Please begin reading if you have found the page.

main clause — no comma

Where does the comma go? Circle the correct sentences.

Example: I love telling jokes, when people laugh.
(I love telling jokes when people laugh.)

12. When people laugh, I tell more jokes.
When people laugh I tell more jokes.
13. I feel embarrassed, if people don't laugh.
I feel embarrassed if people don't laugh.
14. If people don't laugh, I feel embarrassed.
If people don't laugh I feel embarrassed.
15. I should be on TV, because I am so good.
I should be on TV because I am so good.
16. Because I am so good, I should be on TV.
Because I am so good I should be on TV.
17. I don't care, if the chicken crossed the road.
I don't care if the chicken crossed the road.

Score 2 points for each correct answer! SCORE /34   

0-14 16-28 30-34

TARGETING ENGLISH HOMEWORK YEAR 5 © PASCAL PRESS ISBN 978 1 925726 62 6

Phonic & Word Knowledge

AC9E5LY09, AC9E5LY10

Latin suffix 'an' or 'ian'

The Latin suffix –an or –ian means 'characteristic of'. When you add –ian to the ends of words, you often create nouns that are jobs.

Examples from the text: librarian, magician, comedian

A magician is a job connected to magic, a librarian is a job connected to a library and a comedian is a job connected to comedy.

Add the suffix –ian to these words about people.

	Example: person from Australia	Australian
1	person from Italy	
2	person who studies history	
3	person who works with electricity	
4	person who looks after technical equipment	
5	person involved in music	
6	person involved in politics	

Match the –an or –ian words to their meaning.

7	urban	to do with horseriding
8	clinician	to do with suburbs
9	guardian	to do with cities
10	pedestrian	to do with health care
11	equestrian	to do with people and feet
12	suburban	to do with protecting

Confusing words – who's and whose

Some words in English, such as who's and whose, can be easily confused because they sound the same. 'Who' was used as a pronoun in the text.

When 'who' is used as a question word with 'is', it is often contracted to who's. Who's is a contraction meaning 'who is'. The apostrophe shows where the letter 'i' is missing. *Example:* Who's coming to play? = Who is coming to play?

Whose shows ownership. *Example:* Whose book is that?

Circle the correct word to complete these examples.

13. __________ book is that over there?
a Who **b** Who's **c** Whose
14. __________ coming to dinner tonight?
a Who **b** Who's **c** Whose
15. The girl __________ sang smiled widely.
a who **b** who's **c** whose
16. She didn't know __________ jumper she picked up.
a who **b** who's **c** whose
17. __________ the teacher for the next lesson?
a Who **b** Who's **c** Whose
18. Guess __________ dog is having puppies?
a who **b** who's **c** whose

Who's can also mean 'who has'. What meaning does who's have in the examples below?

19. Who's got the ball?
a Who is **b** Who has
20. Jan, who's ill, can't come to practice.
a who is **b** who has
21. Who's been to the beach lately?
a Who is **b** Who has

Score 2 points for each correct answer!

SCORE  /42  0-18  20-36  38-42

Imaginative text – Narrative

The Swimmer

The exhausted child coughed and spluttered for breath. Kicking with all his might, he struggled towards the safety of the wall. It was so close that he could see its pitted surface.

Desperately, he thrust his hand towards the wall. With one last burst of energy, he launched himself forwards and clawed his way along the wall's vertical surface. It had started out as an adventure, some fun in the water; however, the splashing and shrieks of laughter soon turned into panicked gasps for air.

"I have blown the whistle twice. Could you please get out of the pool!" the exasperated teacher called to the child. "And for heaven's sake, stand up! You are at the shallow end of the pool. Seriously! What some people do for attention!"

The child bobbed in the water for a few seconds before gliding towards the steps in the pool. His imagination was on fire as he imagined himself climbing a large mountain.

The exhausted child hauled his body upwards, towards the summit. Gripping each handhold with all his might, he battled his way forward. The summit was so close that he could see its rugged surface.

With flailing arms, the child heaved himself onto the flat surface – a wet, soggy bundle on the cold, hard surface of the summit.

Over the loudspeaker, a crackling voice was heard. "Could all the Year Fives from Wilson Primary School please make their way to the bus. Thank you for your attendance and see you again for swimming lessons tomorrow."

The child sat on the cold tiles for a few seconds before walking towards the bus. His imagination was once again on fire. This time he imagined himself on a quest to fight a large beast that was swallowing his classmates at a very fast rate.

Write the answer or shade the bubble next to the correct answer.

1. **Where does this story take place?**

   ____

2. **Why was the child there?**

   ____

3. **What school does the child attend?**

   ____

TARGETING ENGLISH HOMEWORK YEAR 5 © PASCAL PRESS ISBN 978 1 925726 62 6

4. **The child undertook, or planned to complete, three tasks. One task is named. Name the other two.**

   a reach the wall

   b ______________________

   c ______________________

5. **After reading the story, would you say that the child has:**

   ◯ an active imagination?
   ◯ a desire to get into trouble?
   ◯ no idea how to swim?

6. **What does the teacher think the child is looking for?**

   ____

7. **Find exasperated in the third paragraph. Read the narrative and infer what you think it means. Which word has a similar meaning?**

   ◯ short of breath
   ◯ frustrated
   ◯ delighted

8. **Why would the teacher be exasperated? Write one reason.**

   ____

   ____

9. **What is the large beast that is swallowing the classmates?**

   ____

10. **Where was the mountain and its summit that the child climbed?**

    ____

11. **Was the child really drowning?**

    ◯ Yes
    ◯ No

    Give one reason for your answer.

    ____

12. **When have you felt exasperated? Write two sentences to describe the situation.**

    ____

    ____

    ____

    ____

Score 2 points for each correct answer!

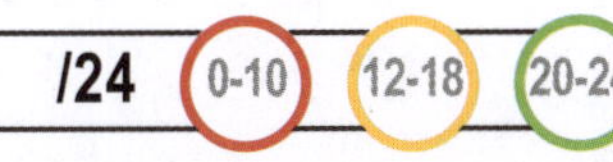

Action verbs

The text contains action verbs that give information to the reader about the level of power or intensity of the action.

Example: The child **heaved** himself onto the flat surface.

A different level of intensity would be achieved with a different verb.

Example: The child **drifted** onto the flat surface.

Read these sentences from the text and circle the answer that best shows the level of power or intensity of the bold verb.

1. Desperately, he **thrust** his hand towards the wall.

   a directed
   b forced
   c guided

2. With one last burst of energy, he **launched** himself forwards …

   a threw
   b put
   c floated

3. … **clawed** his way along the wall's vertical surface.

   a scraped
   b felt
   c sensed

4. Gripping each handhold with all his might, he **battled** his way forward.

   a felt
   b pulled
   c fought

Noun groups

Noun groups provide a fuller description of a person, place or thing. They include words that can come before and/or after a noun.

Example: In the text, the child reaching the summit is described as … a **wet, soggy bundle on the cold, hard surface of the summit.**

TERM 1

Grammar & Punctuation

Circle the noun that is being described in each example.

5. exhausted child
6. pitted surface
7. wall's vertical surface
8. rugged surface
9. crackling voice
10. flailing arms

Complex sentences

Complex sentences have a main clause that can stand alone. They also have a dependent clause that does not make sense on its own. The clauses are joined together by a conjunction.

Circle the dependent clause in these sentences. The conjunction is in bold.

Example: (**After** she blew the whistle,) the exasperated teacher talked to the child in the pool.

11. The child bobbed in the water for a few seconds **before** he glided towards the steps in the pool.
12. The child sat on the cold tiles for a few seconds **before** he walked towards the bus.
13. He was on a quest to fight a large beast **that** was swallowing his classmates at a very fast rate.
14. **If** he killed the large beast, he would be a hero.
15. **As** he climbed into the bus, the child smiled a soft, dangerous smile.

Score 2 points for each correct answer!

Phonic & Word Knowledge

Spelling generalisations

When adding suffixes to words, there are spelling generalisations that you need to know to spell the new word correctly.

Complete the table by writing each word with its suffix in the last column.

	Example: cackle	-ing	cackling
1	glide	-ing	
2	imagine	-ation	
3	behave	-iour	
4	struggle	-ed	
5	safe	-ty	
6	excite	-able	
7	congratulate	-ion	
8	suggest	-ion	

Word building

In the text, the child goes on a quest. 'Quest' comes from Greek, meaning to 'seek or investigate'. It forms the root word of many words in English. Related root words are 'quir' and 'quisit'.

TARGETING ENGLISH HOMEWORK YEAR 5 © PASCAL PRESS ISBN 978 1 925726 62 6

Phonic & Word Knowledge

Write the complete word in the 'new word' column in the table below and match it to a definition (a to e).

Prefix	Root word	Suffix	Suffix	New word	Definition
Example:	quest	–ion		question	e
re–	quest			⑨	
con–	quest			⑩	
re–	quire	–ment		⑪	
in–	quis	–itive		⑫	
	quest	–ion	–(n)aire	⑬	
se–	quest	–er		⑭	

a nosey **b** ask for **c** necessity **d** separate **e** interview **f** survey **g** defeat

Homophones

In previous units, you worked on apostrophes and homophones. This task puts the two together. **Their** is a homophone with **there** and **they're**. They all sound the same but have different meanings:

- their – owned by
- there – at that place
- they're – they are, using the apostrophe to indicate the missing letter.

Complete these sentences with the correct homophone: their/s, there, they're.

The swimming instructor wanted the students to dry off. She asked the teacher, "Where are ⑮ __________ towels?"

The teacher replied, ⑯ "__________ over ⑰ __________."

The instructor looked confused and questioned, "Are you sure those are ⑱ __________ towels?"

The exasperated teacher said rather angrily, "Yes, ⑲ __________ ⑳ __________ towels!"

The instructor replied, "I'll go over ㉑ __________ to make sure everyone gets ㉒ __________ own towel." At that moment, the teacher noticed a child bobbing in the water. She promptly took out her whistle.

Score 2 points for each correct answer! SCORE /44 0-20 22-38 40-44

AC9E5LY04, AC9E5LY05, AC9E5LA01, AC9HS5K08

Persuasive text - Argument

Year Fives Need Chocolate Every Day!

Good afternoon, Madam Chairman, boys and girls. The topic of my debate is that chocolate should be considered a need and not a want for all Year Five students during a school day.

I define the topic as: A need is something that is required to live, such as food, water, shelter and clothing. A want is defined as something that we would like to have but is not necessary to stay alive, such as a bike, iPad or a new pet.

As part of the affirmative team, I believe the statement about chocolate is true, and I will discuss three points to persuade you.

My first point is that chocolate is a food that Year Fives need to sustain them over a day's intense learning. People have different needs and wants because of our differences in age, where we live, and our culture and health. Year Five students are of an age where they need a food that will sustain them over the course of a day's learning. The food that could provide this energy punch is, of course, chocolate. Have you ever felt the afternoon energy drain? Chocolate is the food snack that will revive any child to maximum attention. Chocolate is a high energy food that Year Five students need for energy and concentration. Therefore, chocolate is a need and not a want.

Secondly, chocolate is a special kind of food which has a rich history. It was once considered 'food of the gods' by the ancient Mayans and Aztecs in Mexico and South America. It was a drink only given to the priests and the nobility, or rich people, of the time. Even then, chocolate was seen as something special and used in ceremonies. It was even used as a form of money.

Lastly, chocolate has some beneficial health effects. Chocolate is known to have some healthy fats. It also has chemicals called antioxidants which help blood flow throughout your body, especially if you eat dark chocolate. Of course, chocolate is high in sugar and too much sugar can cause many problems. However, I am suggesting a small amount of chocolate a day.

So, Madam Chairman, boys and girls, in conclusion, chocolate is a need, not a want. It is a food that will sustain Year Fives over a day's learning, it has held a very important role in ancient times, and it has some beneficial health effects. You cannot deny that chocolate must be provided to all Year Five students daily. Ask your teacher for some now.

TARGETING ENGLISH HOMEWORK YEAR 5 © PASCAL PRESS ISBN 978 1 925726 62 6

Reading & Comprehension

Write the answer or shade the bubble next to the correct answer.

The answers to these questions are in the text.

① **What is a need? Give three examples from the text.**

____

____

____

② **What is a want? Give three examples from the text.**

____

____

____

③ **This debate is about:**

- ◯ persuading readers that chocolate is a need and not a want.
- ◯ persuading readers that chocolate has sugar.
- ◯ persuading readers that chocolate was 'food of the gods'.

④ **Who was allowed to drink chocolate or food of the gods in ancient times?**

____

____

Think about this question and search for the answer in the text.

⑤ **What are the three points made in the debate? List them below.**

____

____

____

Use inferencing skills to answer the following questions. The answers are not in the text. Think about what you know and what the author says.

⑥ **If you were on the negative team and had to rebut, or raise an argument against this debate, what point would you make against chocolate being a food Year Fives need?**

____

____

____

⑦ **The text defines the difference between a need and a want. List three things you want that are not considered a need.**

____

____

____

Use your experience and opinions to answer these questions. The answers are not in the text.

⑧ **Do you agree or disagree with this debate? Give two reasons for your answer.**

I agree / disagree with the debate because

____

____

____

______________________________.

⑨ **Would teachers agree or disagree with this debate? Give a reason for your answer.**

Teachers would agree / disagree with the debate because ______________________________

______________________________.

Comprehension Reflections

Look at the top of the opposite page. This text is a P__________ text – A__________.

Write one thing you learned or found interesting:

____

Write one question you have or something you want to find more information about:

____

____

Rating   

Score 2 points for each correct answer! SCORE /18    

TERM 2

Grammar & Punctuation

AC9E5LA01, AC9E5LA03, AC9E5LY03

Persuasive devices

Persuasive devices are language techniques used by authors to convince readers to agree with their point of view. There are several devices used in the text.

Rhetorical questions

Rhetorical questions are a useful technique in persuasive writing. They are asked for a purpose or to make you think. They are not meant to be answered. The answer is already known, and the question is used to make a point.

As there is nobody to answer the question, it is aimed at the reader. It is used to help the reader stop and think about the question.

Example: Have you ever felt the afternoon energy drain? (used in the text to make you think about needing energy in the afternoon)

Read these questions and decide which ones are rhetorical and which ones you would be expected to answer. Circle the rhetorical questions.

1. What were you thinking?
2. What is your favourite movie?
3. Can't you do anything right?
4. What homework do you have?
5. Are you kidding?
6. You don't think I'm that stupid, do you?
7. What's for dinner?
8. Why would you bother?

Read these rhetorical questions and circle the ones you think could be used in the text to help the reader think about the points made.

9. Have you ever wondered about the dangers of sugar?
10. Who cares about chocolate?
11. Have you ever wondered about the history of chocolate?
12. Could you use a high energy snack?
13. Are chocolate wrappers a danger to the environment?

Rule of three

Providing three arguments in a debate or persuasive text is an easy way to help your reader remember your points. More than three points could be difficult to remember. Less than three and your argument is weakened.

Think of three arguments or points you could make for these topics.

14. Cats are better than dogs.
    Argument 1: ______________________________
    ____
    Argument 2: ______________________________
    ____
    Argument 3: ______________________________
    ____

15. Dogs are better than cats.
    Argument 1: ______________________________
    ____
    Argument 2: ______________________________
    ____
    Argument 3: ______________________________
    ____

Modality

Modality means how certain you are of something. High modality words in a persuasive text are more effective in convincing readers to agree with your point of view. High modality words were used in the text to strengthen the points. *Examples:* should, must

Using the bold high modality words, complete the sentences to make a statement with high modality.

16. All Year Five students **have to** ______________________________.
17. All teachers **must** ______________________________.
18. Homework **definitely** ______________________________.
19. All Year Fives **must not** ______________________________.

Score 2 points for each correct answer! SCORE /38 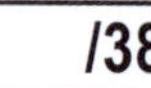 0-16  18-32  34-38 

TERM 2

TARGETING ENGLISH HOMEWORK YEAR 5 © PASCAL PRESS ISBN 978 1 925726 62 6

Phonic & Word Knowledge

AC9E5LY09, AC9E5LY10

Suffix 'ative'

The text is part of a debate for the affirmative team. This is the team that supports or affirms the topic. The word 'affirm' is a verb, but when the suffix 'ative' is added it becomes an adjective. *Example:* affirm (verb) + ative = affirmative (adjective)

The suffixes 'ive', 'ative' and 'itive' all have the same meaning and turn nouns (names of things) and verbs (actions) into adjectives (describing words). These suffixes mean 'connected with' or 'about'.

Complete these sentences with the adjectives listed below.

creative argumentative talkative conservative cooperative

1. Someone who does not like change may be called ____________________.
2. A person who ends up in lots of fights may be called ____________________.
3. If you work well with others, you may be seen as ____________________.
4. Someone who has the power to invent or make something is described as ____________________.
5. If you are very friendly and willing to communicate, you may be seen as ____________________.

Plurals

Most nouns become plural or more than one by adding 's'. *Examples:* boys, girls, gods

However, nouns ending in 's', 'x', 'z', 'ch' and 'sh' have an extra sound added, formed by the 'es' ending.
Example: bus – buses

Write the plurals of the following words.

6. glass ____________________
7. box ____________________
8. lunch ____________________
9. wish ____________________
10. topaz ____________________
11. class ____________________

Words ending in 'y'

With words ending in 'y', the 'y' changes to an 'i' and then add 'es'. *Example:* fly – flies

However, if the letter 'y' follows a vowel, then keep the 'y' and add 's'. *Example:* boy – boys

Some nouns ending in 'f' or 'fe' change to 'ves'. *Example:* knife – knives

Write the plurals of the following words.

12. wolf ____________
13. berry ____________
14. puppy ____________
15. toy ____________
16. city ____________
17. calf ____________

Irregular plural nouns

Some plural nouns are irregular and need to be learned. *Example:* man – men

And some nouns do not change whether they are singular or plural.
Example: one fish – two fish

Write the plurals of the following words.

18. foot ____________
19. woman ____________
20. sheep ____________
21. mouse ____________
22. police ____________
23. furniture ____________
24. goose ____________
25. tooth ____________
26. scissors ____________

Apostrophes showing possession

Remember! Apostrophes can show possession. In the text is the phrase, a day's intense learning. Day's is not the plural of 'day'. The apostrophe means possession, meaning the learning that occurs in that day.

Circle the correctly punctuated sentence in each pair.

27. At the day's end, we will all go home.
    At the days end, we will all go home.
28. Six dog's came running to us.
    Six dogs came running to us.
29. These are two families' train tickets.
    These are two families train tickets.

Score 2 points for each correct answer! SCORE /58 0-28 30-52 54-58

TERM 2

AC9E5LY04, AC9E5LY05, AC9E5LE03, AC9HP6P10

Persuasive text – Argument

Swap a 'Choccy' a Day, Less Sugar, HOORAY!

Many people love the taste of chocolate and enjoy it in many forms. It has a sweet flavour and triggers a feel-good chemical in the brain called dopamine. It is a good source of energy, and if you are hungry, it can make you feel satisfied for a short while. So, what's the problem with eating chocolate every day?

Chocolate is just one of the many foods that has a high level of sugar. Therefore, it is seen by many health professionals as a 'sometimes' food, not necessarily an everyday food. Eating lots of sugar every day is definitely not good for our health. Too much sugar can make us put on weight and can lead to diseases and health issues such as diabetes and high blood pressure. It can even lead to mood changes and depression.

Eating lots of sugar is not good for your teeth as the sugar interacts with bacteria that live around your teeth to form acid. This acid attacks the enamel and dentine of the teeth causing holes or cavities to form. Trips to the dentist may then be needed to repair or remove the decayed teeth.

One step in making better choices for your health is to cut down on your sugar intake. But how? One step could be swap a 'choccy' a day and keep the munchies at bay.

There is little evidence to say that sugar is addictive, but it does have addictive properties in that the more you have, the more you want. Unfortunately, eating chocolate daily can become a hard-to-break habit. This means it will be hard to change the way you think about chocolate and difficult to break the habit of when or how often you want to eat it.

To help break your old habits and create new ones, try removing temptation and changing what you eat for snacks. Swap a 'choccy' a day, less sugar, hooray!

Swap this:

for:

- apple slices with peanut butter on top
- cheese on cracker biscuits
- popcorn or nuts
- fruit e.g. strawberries, grapes, mangoes
- tomatoes and cheese
- hummus dip with veggie sticks
- avocado on toast
- banana smoothie
- yoghurt.

TERM 2

TARGETING ENGLISH HOMEWORK YEAR 5 © PASCAL PRESS ISBN 978 1 925726 62 6

Reading & Comprehension

Write the answer or shade the bubble next to the correct answer.

The answers to these questions are in the text.

1. What is the **feel-good chemical** in our brain?

____

2. What can happen if you eat too much chocolate? List three effects.

____

____

____

3. Swapping chocolate for better snack choices is good for your overall health. Out of the snacks listed, write three you could eat instead of chocolate.

____

____

____

Think about this question and search for the answer in the text.

4. In the text, it states that it could be difficult to swap **a 'choccy' a day** for a healthier choice. Why is that?

____

____

____

____

Use inferencing skills to answer these questions. The answers are not in the text. Think about what you know and what the author says.

5. Think of two healthy snacks that are **not listed** that you could eat instead of chocolate.

____

____

6. One way to break the habit of snacking on chocolate is to snack on healthier foods. What is another way to **break the habit**? (For example, clean your teeth every time you want to eat a chocolate.)

____

____

Use your experience and opinions to answer these questions. The answers are not in the text.

7. Where does chocolate come from? (Choose any that apply.)
   - ◯ It is mined in chocolate mines.
   - ◯ It grows on a bush, and you grind it into a powder.
   - ◯ It comes from the cacao tree.
   - ◯ It is made in supermarkets.

8. Chocolate milk contains a lot of added sugar compared to ordinary milk which contains no added sugar. What **strategies** could help Year Five students reduce how much chocolate milk they drink? (Choose any that apply.)
   - ◯ Reduce the number of brown cows that produce chocolate milk.
   - ◯ Remove chocolate milk from the school canteen and lunch orders.
   - ◯ Give extra homework to Year Five students who drink chocolate milk products.
   - ◯ Educate students about consuming too much sugar.

Comprehension Reflections

Look at the top of the opposite page. This text is a P__________ text – A__________.

Write one thing you learned or found interesting:

____

Write one question you have or something you want to find more information about:

____

____

Rating   

Score 2 points for each correct answer!

SCORE 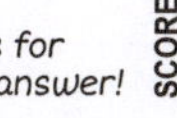

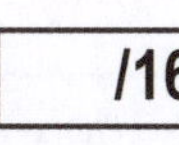

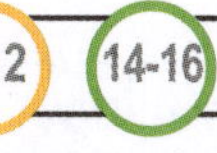

TERM 2

Grammar & Punctuation

AC9E5LY03, AC9E5LE03, AC9E5LA06

TERM 2

Point of view

This unit and Unit 9 have provided different points of view about chocolate. Both agree that chocolate is high in sugar although unit 9 sees this as a positive while this unit sees the high sugar content of chocolate as a negative point.

Noun groups (names of things) and verb groups (action words) have been used in the text to show a point of view. The words from the text that form these groups are listed in the tables below.

Decide whether these are noun groups or verb groups and write them in the spaces in the table.

is seen	old habits	'sometimes' food
	interacts	could be

Auxiliary verb	Verb
	love
	enjoy
	triggers
①	
can	make
can	lead
②	
is	addictive
	attacks
	repair
	remove
③	

Adjective	Noun
sweet	flavour
feel-good	chemical
health	professionals
decayed	teeth
hard-to-break	habit
better	choices
health	issues
addictive	properties
little	evidence
④	
⑤	
everyday	food

⑥ **Use at least one noun group and at least one verb group from the tables to write a sentence from the point of view of a dentist. What would they want to say to Year Five students about eating chocolate?**

____

____

____

____

⑦ **Use at least one noun group and at least one verb group from the tables to write a sentence from the point of view of a Year Five student about eating chocolate.**

____

____

____

____

⑧ **Use at least one noun group and at least one verb group from the tables to write a sentence from the point of view of a chocolate manufacturer.**

____

____

____

____

Language features – Rhyming

Rhyming is a language feature used to emphasise an important idea in this text and create something to remember.

⑨ **The title of the text is a rhyming sentence. What is another rhyming sentence used in the text?**

____

____

⑩ **Create your own rhyming sentence to show your point of view about eating chocolate.**

____

____

____

____

Score 2 points for each correct answer! SCORE /20 0-8 10-14 16-20

TARGETING ENGLISH HOMEWORK YEAR 5 © PASCAL PRESS ISBN 978 1 925726 62 6

Phonic & Word Knowledge

AC9E5LY09

Phobias and definitions

Playing with words can be fun, especially when you come across words you have never heard of before. *Example:* If you had a fear or **phobia of chocolate**, you would name this phobia **xocolatophobia**.

Have fun and match the phobias with their definitions. You will certainly need a dictionary for this task.

Definitions

a fear of dogs
b fear of peanut butter
c fear of fruit
d fear of chocolate
e fear of cooking
f fear of chopsticks
g fear of vegetables
h fear of eating

	Phobias	Definition
1	xocolatophobia	
2	mageirocophobia	
3	cynophobia	
4	cibophobia	
5	lachanophobia	
6	arachibutyrophobia	
7	fructophobia	
8	consecotaleophobia	

High modality word 'definitely'

Persuasive texts use high modality words to express a strong opinion. 'Definitely' is a high modality word, stressing the certainty that something will happen. *Example:* Eating lots of sugar every day is **definitely** not good for our health.

Some words that end in 'ite', like 'definite', are pronounced with an 'it' sound.

However, other 'ite' words are pronounced with the long vowel sound 'i'. *Example:* invite, write, satellite

You need to learn these different pronunciations of 'ite' words.

Place the correct 'ite' words in the sentences. These words all have an 'it' sound.

definite granite infinite opposite composite requisite favourite

If all Year Five students wrote about their (9) ____________ snack foods, would the list be high in sugar? It is not a (10) ____________ that a snack be sweet. There is an (11) ____________ number of choices that can be made. It is not set in (12) ____________ that all students love sugar, in fact it could be the (13) ____________ and savoury foods win out. Some students may have a mix or (14) ____________ list of both savoury and sweet snacks. It is not a (15) ____________ conclusion that chocolate would be the snack of choice for Year Five students.

Words ending with 'ate'

Many words that are spelt with 'ate' have a schwa or 'uht' sound.
Examples: chocolate, climate

(16) **Circle the words where the 'ate' ending of the word has an 'uht' sound.**

plate accurate fortunate
appreciate desperate appropriate
punctuate infiltrate considerate
stipulate

Choose the most appropriate 'ate' word for each sentence.

(17) I was ______________ to win the box of chocolates. fortunate / appreciate

(18) I am ______________ for some chocolate. appropriate / desperate

(19) Does the spelling of chocolate need to be ______________? considerate / accurate

(20) Teachers had to ______________ what was allowed as a healthy snack. stipulate / punctuate

Score 2 points for each correct answer! SCORE /40  0-18  20-34  36-40 

AC9E5LY04, AC9E5LY05, AC9HS5K08

Informative text – Explanation

TERM 2

You Can Have Everything You Want! Or Can You?

What a world it would be if we all got what we wanted all the time. But is that possible? Have you ever had an adult say that you can't have everything you want? Unfortunately, there is a reason behind this statement.

We all have needs and wants. Needs are things we need to survive, such as food, water, clothing and shelter. Wants are things we would like to have but are not necessary to live. If there are things we need and want, we need resources to produce them. Resources are limited, and it is the scarcity or lack of resources that is the reason why we cannot have everything we want.

What are resources? There are three main categories of resources. These are:

- natural resources from the environment, for example, air, water, minerals, land, soil, food that is grown, energy from coal, oil or gas
- human resources, such as workers, business owners, volunteers, managers, teachers
- capital resources, including computers, trucks, tools and machines. These are used to make things. They also include roads, power and water supplies, as well as buildings such as schools and hospitals.

What if the different year levels in your school wanted their own oval at break time to stop arguments and to have unlimited space? Sounds ideal and fair as each year level is catered for. However, land is a natural resource, and your school may not have enough land to do this. This leads to scarcity of land. There are not enough land resources to provide for everyone's wants.

What if each Year Five student in your school could learn or play whatever sport they wanted during PE lessons? There would be a scarcity or lack of human resources in the form of PE teachers. There would not be enough teachers to teach all the different sports in the one lesson and perhaps a scarcity of the playing fields and courts needed.

What if each Year Five class wanted a 3D printer to print more PE teachers? There would be a lack of capital resources which would be the technology and printers required to do so. It is also doubtful that Year Fives would have access to this technology if it indeed exists.

So, can we all have everything we want? The answer is, only if there are enough resources at that point in time to produce what we want. If we all want things at the same time, there will be a scarcity of resources. So, the answer is: NO!

TARGETING ENGLISH HOMEWORK YEAR 5 © PASCAL PRESS ISBN 978 1 925726 62 6

Reading & Comprehension

Write the answer or shade the bubble next to the correct answer.

The answers to these questions are in the text.

1. In the text, what does **scarcity** mean?

____

2. Name the three main categories of **resources**.

____

3. Can we all have everything we want?

   ◯ Yes ◯ No

Think about these questions and search for the answers in the text.

4. If we all want things at the same time, what could happen to the resources?

____

5. The only way we can have **everything** we want is:

   ◯ if there are enough resources at that point in time to produce what we want.

   ◯ if all the resources become scarce.

   ◯ if we make new resources.

Use inferencing skills to answer these questions. The answers are not in the text. Think about what you know and what the author says.

6. At this point in time, are Year Fives able to 3D print more PE teachers?

   ◯ Yes ◯ No

Circle the category for each resource.

7. water in a river

   ◯ natural ◯ human ◯ capital

8. an iPad for all Year Five students

   ◯ natural ◯ human ◯ capital

9. your teacher

   ◯ natural ◯ human ◯ capital

10. the air we breathe

   ◯ natural ◯ human ◯ capital

11. a pizza oven in a pizza shop

   ◯ natural ◯ human ◯ capital

12. If you broaden your thinking to include the whole school, what could **one need** and **one want** be for your school?

   School need:

   ____

   School want:

   ____

13. List four **capital resources** you would find in a school.

   ____

   ____

   ____

   ____

Use your experience and opinions to answer these questions. The answers are not in the text.

Resources can be combined to produce a good or service, for example, the making of a pizza in a pizza shop.

14. List the different **resources** needed to produce a pizza.

   Natural resources could include:

   ____

   Human resources could include:

   ____

   Capital resources could include:

   ____

15. What would it be like if everyone got everything they wanted all the time?

   List one positive point:

   ____

   List one negative point:

   ____

Comprehension Reflections

Look at the top of the opposite page. This text is an I__________ text – E__________.

Write one thing you learned or found interesting:

____

Write one question you have or something you want to find more information about:

____

____

Rating

Score 2 points for each correct answer! SCORE /30 0-12 14-24 26-30

TERM 2

AC9E5LA05

TERM 2

Complex sentences

Complex sentences have a main or independent clause that can stand on its own and a dependent or subordinate clause that does not make sense on its own. These clauses are joined either in the middle or beginning of a sentence with conjunctions. A comma is used if the dependent clause is first in the sentence.

Examples:

Independent clause	Conjunction	Dependent/ subordinate clause
What a world it would be	if	we all got what we wanted all the time.
It sounds ideal and fair	as	each year level is catered for.
It is also doubtful that Year Fives would have access to this technology	if	it indeed exists.
We can satisfy our needs and wants	if	there are enough resources to produce them.
There will be a scarcity of resources	if	we all want things at the same time.

Jigsaw the sentences above so that the conjunction is at the start of the sentence. Write them on the lines below. The first one has been done for you.

Example: If we all got what we wanted all the time, what a world it would be.

1. ______________________________

2. ______________________________

3. ______________________________

4. ______________________________

Underline the conjunctions in these sentences.

5. As soon as the new technology is invented, Year Five students will print more PE teachers.
6. When more land becomes available, there will be ovals for all year levels.
7. Every Year Five student will be able to learn their chosen sport after more PE teachers are printed.

Jigsaw the sentences above and rewrite them by switching the starting clause and moving the conjunction.

8. ______________________________

9. ______________________________

10. ______________________________

Score 2 points for each correct answer! SCORE /20 0-8 10-14 16-20

TARGETING ENGLISH HOMEWORK YEAR 5 © PASCAL PRESS ISBN 978 1 925726 62 6

Phonic & Word Knowledge

Word building with 'tech/techni'

Technology is a word from the text. It has the root word 'tech' or 'techni', which comes from the Greek language meaning skill or ability.

How many words can you correctly make from the root word tech or techni? Write the words below the table and write your total number of words made.

Prefixes	Root word	Suffixes
nano		cian
micro		cal
bio	**tech**	que
	techni	colour
		cally
		nological
		nology

1. New words: ______________________________

____

____

____

Total number of words: ______________

Syllables part 1

All words have syllables. It is important to recognise syllables in words as it helps you learn to spell words correctly. When you say a word one syllable at a time, spelling becomes much easier.

One way to find how many syllables are in a word is to place your hand under your chin and then count the number of times your jaw drops as you say a word.

How many syllables in the following words?

2. resources _____
3. necessary _____
4. scarcity _____
5. unfortunately _____
6. unkindly _____

AC9E5LY09

Rules to find syllables

Every syllable must contain at least one vowel sound: a, e, i, o, u and y (a consonant that wants to be a vowel). Here are some rules to help:

- Divide after a prefix and before a suffix. *Examples:* re/write, friend/ly
- Divide between compound words. *Example:* birth/day

Practise these rules by drawing lines where the syllables are.

7. includes
8. evermore
9. statement
10. during
11. revealed
12. doubtful
13. unkindly

Another rule to help find syllables:

- Divide between two middle consonants: VC/CV. *Example:* bas/ket

However, keep th, sh, ch, qu and wh together.

Practise this rule by drawing lines between the syllables.

14. lesson
15. supplies
16. fantastic
17. splendid
18. answer
19. survive
20. access

And another rule to help find syllables:

- Divide after the consonant when the first vowel is short: VC/V. *Example:* cab/in

Practise this rule by drawing lines between the syllables.

21. level
22. limit
23. limited
24. finish
25. practise
26. shelter
27. example

And the last rule to help find syllables for now:

- Divide before the consonant when the first vowel is long: V/CV. *Example:* ba/sic

Practise this rule by drawing lines between the syllables. (Hint: 'ea' is one long vowel sound and 'ch' is one consonant sound.)

28. human
29. enough
30. student
31. clothing
32. cater
33. resource
34. teacher

Score 2 points for each correct answer! SCORE  /68  0-32  34-62  64-68

TERM 2

AC9E5LY04, AC9E5LY05, AC9S5U04

Informative text – Report

TERM 2

DANGEROUS LIQUID FOUND IN AUSTRALIA

Reported by Vand Wasser for the Primary Times

A dangerous liquid chemical compound has been found as the cause of many incidents in Australia.

Leading Australian chemist, W. Tappet, has sent an urgent message to all Australians to be mindful of the dangers of this liquid, known only as Liquid X.

Professor Tappet has explained that matter makes up everything on Earth, including us. She further explained that matter can exist in three different states: solid, liquid and gas. Each of these has different properties which are explained by how the particles they are made of are arranged and move.

In a solid, the particles have less energy and take up a set volume and shape. In a liquid, the particles have more energy and still take up a set volume but can change shape. A gas has particles with a lot of energy and so does not take up a set volume or shape.

However, Liquid X can change between all three states of matter. It can be a solid, liquid or gas, but the main source is found in a liquid form or state. If heat is taken away from it, Liquid X can turn into a solid compound. If heat is added to Liquid X, it can readily turn into a gas.

It is colourless, odourless and tasteless, and has been linked to the erosion of natural landscapes and loss of people's houses in times of natural disasters. It has caused severe burns to people and is dangerous if you breathe it in.

Liquid X is everywhere. It has been found in our rivers, lakes, oceans and streams. Athletes have been using Liquid X to enhance their performance, and it has been used as an additive in certain 'junk foods' and other food products.

Year Five students have been known to willingly consume Liquid X daily and even been told to do so by teachers. Parents have knowingly bought Liquid X for their children.

The Australian Government is looking into the handling of Liquid X and has plans in the future for the storage of this dangerous liquid compound. Be aware of how you handle it and where you come across it.

TARGETING ENGLISH HOMEWORK YEAR 5 © PASCAL PRESS ISBN 978 1 925726 62 6

Reading & Comprehension

Write the answer or shade the bubble next to the correct answer.

The answers to these questions are in the text.

1. **What is the name of the newspaper?**

   ____

2. **In what state of matter is Liquid X usually found?**

   ____

3. **If heat is applied to Liquid X, what does it turn into?**

   ____

Think about these questions and search for the answers in the text.

4. **Which particles have more energy?**
   - ◯ solids
   - ◯ liquids
   - ◯ gases

5. **Name two places where Liquid X has been found.**

   ____

   ____

6. **Who has consumed Liquid X? Name two groups of people.**

   ____

   ____

7. **According to the report, Liquid X is considered dangerous. Give two reasons why.**

   ____

   ____

Use inferencing skills to answer these questions. The answers are not in the text. Think about what you know and what the author says.

8. **What is Liquid X?**

   ____

9. **How can Liquid X be dangerous if you breathe it in?**

   ____

   ____

10. **How could Liquid X be responsible for destroying houses in a natural disaster?**

    ____

    ____

Use your experience and opinions to answer these questions. The answers are not in the text.

11. **Where would Liquid X be found in the world in its solid form?**

    ____

    ____

12. **Where would Liquid X be found in the world as a gas?**

    ____

    ____

13. **Do you consider Liquid X to be dangerous? Give two reasons for your answer.**

    ____

    ____

14. **How would the government store Liquid X in Australia?**

    ____

    ____

TERM 2

Comprehension Reflections

Look at the top of the opposite page. This text is an I__________ text – R__________.

Write one thing you learned or found interesting:

____

Write one question you have or something you want to find more information about:

____

____

Rating   

Score 2 points for each correct answer!

SCORE 

Grammar & Punctuation

AC9E5LA08

TERM 2

Double negatives

The Year Five student pleaded with the teacher, "I didn't do nothing! I don't have no Liquid X. I did not bring no Liquid X to school!" The teacher sent the child to the principal. Why?

The student used double negatives. *Examples of negative words:* no, not, nothing, nobody, hardly, neither, never, scarcely, or any word that ends in **n't** such as did**n't**, should**n't**

A double negative is a sentence that contains two negatives like those underlined above. These cancel each other out and form a positive. So, it seems the student is saying, "I did do something. I do have Liquid X. I brought Liquid X to school."

To correct a double negative, you should change one of the negative words. So, the student should have said, "I didn't do anything! I don't have any Liquid X. I did not bring Liquid X to school!" There is only one negative per sentence and no trip to the principal!

Help this Year Five child with their sentences. Circle the negative words and decide if the sentence is correct. If there are two negatives, rewrite the sentence with only one negative word.

Example:

At school, I (haven't) drunk Liquid X (hardly) at all.

correct / (incorrect)

At school, I haven't drunk Liquid X at all.

1. In fact, I didn't buy no Liquid X.
   correct / incorrect

2. No-one saw nothing, so I am innocent!
   correct / incorrect

3. However, I don't want to be left out of the Year Five contest.
   correct / incorrect

4. I haven't yet received no answer to my request to enter.
   correct / incorrect

5. No-one wants to miss out on the Year Five chocolate-eating contest.
   correct / incorrect

6. Last time, I did not hardly come close to being a winner.
   correct / incorrect

7. Not neither of my contest results over the term were high enough to let me win.
   correct / incorrect

8. If I can always break the record, it is not scarcely a challenge.
   correct / incorrect

9. I will not never break the chocolate-eating record for Year Five unless I use Liquid X to help wash it all down. Just don't tell the teachers.
   correct / incorrect

Score 2 points for each correct answer!

SCORE /18   0-6 8-14 16-18

TARGETING ENGLISH HOMEWORK YEAR 5 © PASCAL PRESS ISBN 978 1 925726 62 6

Phonic & Word Knowledge

AC9E5LY09

Silent letters

Some words include letters which are not pronounced when the word is spoken. The word breathe from the text has a silent 'e' at the end. Without the 'e', the word becomes breath pronounced 'breth', which is a different word. It can be tricky to remember silent letters.

Circle the silent letter in each word below.

Example: Wednesday

1. sign
2. ghost
3. science
4. doubt
5. often
6. column
7. mortgage
8. knife
9. island

Choose words from the activity above to complete the text below.

It was on (10) ______________ that I read the newspaper article about Liquid X. I had to read each (11) ______________ of the article twice to make sure I understood it.

I do not (12) ______________ that Liquid X is dangerous. I don't (13) ______________ become scared, but I am this time. I may have to visit the bank to take out a (14) ______________ to buy an (15) ______________ in the Pacific Ocean to escape Liquid X. Or would I escape it?

Syllables part 2

Continuing from Unit 11, it is important to recognise syllables in words as it helps you learn to spell words correctly. You looked at dividing a word after a long vowel V/CV. However, if the vowel is short, it takes a friend for protection, so you divide after the consonant VC/V or VC/C.
Example: un/able, ac/cept

Practise the syllable rules by dividing the words below.

16. enhance
17. athletes
18. limit
19. exhale
20. undo
21. properties
22. volume
23. explained

More rules

- If two vowels are next to each other, but they are not a pair (make one sound), split between them V/V. *Example:* li/on
- However, if two letters make one sound, they are counted as one, such as 'er', 'or', 'ie', 'ee'. *Example:* or/der
- For words that end in a consonant and 'le' such as 'ble', you count back three or divide before the consonant. *Example:* ta/ble
- However, if it is a 'ckle' word, you count the 'ck' sound as one. *Example:* pi/ckle

Practise these rules by dividing the words below.

24. being
25. whistle
26. trickle
27. riddle
28. fluid
29. media
30. biology
31. castle

You dropped something

Many words drop a letter when adding a suffix, but it is not always the final letter.
Example: disaster – disas**trous** ('e' dropped)

Complete the table below by writing what suffix is added and what letter was dropped.

	Base word	New word	Suffix added	Letter dropped
	e.g. disaster	disastrous	ous	e
32	argue	argument		
33	proceed	procedure		
34	humour	humorous		
35	administer	administration		
36	repeat	repetition		

Unscramble these words where the syllables have been mixed around and write them on the line. The words appear somewhere on this page.

37. trous-as-dis ______________
38. ties-prop-er ______________
39. on-li ______________
40. nant-so-con ______________
41. tra-tion-min-ad-is ______________
42. e-tion-ti-rep ______________

Score 2 points for each correct answer! SCORE /84 0-40 42-78 80-84

TERM 2

Persuasive text – Discussion

Should Year Five Students be Allowed to Drive to School?

Currently, students need to be aged 16 or over before they can learn to drive. What if the driving age was lowered for Year Five students so they could drive as far as the local school and back? There are advantages and disadvantages to this proposal. Many parents and caregivers find school drop-offs and pick-ups stressful and would be happy to find a solution to the morning rush. But do Year Five students have the maturity to handle driving a car for even such a short distance? There are two sides to the argument.

On the one hand, if Year Five students drove to school, parents would not have to pick up or drop off students. This would give parents more freedom in their work and life schedules and make for a happier home. There would be no blaming of parents for students being late to school as students would need to organise their own way to school. This would certainly help students develop time-management skills as well as a feeling of independence and responsibility. It would even be an incentive to attend school and would decrease the number of absences.

Finally, Year Five students would start to develop a lifelong skill, as driving is something that would stay with them for the rest of their lives. The earlier you become good at it, the more experienced and responsible a driver you will end up being.

On the other hand, it may seem reckless and dangerous to put a powerful machine in the hands of primary school students. Year Five students can be easily distracted and would find it difficult to maintain concentration during busy times on the road. They are not mature enough to make the quick decisions necessary when under pressure in traffic. This is especially the case at school drop-offs and pick-ups, which are usually very busy times around schools.

If students were allowed to drive, schools would have to provide enough parking spaces for student parking. This may not be possible for many schools.

In conclusion, it seems safer to keep the driving age at the present age of 16 and not allow Year Five students to drive to school. Even though learning to drive is a lifelong skill, students in Year Five may need time to develop the maturity and responsibility required to handle a car on the road.

Reading & Comprehension

Write the answer or shade the bubble next to the correct answer.

The answers to these questions are in the text.

1. **What age do you need to be to learn to drive?**

   ____

2. **When are the stressful times of the day for parents and caregivers?**

   ____

   ____

3. **What would help students develop time-management skills as well as a feeling of independence and responsibility?**

   ____

   ____

4. **What are the benefits of learning to drive at an early age?**

   ____

   ____

Think about these questions and search for the answers in the text.

5. **Does the author of the text think Year Fives should drive to school?**

   ◯ Yes ◯ No

6. **Which row shows how this argument is organised?**

	Beginning	Middle	End
◯	Introduction	All points that agree with Year Fives driving	Conclusion
◯	Introduction where the topic and some points are introduced	Points that agree with Year Fives driving and points that disagree with Year Fives driving	Conclusion where the author gives their opinion
◯	Points that agree with Year Fives driving	Points that disagree with Year Fives driving	Conclusion where the author gives their opinion

Use inferencing skills to answer these questions. The answers are not in the text. Think about what you know and what the author says.

7. **Why could learning to drive be an incentive to attend school and possibly decrease the number of absences?**

   ____

   ____

8. **Do you agree or disagree with the following statement from the text?**

   Year Five students can be easily distracted and would find it difficult to maintain concentration during busy times on the road.

   ◯ Agree ◯ Disagree

   Write one sentence to explain your thinking behind your answer.

   ____

   ____

Use your experience and opinions to answer these questions. The answers are not in the text.

9. **Put on your thinking cap. What is one possible new point as to why Year Five students should be allowed to drive to school?**

   ____

10. **What is one possible new point as to why Year Five students should not be allowed to drive to school?**

    ____

Comprehension Reflections

Look at the top of the opposite page. This text is a P__________ text – D__________.

Write one thing you learned or found interesting:

____

Write one question you have or something you want to find more information about:

____

____

Rating   

Score 2 points for each correct answer! SCORE 

Grammar & Punctuation

AC9E5LA08, AC9E5LA05, AC9E5LY03

Complex sentences

Complex sentences have dependent and independent clauses joined together by a conjunction. The conjunction can go at the start of the sentence or in the middle.

If the sentence starts with the dependent clause, it is followed by a comma.

You can jigsaw a complex sentence to start with a different clause. Put a circle around the dependent clause in each set of sentences and underline the conjunction.

Example:

Students need to be aged 16 or over before they can learn to drive.

Before they can learn to drive, students need to be aged 16 or over.

1. After they learn to drive, students develop a feeling of independence and responsibility.
   Students develop a feeling of independence and responsibility after they learn to drive.
2. Year Fives are not mature enough to make the quick decisions necessary when they are under pressure in traffic.
   When they are under pressure in traffic, Year Fives are not mature enough to make the quick decisions necessary.
3. If students were allowed to drive, schools would have to provide enough parking spaces for student parking.
   Schools would have to provide enough parking spaces for student parking if students were allowed to drive.

Persuasive devices – Emotive language

A persuasive text uses persuasive devices to sway the reader to a particular point of view. In this text, the author has used emotive language to influence the reader.
Examples: stressful, happily, blaming, need, incentive, lifelong, earlier

Find emotive words in the text to complete the following sentences.

This would give parents (4) ______________ in their work and life schedules and make for a (5) ______________ home.

On the other hand, it may seem (6) ______________ and (7) ______________ to put a (8) ______________ machine in the hands of primary school students.

Circle which emotive words you would use to persuade readers that Year Fives are capable of driving.

9. The __________ Year Five student sat behind the steering wheel of the car.
   responsible / rebellious / distressed
10. She __________ drove the car up the road towards the school.
    recklessly / haphazardly / vigilantly
11. As she drove, she had __________ look upon her face.
    an absorbed / an evil / a ruthless
12. The student made sure she drove in __________ manner.
    an erratic / a focused / a dazed
13. As she neared the school, the student __________ around the corner to the car park.
    screeched / drifted / navigated
14. A teacher's car was approaching the same parking spot, so the student did the right thing and __________ the park.
    relinquished / snaffled / seized

Score 2 points for each correct answer! SCORE /28   

TARGETING ENGLISH HOMEWORK YEAR 5 © PASCAL PRESS ISBN 978 1 925726 62 6

Phonic & Word Knowledge

UNIT 13

AC9E5LY09

Context clues

To figure out the meanings of words in a text, you need to use context clues. This means looking at the words and phrases around the word you are looking at to get ideas about what it could mean.

Circle the best word to replace the bold word in each sentence. Use context clues, not a dictionary.

1. The Year Five student drove **erratically** around the streets. One minute she was on the right side of the road and the next she was on the footpath and heading for a teacher's car.
   safely / quickly / unsteadily
2. The teacher was **parsimonious** and had refused to spend money on the upkeep of his car. It looked dented and uncared for; however, it was now in the path of the approaching Year Five driver.
   stingy / helpful / happy
3. The student let out a **histrionic** groan. She threw her arms in the air and pulled her hair. She closed her eyes and waited for the impact.
   quiet / dramatic / squeaky
4. With great **dynamism** the teacher leapt into action. He leapt through the open window of the approaching car and grabbed the steering wheel just in time to miss his own car.
   energy / terror / humour
5. With a feeling of **trepidation**, the student got back behind the wheel. Even though her hands shook, and her stomach felt queasy, she continued the drive back to school.
   sorrow / relief / nervousness

Syllables

In previous units, you have looked at some of the rules for dividing words into syllables. You may need to look back at Units 11 and 12 to help you in the next activity.

Circle the correct division of syllables for each word.

6. **experienced**
   ex-per-i-enced | ex-per-i-ence-d | exp-eri-enced
7. **management**
   man-a-ge-ment | man-age-ment | manage-ment
8. **concentration**
   conc-en-tra-tion | concen-tra-tion | con-cen-tra-tion
9. **disadvantages**
   dis-ad-van-tag-es | dis-ad-van-ta-ges | dis-ad-van-tages

Accented syllables

When a word has more than one syllable, one of the syllables is always a little louder than the others. The louder syllable is called an accented syllable as it has the most stress put on it.

Example: 'Banana' in syllables is ba-na-na. The middle syllable is accented or said slightly louder than the other syllables and more stretched out: ba-**NA**-na.

Identifying accented syllables is important in successfully reading longer words.

Circle the word with the correctly accented syllable.

Example: ta-BLE — TA-ble (circled)

10. AL-bum — Al-BUM
11. RAB-bit — rab-BIT
12. IN-sist — in-SIST
13. UN-less — un-LESS
14. SAD-ness — sad-NESS
15. COL-lect — col-LECT

Score 2 points for each correct answer!

SCORE /30    

0-12 | 14-24 | 26-30

TERM 2

Informative text – Explanation

TERM 2

Would You Freeze Without a Spacesuit?

What would happen to you if you found yourself outside the International Space Station without a spacesuit? Would you freeze? Not at first. It would take 18 to 36 hours to freeze in space. Would you explode?

Fun fact!

A human body would expand, but the skin would be elastic enough to cope with the pressure change, so you would not explode. One handy tip is to not take a big breath and hold it because your lungs would explode. Instead, expel or blow out all the air in your lungs first. You would, however, still die, and very quickly, due to a lack of oxygen to the brain. You would become unconscious in 15 seconds and have one more minute before dying. So, do not find yourself outside a spacecraft without a spacesuit.

Now, back to freezing! Everything is made of matter, including us. However, in space, next to the International Space Station, there is no matter. It is a vacuum. Because there is no matter to transfer heat (take or give heat away), space is neither cold nor hot. Spaceships and satellites do not freeze in space; however, your body would eventually freeze if you were without a spacesuit.

Freezing is the process where a liquid turns into a solid. This happens when the particles that make up a liquid lose energy, so they move less and stick together to form a solid. This is called heat transfer. However, this is a reversible change. The particles can be given heat by heat transfer, causing them to move more quickly to form a liquid. This process of a solid turning into a liquid is called melting.

Why do the liquids in our bodies take so long to freeze in space? There are three main ways to transfer heat: conduction, convection and radiation. Conduction occurs when heat is transferred from one solid object to another through direct contact, such as burning your hand if you touch a hot stove. But since you are floating out in space and not touching anything, as it is a vacuum, you will not lose heat this way.

Convection is when heat is transferred through air or water. For example, you can cool down the temperature of your body by turning on a fan. But space is a vacuum and there is no air or water to allow heat to be taken away or transferred from you.

Finally, there is radiation – and this is really the only way you can freeze in space. Radiation occurs when you lose heat from your body by sending out heatwaves, like a stove giving off heat. This is a much slower transfer of heat energy.

So, if in the future you are travelling in space, watch which door you step through and make sure a spacesuit is handy.

TARGETING ENGLISH HOMEWORK YEAR 5 © PASCAL PRESS ISBN 978 1 925726 62 6

Reading & Comprehension

TERM 2

Write the answer or shade the bubble next to the correct answer.

The answers to these questions are in the text.

1. How long would it take for you to **freeze** in space without a spacesuit?

2. Why should you not take a big breath of air before you find yourself outside a spaceship without a spacesuit?

3. What will you eventually die from if stranded in space without a suit?

4. What is **heat transfer**?

5. What are the three main ways to transfer heat?

Think about these questions and search for the answers in the text.

6. Which of the three ways of heat transfer will eventually **cool our body** in space?

7. Why does being in a vacuum in space stop the other two methods of heat transfer?

8. What is the difference between **freezing** and **melting**?

Use inferencing skills to answer these questions. The answers are not in the text. Think about what you know and what the author says.

9. If you are melting chocolate, what happens to the chocolate molecules?

10. Once you have melted chocolate, can you **reverse** the change?

 ◯ Yes ◯ No

11. Explain your answer.

Use your experience and opinions to answer this question. The answer is not in the text.

12. If you put the melted chocolate outside the International Space Station, would it change state? Explain your thinking.

Comprehension Reflections

Look at the top of the opposite page. This text is an I__________ text – E__________.

Write one thing you learned or found interesting:

Write one question you have or something you want to find more information about:

Rating   

Score 2 points for each correct answer! SCORE /24   

UNIT 14

Grammar & Punctuation

AC9E5LA08, AC9E5LA05, AC9E5LY06

TERM 2

Present tense

An explanation is non-fiction writing that explains how or why things happen. This text explains three different forms of heat transfer and why you wouldn't freeze in space straightaway without a spacesuit.

Explanations are written in present tense, but there are different forms of present tense.

Simple present	Present continuous	Present perfect	Present perfect continuous
Just the verb (no helping verb)	Helping/ auxiliary verb: **am/ is/are** + -ing verb	Helping/ auxiliary verb: **have/has** + past participle	Helping/ auxiliary verb: **have/has** + been + -ing verb
I **go** to outer space.	The ice **is melting** slowly.	The fan **has cooled** me down.	They **have been waiting** for you.
She **flies** a space-ship.	If you **are travelling** in space, wear a suit.	You **have worn** a spacesuit today.	Chris **has been checking** the suits for leaks.

Write which form of present tense is in each sentence. The verbs are bold for the first three sentences, then find the verbs on your own.

1. I **love** anything to do with space.
   ____
2. I **have been practising** my spacewalk moves for the camera. ______________________
3. I **have chosen** the green spacesuit for the event. ______________________
4. Hmmm, a spacesuit is unnecessary.
   ____
5. The astronaut is floating in space.
   ____
6. I have decided, no suit.
   ____
7. I am standing in the airlock of the ship.
   ____
8. I have worn a onesie for the cold weather.
   ____
9. I have taken a large breath of air into my lungs. ______________________
10. The cameras have been filming me this whole time. ______________________
11. I step out of the airlock with care.
    ____
12. My lungs are expanding!
    ____

Cause and effect

An explanation has many complex sentences that are used to show cause and effect. The clauses in a complex sentence are linked by a conjunction or joining word.

conjunction ↓   cause {between brackets} ↓

Example: Because {there is no matter to transfer heat,} {space is neither cold nor hot.}

↑ effect {between brackets}

The complex sentences from the text show cause and effect. Circle the cause, underline the effect and put a box around the conjunction.

13. Your body will eventually freeze if you are without a spacesuit.
14. If you take a big breath and hold it, your lungs will explode.
15. As there is no matter in space, space is a vacuum.
16. A liquid turns into a solid because the liquid particles lose energy and move less.

Score 2 points for each correct answer! SCORE 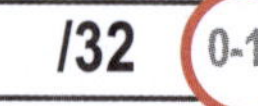 /32  0-14  16-26  28-32

TARGETING ENGLISH HOMEWORK YEAR 5 © PASCAL PRESS ISBN 978 1 925726 62 6

Phonic & Word Knowledge

AC9E5LY09

Tricky words with double letters

The word vacuum has the rare double 'u'. The word comes from the Latin 'vacuus', meaning empty. Some words with double letters are tricky to spell and need practise to learn.

Look, cover, write and check the tricky words listed below. Do this three times for each word.

1. embarrass

 ______ ______ ______

2. success

 ______ ______ ______

3. disappear

 ______ ______ ______

4. necessary

 ______ ______ ______

5. occurred

 ______ ______ ______

6. possession

 ______ ______ ______

Use the words above to complete the paragraph.

I stepped out into the vacuum of space and then it (7) ______________ to me that I should have put a spacesuit on. I tried to get back inside the spaceship, but I had no (8) ______________. I thought it was not (9) ______________ to use a suit as I would not freeze immediately or explode; however, I didn't want to (10) ______________ into the blackness of space. I also didn't want to (11) ______________ myself and call for help although I did have a radio in my (12) ______________ that I could have used.

Tricky words to pronounce

When you come across a word that is tricky to pronounce, sound it out from the start to the end. Breaking it up into syllables will help you sound it out.
Example:
supercalifragilisticexpialidocious

13. **Sound out each of the 14 syllables. Pronounce it correctly to an adult and circle 'completed' when you have finished.**

 su-per-cal-i-frag-i-lis-tic-ex-pi-al-i-do-cious

 completed / not completed

Many English words have come from other languages and may be difficult to say. Complete the table below and tick the column when you have successfully pronounced the word to an adult three times.

	Word	Meaning	Correctly pronounced 3 times to an adult	✓
14	asthma	a condition that affects the airways	as-muh (don't say the 'th')	
15	anemone	a sea animal that looks like a flower	uh-neh-muh-nee	
16	colonel	a rank of officer	ker-nuhl	
17	mischievous	causing trouble in a playful way	mis-chuh-vuhs	
18	epitome	a perfect example	uh-pi-tuh-mee	
19	juror	member of a jury	juor-ruh	
20	hyperbole	an exaggeration	hai-per-buh-lee	

Score 2 points for each correct answer! SCORE /40    

TERM 2

AC9E5LY04, AC9E5LY05, AC9HS5K08

Informative text – Procedure

Making an Informed Decision on What to Buy

Happy birthday! You have just been given $45 birthday money to spend. So, what needs or wants would you like to satisfy? It just so happens that the latest thing you want is on sale at two different places. You need to make an informed decision.

To make an informed decision, you need to follow 5 steps:

1. Work out what you want.
2. Do some research to find out where you can get it.
3. Evaluate or assess each product you find. Look at cost and whether it satisfies your needs.
4. Purchase (buy) it.
5. See if it is what you want or return it.

How does that process work when buying a homework machine?

Step 1: Work out what you want. You want a homework machine. This, you know for sure.

Step 2: Where can you get it? You have found two adverts (below) that tell you the price and some of the conditions if you purchase the product. Each advert uses different persuasive devices to convince you to buy the product.

You are up to Step 3: Evaluate and work out which machine is the best for you, the Relaxo or the FFYF. Do you have a budget? A budget is a plan for saving and spending. It looks at the money you have and the money you want to spend. So, how much of your birthday money do you want to spend?

Step 4: Which machine will you buy, the Relaxo or the FFYF?

Step 5: Is the machine what you wanted after all? Does it work for you? Will you keep it or return it?

The five steps can be used for simple decisions such as what to buy for your lunch or more complex decisions such as buying clothes, an iPad or a present for a friend.

So, next time you are assigned homework, will you wish you had bought one of the homework machines?

TERM 2

TARGETING ENGLISH HOMEWORK YEAR 5 © PASCAL PRESS ISBN 978 1 925726 62 6

Reading & Comprehension

Write the answer or shade the bubble next to the correct answer.

The answers to these questions are in the text.

1. How many steps do you need to follow to make an informed decision?

____

2. How much birthday money were you given?

____

3. What does **FFYF** stand for?

____

4. What is a **budget**?

____

Think about these questions and search for the answers in the text.

To help you do Step 3 and analyse the products, complete the table for each product.

	Criteria	Relaxo	FFYF
5	price		
6	change from your birthday money		
7	how long the offer lasts		
8	waiting time to buy it		
9	guarantee provided		
10	the message the advert is giving		
11	the advert that appeals to you more		

Use inferencing skills to answer these questions. The answers are not in the text. Think about what you know and what the author says.

12. Which **step** in the process do you think is the most important and why?

____

____

____

13. What does the advert imply or suggest if you **do not buy** the FFYF machine?

____

____

14. Based on the information in the table and depending on which advert appeals to you, which machine would you buy?

◯ Relaxo ◯ FFYF

Why did you pick the one you did? Write a sentence explaining your choice.

____

____

Use your experience and opinions to answer these questions. The answers are not in the text.

15. Write a sentence explaining why a homework machine **would be a good idea.**

____

____

____

16. Write a sentence explaining why a homework machine **would not be a good idea.**

____

____

____

Comprehension Reflections

Look at the top of the opposite page. This text is an I__________ text – P__________.

Write one thing you learned or found interesting:

____

Write one question you have or something you want to find more information about:

____

____

Rating   

Score 2 points for each correct answer! SCORE /32  0-14  16-26  28-32

TERM 2

AC9E5LA08, AC9E5LA03

TERM 2

Advertising and persuasive devices

Advertising is a form of persuasive text, so it uses many persuasive devices. Part of an advertisement includes a brand name. The name needs to be short and snappy as well as reflect what you want your audience to think about when they hear or see the name. If you were to buy laundry detergent, would you buy one called 'Grind' or 'Dash'? Probably 'Dash' as the name suggests it will work fast and you will finish the laundry quickly.

Circle the most appropriate name for the products listed.

1 **cat food** Frisky Gutso Picky Filler

2 **deodorant** Pong Fresh Itchy Dead Zone

3 **toothpaste** Scour Squeeze Bright Fang

Choose the best name for your team on sports day that reflects your team's strength and determination.

4 **An animal name**
Koalas Wildcats Sloths Cougars

5 **An insect name**
Ants Hornets Dragonflies Aphids

6 **A bird name**
Sparrows Pigeons Falcons Pelicans

7 **Which name would you finally choose out of all those listed? Why?**

____

____

Alliteration

The advert for the FFYF machine uses an alliteration as a persuasive device: Freedom For Year Fives. It makes the brand more memorable for the reader, and the key idea remains in their minds.

Alliteration happens when words that start with the same **sound** – not necessarily the same letter – are repeated within the same phrase or sentence. The words do not have to be right next to each other. *Example alliteration for a car advert:* Don't dream it, drive it!

Create your own advertising alliterations for each product by adding at least two more words with the same sound.

Example:
shampoo **sh**immer and **sh**ine with **sh**ampoo

8 soda ______________________________

____

9 doughnuts ______________________________

____

10 pies ______________________________

____

Imperatives

The FFYF advert also uses imperative sentences as a persuasive device. This means they make direct requests and commands. *Examples:* Be cool like me. Don't be a loser, be a groover, like me!

You hear imperative sentences every day. *Examples:* Clean your room. Close the door. Please pass the salt.

11 **Write two imperative sentences you would hear from your teacher.**

____

____

____

____

12 **Write two imperative sentences you would hear from your parent/s or caregiver/s.**

____

____

____

____

13 **Write an imperative sentence you would hear from your friends.**

____

____

Score 2 points for each correct answer! SCORE /26  0-10  12-20  22-26

TARGETING ENGLISH HOMEWORK YEAR 5 © PASCAL PRESS ISBN 978 1 925726 62 6

Word building with 'cide' and 'cise'

The word decision in the text comes from the Latin base word 'cide' or 'cise', meaning cut, and the prefix 'de', meaning off. So, a decision means to cut off everything except what is most important.

Use the table to build words using the base words 'cide' and 'cise'. The 'e' is dropped when certain suffixes are added.

Prefix	Base word	Suffix 1	Suffix 2	New word
in	cide	ent		*Example:* **incident**
in		ent	al	1
co in				2
homi				3
pesti				4
de				5
herbi				6
ac		ent		7
con	cise			8
in		ive		9
in		ion		10
de		ion		11

Choose words you made from the table to complete these sentences.

12. You must make a ____________ about which homework machine you would like to buy.
13. Your improved marks for homework should happen at the same time, or ____________ with the time you started using the homework machine.
14. Just make sure your teacher doesn't find out or something unpleasant, like an ____________, may happen.

Comparative and superlative adjectives with 'er' and 'est'

When comparing two things, you use the suffix 'er' to make the comparative adjective.
Examples: The FFYF machine is cheap**er**. The Relaxo is nic**er**.

When comparing more than two things, you use the suffix 'est' to make the superlative adjective.
Example: The FFYF is the great**est** thing I've ever bought for myself.

For adjectives that end in 'y', change the 'y' to an 'i' and add 'er' or 'est'.
Examples: nois**y** – nois**ier**/nois**iest**
happ**y** – happ**ier**/happ**iest**

Circle the correct word for each sentence.

15. My dog is ____________ than your cat. cleaner / cleanest
16. Oh yeah? My cat is the ____________ in the whole street. faster / fastest
17. Your cat is the ____________ of our two pets. noisier / noisiest
18. Well, you are the ____________ kid in the class. noisier / noisiest

Comparing with 'more' and 'most'

If the comparison word you use has three syllables or more, you do not add 'er' or 'est'. You add more for comparing two things and most when comparing more than two. *Example:* Attractive is a three-syllable word (at-trac-tive). Your cat is the **more attractive** of our two pets. However, my dog is the **most attractive** out of all the dogs in the neighbourhood.

Circle the correct word for each sentence.

19. It is ____________ important to complete our homework than watch TV. more / most
20. Really? Then the ____________ important decision of all is to get the right homework machine. more / most

Score 2 points for each correct answer! SCORE /40    

Reading & Comprehension

AC9E5LY04, AC9E5LY05

Imaginative text – Narrative

The Ship

"Listen!" she whispered, her body rigid with fear. "There's something in here!" The decaying, grey and battered ship was moored by the shore. Chris and her two friends had decided to paddle to the ship on their boards to take a closer look at the strange, three-masted sailing ship. It seemed to have magically appeared overnight.

While exploring the decks of the ancient ship, their talk turned to stories of scarred and bloodthirsty pirates. Chris told the story that pirates would hire sailors to join their crew for the price of a golden coin. That afternoon, their imaginations and conversations were full of treasure and sword fights as they clambered downstairs to the lower deck.

An explosion of noise brought them back to the stairs, but they found themselves trapped below deck. The old, wooden hatch had slammed shut, trapping them in the dark and damp cabin. That was when they felt it. The air became as cold as a grave, and as quiet. Their breath came out in little clouds of condensation as the temperature plummeted in the cabin. Water that had been dripping from the cabin roof lost all energy and changed into icicles that hung like jagged arrows from above.

A slow and steady scraping noise was heard inside the cabin. This was when Chris alerted her friends that something was in the cabin with them. She watched with alarm as her friends desperately lunged and pulled at the hatch. They finally splintered the old wood and gained their freedom.

The water had been tranquil and glassy when they started out, but over the previous hour, while they had been exploring, the sea had turned murderous. Crested waves tumbled to the shore, making it impossible to paddle back safely.

******

The next morning, the sea was quiet and peaceful. The sun rose higher into the soft blue sky and with it came the heat of another glorious summer day. The old ship shimmered in the heat and seemed to melt, slowly becoming part of the sea itself and disappearing from view. Floating on the water where the ship had been was a child's board, bobbing gently on the tide. A crab was perched on top, slowly making its sideways journey to the edge of the board. It made a slow and steady scraping sound as it moved until it slipped silently into the sea. On the board, it left three golden coins shimmering in the sun. A pirate's flag was printed clearly on the face of each coin.

TERM 2

TARGETING ENGLISH HOMEWORK YEAR 5 © PASCAL PRESS ISBN 978 1 925726 62 6

Reading & Comprehension

Write the answer or shade the bubble next to the correct answer.

The answers to these questions are in the text.

① How many people paddled to the ship?

② Where were they trapped?

③ What time of year was it?

○ spring ○ summer ○ winter

④ Why could they not paddle back to the safety of the shore?

Think about these questions and search for the answers in the text.

⑤ How does the author let you know that it was **very cold** below deck? List three clues from the text.

⑥ How did they **escape** to get back up to the deck of the ship?

Use inferencing skills to answer these questions. The answers are not in the text. Think about what you know and what the author says.

⑦ What was in the cabin making the **scraping noise**?

⑧ What do you think happened to Chris and her friends?

⑨ Why were **three gold coins** left on the board?

⑩ The sea had turned **murderous**. Why would it have been described that way?

⑪ Find **plummeted** in the third paragraph. The sentences around it give you an idea of its meaning. Which word has a similar meaning?

○ fell ○ climbed ○ wobbled

Use your experience and opinions to answer these questions. The answers are not in the text.

⑫ Why would pirates be **scarred**?

⑬ Was it okay for the children to paddle out and explore the ship? Give a reason for your answer.

Comprehension Reflections

Look at the top of the opposite page. This text is an I__________ text – N__________.

Write one thing you learned or found interesting:

Write one question you have or something you want to find more information about:

Rating

Score 2 points for each correct answer! SCORE /26 0-10 12-20 22-26

TERM 2

Grammar & Punctuation

AC9E5LA06, AC9E5LA08

TERM 2

Noun groups

Remember! A noun is the name of a person, place or thing. When you want to describe a noun, you can add describing words (adjectives) before or after it to form a noun group.

Draw lines to match the adjectives to the noun to form a noun group. You may need to look back at the text.

Adjectives	**Noun**
Example: dark and damp	cabin
(1) decaying, grey and battered	pirates
(2) glorious summer	noise
(3) quiet and peaceful	day
(4) soft blue	journey
(5) scarred and bloodthirsty	ship
(6) explosion of	sky
(7) sideways	sea

Write two of your own descriptive adjectives for each underlined noun.

Example: The coins were **circular** and **golden**.

(8) The ________________ and ________________ waves pounded the shore.

(9) The pirate's face was ________________ and ________________.

(10) The ________________ and ________________ crab sat on the board.

Similes for description

Similes are used in descriptions to compare one thing to another using like or as.

There are two similes in the text. Write them below.

(11) ____

____

(12) ____

____

Verb groups – Auxiliary verbs

Verb groups can contain a main verb on its own or a main verb with a helper, called an auxiliary verb. These underlined main verbs from the text have helpers or auxiliary verbs.

Examples:

was moored — was: auxiliary verb; moored: main verb
would hire — would: auxiliary verb; hire: main verb
had turned — had: auxiliary verb; turned: main verb

Find the following verbs in the text and write the auxiliary verbs in the spaces provided.

Example: **was** heard

(13) ____________ decided

(14) ____________ slammed

(15) ____________ exploring

(16) ____________ heard

(17) ____________ perched

(18) ____________ printed

Adverbs ending in 'ly'

Verb groups can also contain adverbs that describe the action. Often these adverbs end in 'ly' but not always. *Examples:* quick**ly**, week**ly**, always, never

Find the adverbs in the text that describe the verbs listed below. Write them in the spaces provided.

Example: **magically** appeared

(19) ______________ lunged

(20) bobbing ______________

(21) ______________ splintered

(22) slipped ______________

(23) printed ______________

Think of adverbs ending in 'ly' to describe the following underlined verbs.

Year Five students sing (24) ______________ly as well as dance (25) ______________ly.

Score 2 points for each correct answer! SCORE /50 0-22 24-44 46-50

TARGETING ENGLISH HOMEWORK YEAR 5 © PASCAL PRESS ISBN 978 1 925726 62 6

UNIT 16

Phonic & Word Knowledge

AC9E5LY09

Spelling generalisations – Double letters

When you add a suffix to a word, how do you know when to double the last letter? Look out for words that:

- have one syllable
- have one short vowel sound (a, e, i, o, u)
- end in one consonant (the other letters).

This only applies when you add the suffixes: ed, ing, er, est, y, ish.

Complete the tables by adding the suffix provided. One table contains words that are from the text and the other does not.

	Root word	Suffix	New word (from the text)
	Example: slam	ed	slammed
1	trap	ed	
2	drip	ing	
3	bob	ing	
4	slip	ed	
5	jag	ed	

	Root word	Suffix	New word (not from the text)
6	drip	ed	
7	slip	er	
8	sad	est	
9	red	ish	
10	star	y	
11	sun	y	
12	snob	ish	

Spelling generalisations – No doubling

When adding the suffixes full, ness, ly, ment, DO NOT double the last letter. Just remember that when you add full as a suffix, take off one 'l' so the suffix becomes ful.
Example: care + full = careful

Complete the table by adding the suffix provided.

	Root word	Suffix	New word
	Example: fit	full	fitful
13	sad	ly	
14	red	ness	
15	ship	ment	
16	cap	full	

Latin suffix 'ous'

In the text, the words murderous and glorious are used to describe the sea and the summer's day. Adding the Latin suffix 'ous' to the end of the root word turns a noun into an adjective (describing word). It changes the word's meaning to mean 'full of'.

However, some words do not have an obvious root word to begin with.
Example: enormous

Complete the paragraph with the missing 'ous' words. Use the list of words below. You may need to use a dictionary to help you.

adventurous, curious, dangerous, outrageous, enormous, furious, courteous

The Year Fives were (17) ______________ about the new student, Chris, who joined the class. Chris had a large or (18) ______________ parrot on her shoulder that was not very nice or (19) ______________ as it kept calling out for everyone to, "Walk the plank!" The teacher was (20) ______________ because the parrot copied everything he said. The students, on the other hand, were captivated by the very sharp and (21) ______________-looking sword Chris had strapped to her side. The principal, however, thought it was (22) ______________ that a Year Five student would bring a sword to school. Everyone agreed that the new student must live an (23) ______________ life.

Score 2 points for each correct answer! SCORE /46  0-20  22-40   42-46

TERM 2

Persuasive text – Argument

The 4 Cs - Classic Class Fun at Creek Camp

Have you ever wanted to escape school and go on camp with your friends? Then this is the camp for you.

To begin with, Year Fives need to experience a school camp to disconnect with technology and make connections with other students and with their teachers. You will not need to go online as you will be too busy having new experiences.

For instance, at the 4 Cs, you will learn how to climb across rope bridges, learn to be proficient at rockclimbing and use the flying fox. You will also be introduced to the sport of abseiling. Abseiling is the opposite of climbing because you are going down a rock face using a rope rather than climbing up. Our expert team will coach and instruct you on the safety procedures and support you to 'have a go' and try all the activities offered.

We want you to have fun but also to challenge yourself. It is crucial to remember that every challenge you overcome helps you build resilience and self-confidence.

In addition, school camp is the place where your social skills grow and develop. This is because most activities we offer involve teamwork, communication and listening.

Finally, you must come to the 4 Cs as we are set in beautiful grounds in a small, green, wooded valley that will take your breath away. We have a natural watercourse where you will experience raft building, canoeing and other water activities.

We are lucky enough to have a cave system on our site, so cave exploration with our expert instructors is one of the activities offered. Immerse yourself in life underground.

Leave the classroom behind and enjoy the outdoor environment.

You know you want to!

TARGETING ENGLISH HOMEWORK YEAR 5 © PASCAL PRESS ISBN 978 1 925726 62 6

Reading & Comprehension

Write the answer or shade the bubble next to the correct answer.

1. **What do the 4 Cs stand for?**

   ____

   ____

2. **Why will you not need to go online?**

   ____

   ____

3. **What is abseiling?**

   ____

   ____

4. **What does every challenge you overcome help build?**

   ____

   ____

5. **Why will your social skills grow and develop at the 4Cs?**

   ____

   ____

6. **How many specific activities are listed in the brochure?**

   ____

7. **Describe the setting of the 4 Cs site. From the text, what natural features do you think it has?** ______________

   ____

   ____

   ____

   ____

8. **What activity do you think Year Five students will consider as the most challenging at the 4 Cs?**

   ____

   Write one sentence to explain why.

   ____

   ____

   ____

   ____

9. **Find resilience in the fourth paragraph. You may have heard this word at school. Read the text and infer what you think it means.**

   - ○ ability to bounce back after challenges and tough times
   - ○ ability to do the things you want
   - ○ ability to live or reside anywhere

10. **Do the instructors expect you to complete all activities?**

    - ○ Yes
    - ○ No

    Explain your answer.

    ____

    ____

    ____

    ____

11. **What important information is lacking in this brochure that you and your parents or caregivers would need to know?**

    ____

    ____

    ____

    ____

12. **Which activity would you like to do most? Write a sentence to explain your answer.**

    ____

    ____

    ____

    ____

TERM 2

Score 2 points for each correct answer! SCORE /24

Grammar & Punctuation

Verb groups and tense

Some verbs in the text consist of a verb and an auxiliary verb (helper) either in future tense or present tense.
Example: will learn (future tense)
are set (present tense)

Complete the tables by writing the verb groups where they belong, either future or present.

will coach and instruct
have abseiled   will be introduced
will study   are going   is not climbing

Future Tense: auxiliary verb	main verb
will	take
will not	need
①	
②	
③	

Present Tense: auxiliary verb	main verb
is	offered
has	read
④	
⑤	
⑥	

Choose present or future tense verbs for these sentences.

⑦ The teachers _____ our camp right now.
are planning / will have planned

⑧ I _____ my best friend to be in the same cabin with me when the teachers ask us for cabin buddies tomorrow.
have asked / will ask

⑨ I _____ my bags already.
have packed / will be packing

⑩ I bet teachers _____ us not to take our teddies.
have been asking / will be asking

⑪ Poor Ted _____ to go on camp all year.
has been waiting / will wait

⑫ I _____ to secretly pack Ted in my pillowcase.
am planning / will have been planning

⑬ I _____ Ted home alone!
have not left / will not leave

⑭ I wonder if Ted _____ inside my pillowcase?
can breathe / will have breathed

Noun groups

Noun groups include words that can come before and after the noun.

Underline the noun in these noun groups that are from the text.

⑮ beautiful grounds
⑯ small, green, wooded valley
⑰ natural watercourse
⑱ water activities
⑲ new experiences
⑳ school camp
㉑ rope bridges

Complex sentences

Complex sentences have one independent clause that stands alone and one or more dependent (or subordinate) clauses that do not make sense on their own. The clauses are joined by a conjunction.

Rewrite these sentences with the conjunction (underlined) at the beginning with the dependent clause. Don't forget the comma!

Example: Your social skills grow and develop <u>because</u> most activities involve teamwork.

<u>Because</u> most activities involve teamwork, your social skills grow and develop.

㉒ Abseiling is the opposite of climbing <u>because</u> you are going down a rock face.

____
____
____
____

㉓ You must come to the 4Cs <u>as</u> we are set in beautiful grounds in a small, green, wooded valley.

____
____
____
____

Score 2 points for each correct answer! SCORE /46   

0-20 22-40 42-46

TARGETING ENGLISH HOMEWORK YEAR 5 © PASCAL PRESS ISBN 978 1 925726 62 6

Phonic & Word Knowledge

Spelling generalisations – Syllables

Syllable rules:
- Divide between compound words, prefixes and suffixes.
- Divide between two consonants that do not make one sound VC/CV.
- If the first vowel is short: VC/V. If the first vowel is long: V/CV. However, keep vowel teams together such as 'ar', 'er', 'ea' and blends such as 'cr'.
- If two vowels are next to each other, but they are not a pair (make one sound), split between them V/V.
- For words that end in a consonant and 'le' (C-le), you count back three or divide before the consonant; however, you count the 'ck' sound as one.

Test your knowledge of syllables with the following tricky words.

The third rule will help you:

(1) secret ______________

(2) rocket ______________

(3) gather ______________

The second rule will help you:

(4) basket ______________

(5) costume ______________

Sometimes 'y' also wants to be a vowel:

(6) February ______________

(7) syllable ______________

(8) cyclone ______________

Stressed syllables

A stressed syllable has a longer, louder, higher sound than the other syllables in the word.

Prefixes and suffixes are not usually stressed.
Example: WALK -ing (walk is stressed)

Underline the stressed syllable in each word.

(9) un - clear

(10) thought - ful

(11) help - less

(12) im - pos - si - ble

Some words are usually stressed on the syllable just before the suffix.

Example: in – for – MA - tion.

Underline the stressed syllable in these words.

(13) suc - cess - ful

(14) re - la - tion

Homonyms and homographs

Homonyms are words that look and sound the same but have a different meaning. Homographs look the same but sound different depending on which syllable is stressed.

These sentences have present in them, but it has a different meaning in each sentence. Circle the correct stressed syllable for each meaning.

(15) Everyone in our class is present today.
(means 'here') PRE - sent / pre - SENT

(16) She gave her friend a lovely present.
(means 'gift') PRE - sent / pre - SENT

(17) I will present my speech on Monday.
(means 'give') PRE - sent / pre - SENT

Vowels

A, E, I, O, U, and sometimes Y, are vowels. In the text, the word canoeing has three vowels all in a row. Other examples of words with three vowels in a row include beautiful, serious and delicious (in fact, any word ending in 'ious').

Fill in the three missing vowels in each word contained in the paragraph.

I was feeling a bit (18) q _ _ _ sy on the bus to camp. I was (19) consc _ _ _ s of my stomach cramping. So, I sat (20) q _ _ _ tly, not speaking, (21) s _ _ _ng if I could last the trip. I thought I was (22) victor _ _ _ s until I felt a rumbling. With a (23) sq _ _ _ l of brakes, I was soon out the door and …

Score 2 points for each correct answer! SCORE  /46  0-20  22-40  42-46

TERM 2

Imaginative text – Report & Poetry

INTERVIEW WITH AN ALIEN - 2240

Transcript from the broadcast *In your shoes!*

Chris: I wish to welcome Sam to the program *In your shoes!* Sam lives in a colony on Mars and was born there. He is now officially classified as a 'Martian'. We are linked via satellite connection to Sam.

Chris: Now, Sam, you say that you feel and look different to us here on Earth. You have been a part of the colonisation of Mars and, in fact, were born on Mars. Our viewers would like to know: How have the new 'Martians' adapted or changed to live on Mars?

Sam: Thank you, Chris. When the first colonists arrived many generations ago, we struggled to survive. Over many years, we have slowly adapted to the environment. I identify as a Martian; in fact, I have phrased this feeling as:

No Earthling am I,
Body changing to survive,
Adaptation, Mars.

A Haiku, for our viewers, is a three-line Japanese poem with a pattern of 5 syllables line 1; 7 syllables line 2; 5 syllables line 3.

It's a little Haiku poem that states we had to adapt. We adapted in three ways:

1. Behavioural adaptations. We had to learn to live underground in caves to escape the dangerous UV rays from the Sun.
2. Physiological adaptations. Those now born on Mars have changes inside us to help us live on Mars. We have denser bones to help with the effect of lower gravity, and our blood is at a lower temperature to cope with the lower pressure and colder temperature of the planet.
3. Structural adaptations. These are the changes to our physical appearance. We Martians are taller because of the low gravity – we only have 1/3 of Earth's gravity. And we have larger eyes to collect more light from the dark environment.

Because Mars is low in oxygen, we still need to use spacesuits to go onto the surface of the planet but have the technology to make oxygen in our living quarters and cities.

Because of the adaptations to the Martian environment, I cannot easily visit Earth and walk around. However, I don't miss Earth as I'm a Martian. I want you to see Mars how I see it.

Canyons, clouds and wind,
Raging dust storms, dry lake beds,
Danger, beauty, Mars.

Chris: That is fascinating, Sam. We wish you Martians all the best from Earth.

TARGETING ENGLISH HOMEWORK YEAR 5 © PASCAL PRESS ISBN 978 1 925726 62 6

Reading & Comprehension

Write the answer or shade the bubble next to the correct answer.

The answers to these questions are in the text.

① What are the rules for writing a **haiku poem**?

② Where on Mars does Sam live?

③ **Adaptation** means:

- ◯ changing where you live, especially different planets.
- ◯ changes in body and behaviour to survive an environment.
- ◯ changing how you think about a place or environment.

④ In what year was the **interview** conducted?

Think about these questions and search for the answers in the text.

⑤ What are the three different **types of adaptations**?

⑥ Adaptation happens very quickly.

◯ True ◯ False

⑦ What makes you think that?

⑧ From what you have read in the text, what are some of the **similarities** and **differences** between Earth and Mars?

Similarities

Differences

Use inferencing skills to answer these questions. The answers are not in the text. Think about what you know and what the author says.

⑨ If new 'Martians' have adapted to Mars, why do you think Sam would find it hard to visit Earth?

⑩ If, in the future, humans developed lungs to breathe on Mars, what form of **adaptation** would that be?

Use your experience and opinions to answer this question. The answer is not in the text.

⑪ If Mars is a dangerous environment, why would we want to **colonise** it?

Comprehension Reflections

Look at the top of the opposite page. This text is an I_________ text – R_________ & P_________.

Write one thing you learned or found interesting:

Write one question you have or something you want to find more information about:

Rating   

Score 2 points for each correct answer! SCORE /22 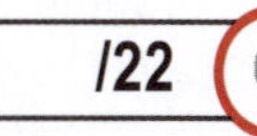  

TERM 3

Grammar & Punctuation

AC9E5LA09

Apostrophes of possession

Apostrophes of possession (ownership) indicate that a noun owns something. *Example from the text:* Earth**'s** gravity (The Earth owns the gravity.)

You do not add an apostrophe to show more than one thing or plural. *Example:* colonists (plural noun with no apostrophe)

Rules for single nouns

With single nouns, we add apostrophe s. *Examples:* Fred**'s** lunch, Joy**'s** recess

For single nouns that end in 's', add apostrophe s. *Examples:* Jame**s's** book, Joy Cros**s's** bag, Mar**s's** moon

Practise these rules by choosing the correct spelling.

1. ________ legs are longer than ours on Earth.
   Sam / Sams's / Sams' / Sam's
2. _______ gravity is only 1/3 that of Earth.
   Mars / Mars's / Mars' / Mar's
3. A _________ blood is different to ours.
   Martian's / Martian / Martians' / Martians's

Rules for plural nouns

For plural nouns not ending in 's', add apostrophe s. *Examples:* children's playtime, the fish's scales

For plural nouns ending in 's', add an apostrophe only at the end after the s. *Examples:* the students' desks, the teachers' cars

Practise these rules by choosing the correct spelling.

4. Sam is so tall that normal ______ clothing will not fit.
   men / men's / mens' / mens's
5. Sam couldn't drive any of the ______ cars unless the seat was in the boot.
   teacher / teacher's / teachers' / teachers's
6. On Mars, all ______ seats must be a long way from the front.
   driver / driver's / drivers' / drivers's

More than one thing or person?

If an item belongs to more than one person/thing, only add an apostrophe of possession to the last person/thing in the group. *Example:* This is Fred and Joy**'s** book about Martians. They wrote a book together.

What if they wrote a book each? *Example:* These are Fred**'s** and Joy**'s** book**s** about Martians. (notice 'book' now becomes 'books')

Practise these rules by choosing the correct spelling.

7. Sam and Jo own a car together on Mars. ______ car is red, like the planet.
   Sam and Jo / Sam's and Jo's / Sam and Jo's
8. Sam and Jo each have their own spacecraft though. ______ spacecrafts are red so that they can go really fast.
   Sam and Jo / Sam's and Jo's / Sam and Jo's

9. **Sam wants to sell his car. He has made a for sale sign, but he has made some mistakes. Help Sam out. Write it again in the box without the mistakes.**

Score 2 points for each correct answer! SCORE /18   

TERM 3

TARGETING ENGLISH HOMEWORK YEAR 5 © PASCAL PRESS ISBN 978 1 925726 62 6

Phonic & Word Knowledge

UNIT 17

AC9E5LY09

Greek base word 'phys'

The word physiological is in the text, describing the changes or adaptations that occurred inside the Martians. The word part 'phys' is a Greek base word, meaning study of nature. *Examples:* **phys**ical, **phys**iotherapy, **phys**ics and **phys**iognomy

Using context clues (hints found in a sentence that help you to understand the meanings of words), circle the correct meaning of the bold word in these sentences.

1. I could tell the teacher was angry because of his **physiognomy** – the flared nostrils and the clenched teeth.
   words / walk / face / body
2. The Martian's **physique** is so different to ours. Sam is tall and thin but muscular.
   words / walk / face / body
3. I needed **physiotherapy** after visiting Mars to fix my muscle problems with exercise and stretches.
   water / treatment / food / relaxation
4. **Physicians** are very helpful in diagnosing and treating illnesses and injuries of patients.
   machines / scientists / doctors / physics teachers

Soft c and g

Why bother about them? Soft c and g are often found in Greek and Latin roots, so they tend to appear in more complex words that have lots of syllables. Understanding how to make sense of the different sounds of 'c' and 'g' helps you to read very complex words. Here are some rules to help:

- When 'c' is in front of i, y, e, it is soft and says /s/. *Examples:* **c**ities, **c**ycle, ra**c**e
- When 'c' is in front of any other letter, it is hard and says /k/. *Examples:* **c**amera, **c**ar
- When 'g' is in front of i, y, e, it is soft and says /j/. *Examples:* **g**iant, **g**ypsy, **g**em
- When 'g' is in front of any other letter, it is hard and says /g/. *Examples:* **g**o, **g**ave, **g**ravel
- However, there are words that have a hard 'g' sound that are exceptions. *Examples:* **g**et, **g**ive, bu**gg**y, bi**gg**er

Tick if the bold letter is hard or soft in the tables below.

	Root word	Hard	Soft
5	**c**astle		
6	**c**ancel		
7	dan**c**e		
8	**c**rystal		
9	**c**ircumference		
10	re**c**ent		
11	**c**ity		
12	**c**ereal		
13	biologi**c**al		
14	**c**ircumspect		

	Word (some exceptions to the rule)	Hard	Soft
15	**g**iraffe		
16	an**g**le		
17	an**g**el		
18	brid**g**e		
19	**g**yroscope		
20	biolo**g**ical		
21	**g**irl		
22	**g**ym		
23	**g**et		

Score 2 points for each correct answer! SCORE /46 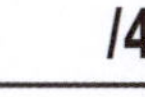 0-20  22-40  42-46

TERM 3

Informative text – Report

Adaptation

Plants and animals adapt in three ways: behaviourally, physiologically, and structurally or physically. Adaptations are the special features that enable plants and animals to be successful in a particular environment. For animals closer to the bottom of the food chain, adaptations for self-defence are important.

To understand that point, you need to understand what a food chain is. We asked some typical students (below) their thoughts about a food chain.

Every living plant and animal must have energy to survive. Plants rely on the soil, water and sun for energy. Animals rely on plants as well as other animals for energy. A food chain describes how different organisms eat each other, starting out with a plant and ending with an animal. In this case, you.

Student 1: Cat

Student 2: Purple

Sun → grass → cow → butcher → supermarket → you

Sun → wheat → baker → supermarket → you

Plants and animals at the beginning or lower end of the food chain will have to protect themselves from being eaten. Structural or physical adaptations help them hide, scare predators away or even taste bad so that predators avoid them. An example of a physical adaptation is the meerkats' fur colour. They have dark fur around their eyes to reduce the glare of the sun so that they can see danger coming from every angle.

Many animals have developed the ability to run fast to protect themselves from predators. Animals have adapted camouflage to blend in with their surroundings and so avoid being hunted. A great example of this is the leafy stick insect that looks – yes – like a stick.

Animals at the higher end of the food chain also have adaptations, but these adaptations are to help them catch prey. For example, the tiger's stripes help it camouflage or blend into the shadows of the jungle so that it can sneak up on its prey.

Of course, adaptation doesn't happen overnight. It can take thousands of years. Over time, animals that are better adapted to their environment survive and breed. Animals that are not well adapted to an environment may not survive.

Reading & Comprehension

Write the answer or shade the bubble next to the correct answer.

The answers to these questions are in the text.

1. What is a **food chain**?

2. Why is **adaptation** important for animals or plants closer to the bottom of the food chain?

3. What does every living animal and plant need to survive?

4. Why have animals adapted **camouflage**?

5. What two foods is Purple describing in its food chains?

Think about these questions and search for the answers in the text.

6. Why do you think **the Sun** is at the start of the food chain?

7. Why would **stripes** help an animal?

8. What adaptation does the **leafy stick insect** use and what is the purpose?

9. **Camouflage** is an adaptation used:
   - ◯ only by animals on the lower end of the food chain to avoid being eaten.
   - ◯ by animals high and low on the food chain.
   - ◯ only by animals on the higher end of the food chain to help catch their prey.

Use inferencing skills to answer this question. The answer is not in the text. Think about what you know and what the author says.

10. Arrange these **food chains** in the right order.

    plants, foxes, insects, small birds, Sun

    insects, snakes, plants, kookaburras, Sun, frogs

Use your experience and opinions to answer these questions. The answers are not in the text.

11. What animal (excluding humans) do you think would be in the **higher end** of the food chain in:
    - ◯ an African jungle? ________________
    - ◯ the ocean? ________________
    - ◯ Australia's desert or inland region? ________________

12. Food chains do not finish with the death of an animal or plant. If an animal higher in the food chain dies, what do you think would feed off it? Think of two suggestions.

    Tiger dies ⟶ ________________, ________________

Comprehension Reflections

Look at the top of the opposite page. This text is an I__________ text – R__________.

Write one thing you learned or found interesting:

Write one question you have or something you want to find more information about:

Rating   

Score 2 points for each correct answer! SCORE /24   

TERM 3

Grammar & Punctuation

AC9E5LY06

Quotation marks

In the text, the students were asked about a food chain and their answers were in speech bubbles. If their answers were written in text, you would need to use quotation marks.

Rules to follow when using quotation marks:

- No two people speak on the same line.
- Quotation marks go around the exact words said.
- When a person starts speaking, use a capital letter.
- A punctuation mark of some kind must go before every quotation mark unless it is at the start of a sentence. *Example:* I shouted, "Please, help me!"

Put the punctuation marks in each sentence. Use the punctuation in brackets.

The conversations about food chains may have gone like this:

1. What You want me to tell you about food chains Cat asked (**Use ? ? " " .**)
2. Purple excitedly interrupted I know what they are, and I can even list the food chain for my burger (**Use , " " .**)
3. Cat looked up briefly and stated very loudly It's the supermarket. Everyone knows that's where our food comes from (**Use , " " !**)

Now it's harder with no clues. Add the punctuation including apostrophes for contractions (e.g. can't).

4. Purple looked up in alarm Oh Cat, dont you know thats not where food comes from originally
5. Yeah, yeah, I suppose it involves a farm of some sort said Cat
6. Purple smiled Well it always starts with a plant at least, thats for sure

Nominalisation

Nominalisation is where verbs (actions or events) or adjectives (describing words) are changed into nouns (things or ideas). This can be done by adding certain suffixes or changing the spelling. Why do it? Using nominalisation adds more sophistication and detail to your writing, especially in non-fiction texts such as reports and explanations.

In the text, the word adaptation is used as a noun to name a process, in place of adapt which is a doing word or verb.

Example: For animals closer to the bottom of the food chain, **adaptations** (noun) for self-defence are important.

Read these sentences and change the verb or adjective in brackets to a noun by adding a suffix or a different spelling.

Example: With Cat and Purple's **assistance**, (assist) we set up an interview about food chains.

7. Cat showed little _______________ (anxious) about being interviewed.
8. There was a significant _______________ (different) in understanding food chains between Cat and Purple.
9. Cat's answer lacked _______________ (deep) in his explanation of a food chain.
10. After reading the text, my _______________ (expect) is that Cat will be better informed.
11. Then again, the _______________ (prove) will be in the way Cat answers the question if asked again.
12. Purple seems to understand how _______________ (adapt) are important for the _______________ (survive) of animals and plants along the food chain.
13. My _______________ (assess) of their answers will be in their reports. Poor Cat!

Score 2 points for each correct answer! SCORE /26

TERM 3

TARGETING ENGLISH HOMEWORK YEAR 5 © PASCAL PRESS ISBN 978 1 925726 62 6

Phonic & Word Knowledge

AC9E5LY09, AC9E5LY10

Suffix 'al'

The suffix 'al' means 'relating to'. When 'al' is added to a noun, the noun becomes an adjective. Remember, adjectives describe a noun. In the text, behavioural, physiological, structural and physical are adjectives that describe the noun adaptation.

To help with the spelling, remember that when the root word ends in a consonant, you usually just add the suffix. *Example:* behaviour + al = behaviour**al** (means relating to behaviour)

When the root word ends in 'e', remove the 'e' and add the suffix. *Example:* structur**e** + al = structur**al** (means relating to the structure of something)

Write the new word in the table after adding the suffix 'al'.

Example: structure + al =	structural
nature + al =	①
emotion + al =	②
globe + al =	③
capit (Latin for head) + al =	④
nation + al =	⑤
accident + al =	⑥
season + al =	⑦

Complete the passage with these new words.

emotional global natural seasonal national

Hamburgers are a ⑧ ______________ snack, known around the world. In America, it is almost a ⑨ ______________ dish, being a ⑩ ______________ choice for a snack or meal. You can eat hamburgers all year round. They are not a ⑪ ______________ snack. For many burger fans, it becomes an ⑫ ______________ event when they get the perfect burger.

Borrowed words

English has many words that come from Latin and Greek languages. However, the word camouflage in the text is borrowed from the French language. The English language, as spoken today, has borrowed heavily from many languages.

Write the 20 words under their country of origin in the table. You may need to use a dictionary.

⑬ – ㉜

camouflage, broccoli, shampoo, kindergarten, ninja, pyjamas, tsunami, cartoon, pretzel, ballet, beef, hamburger, karate, spaghetti, jungle, poodle, menu, origami, cauliflower, veranda

France	Germany

Italy	Japan

India

Score 2 points for each correct answer! SCORE /64    

AC9E5LY04, AC9E5LY05, AC9S5U01

Informative text – Report

Blobfish and Vampire Bats

The world is full of amazing and very diverse or different environments. It has taken millions of years for plants and animals to adapt or change to survive the environments they inhabit. The table below shows the different types of adaptations of two animals to their environments.

Animal	Behavioural adaptations	Physiological adaptations	Structural adaptations
Vampire bat	• can fly, jump, run and walk, which aids it in finding its prey, then attaching to it for feeding	• bacteria in its gut help digest blood • stretchy stomach to hold large quantities of blood • anticoagulants in saliva so it can drink blood without it clotting	• sharp teeth to make small cuts into prey • heat sensors on nose to locate prey • strong hind legs, and thumbs to help climb onto prey
Blobfish	• stays largely still and uses as little energy as possible • does not swim but drifts with the movement of water	• soft bones and very little muscle to survive in a high-pressure habitat	• squishy jelly-like body to help it survive in a high-pressure habitat • fatty body helps it float as it does not have a swim bladder like other fish

- At sunset, in the rainforests and deserts of Mexico and Central and South America, **vampire bats** emerge or come out of their dark caves, mines, tree hollows and abandoned buildings in search of food.
- Vampire bats' ability to sense an animal's breathing helps them find their prey. They use the heat sensors on their noses to find the best spot on their prey's body to feed from. Their teeth cut through the animal's skin and their tongue laps up the blood flow for about 30 minutes. The bat is very light and agile, so it's possible their prey doesn't even know it's happening!
- The bats have adapted to a blood diet rich in iron and protein but with minimal fats or carbohydrates and are the only mammals that can survive on a diet of just blood.
- **Blobfish** have been unfairly named as one of the world's ugliest animals. They only look like a big blob of jelly when removed from their natural environment.
- Blobfish live in some of the deepest parts of the ocean between Australia and New Zealand. At around 1200 m deep, you need a submarine to be able to see them alive. They live on the bottom of the ocean feeding on whatever passes them by. They stay mostly still as a survival strategy and to conserve energy while they lie in wait for any prey to swim by.
- Underwater, blobfish look like fish or very large tadpoles. They have adaptations to survive the pressure and weight of the water surrounding them. However, if they are brought to the surface, decompression or the lack of pressure can make them expand and causes their skin to relax, distorting their features. On the surface, their jelly-like body does not hold its shape and so it collapses into a shapeless jelly blob.

TERM 3

TARGETING ENGLISH HOMEWORK YEAR 5 © PASCAL PRESS ISBN 978 1 925726 62 6

Reading & Comprehension

Write the answer or shade the bubble next to the correct answer.

The answers to these questions are in the text.

1. **When do vampire bats come out to feed?**

____

2. **Name one structural adaptation of the vampire bat.**

____

3. **Vampire bats suck blood out of their prey.**

◯ True ◯ False

4. **How do vampire bats stop the blood from clotting?**

____

____

5. **What physiological adaptations does the blobfish have to live in deep water?**

____

____

Think about these questions and search for the answers in the text.

6. **How do blobfish differ from other fish?**

____

____

7. **How did the blobfish get its name?**

____

____

8. **What adaptation helps the vampire bat climb onto its prey?**

____

____

9. **From the text, vampire bats are:**

◯ a large, flying species of bat with large, strong limbs.
◯ a very light, small species of bat.
◯ one of the larger species of bat to be able to fight and overcome their prey.

Use inferencing skills to answer these questions. The answers are not in the text. Think about what you know and what the author says.

10. **Why would it be difficult to keep vampire bats as pets?**

____

____

11. **Why could you not keep blobfish in an aquarium?**

____

____

Use your experience and opinions to answer this question. The answer is not in the text.

12. **Vampire bats are the only mammals to live on blood alone. Name two other animals (insects) that live entirely on blood.**

____

____

Comprehension Reflections

Look at the top of the opposite page. This text is an I__________ text – R__________.

Write one thing you learned or found interesting:

____

Write one question you have or something you want to find more information about:

____

____

Rating   

Score 2 points for each correct answer! SCORE 

TERM 3

Grammar & Punctuation

AC9E5LY06

Dialogue tags mid-sentence

Remember the rules for direct speech:

- No two people speak on the same line.
- Quotation marks go around the actual spoken words.
- When a person starts speaking, you use a capital letter.

Dialogue tags tell us who has spoken the words and how they have been spoken. Dialogue tags can appear before the spoken words, but they must be followed by a comma.
Example: **I shouted,** "Please, help me!"

Or they can be written after the spoken words followed by a full stop.
Example: "Please, help me!" **I shouted.**

But dialogue tags can also be written mid-sentence. Note that there is a comma before and after the dialogue tag and there is only a capital letter at the beginning of the sentence.
Example: "Please," **I shouted,** "help me!"

If there are two sentences spoken by that speaker, use a full stop after the dialogue tag. Note that there is a capital letter to start each sentence.
Example: "Please, help me!" **I shouted.** "There's a vampire bat after me."

Place the following punctuation " " , ? ! . where needed in these sentences.

1. I have become an internet sensation continued Blobfish and I am famous.
2. You see shouted Vampire Bat you could have your own blog and fan club.
3. Blobfish smiled a jelly-like smile You really think so he wondered.
4. You could Vampire Bat said excitedly become a seafood expert or an influencer.
5. Ah, my own recipe of crustacean pie Blobfish replied I have always wanted to be a chef.
6. Personally said Vampire Bat I like something a little juicier.

Dialogue tags

When writing conversations, often the word 'said' is overused. There are many alternative dialogue tags that can be used to show more meaning.
Example: "There's no way I'm walking through the bush," **complained** Pat.

TERM 3

Match the dialogue tag with the way the words are spoken. There can be more than one answer, so use a different word for each sentence.

	Dialogue			Choose a dialogue tag	
Example:	"Look out, there's a snake!"	**shouted**	Pat.	pleaded	stated
7	"Don't be silly. It's a stick,"		Sandy.	ordered	shouted
8	"Are you sure? It seems to have a flicking tongue,"		Pat.	explained	replied
9	"I know a snake when I see one, thank you very much,"		Sandy.	screamed observed	
10	"Hang on! It's moving!"		Pat.	announced questioned	
11	"Wait for me!"		Sandy.	commented	

12. Write your own conversation between Blobfish and Vampire Bat. Use dialogue tags other than 'said'. If using 'said', think how it was said. For example, said tiredly, said nervously, said angrily etc. Remember, no two people speak on the same line.

____

____

____

____

Score 2 points for each correct answer! SCORE /24   0-10  12-18  20-24

TARGETING ENGLISH HOMEWORK YEAR 5 © PASCAL PRESS ISBN 978 1 925726 62 6

Phonic & Word Knowledge

UNIT 19

AC9E5LY09

Word patterns with 'dge' and 'ge'

Can you think of a word that ends in the letter 'j'?

In the English language, the letter 'j' never ends a word; however, the 'j sound' often does.

Both 'dge' and 'ge' make the sound 'j', but which one to use? Look at this flow chart. If the word answers 'yes' to the two questions, then it is likely to end in 'dge'. If one or two answers are 'no', then it is likely to end in 'ge'.

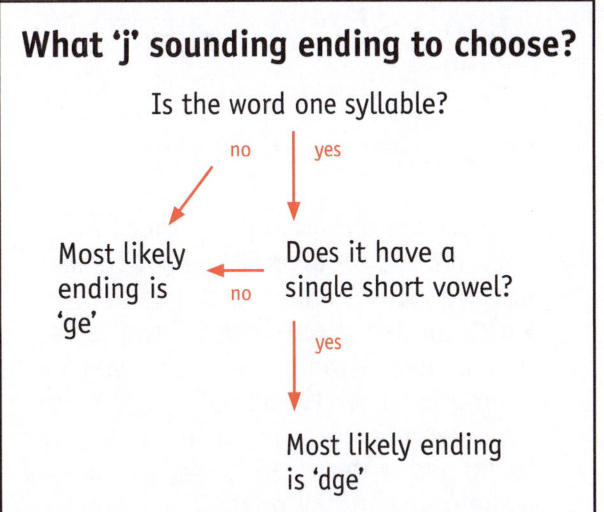

Use the flow chart to work out why the words in the table end in 'ge' or 'dge'.

	Word	Has one syllable	Single short vowel	Which ending – 'ge' or 'dge'?
	Example: change	yes	no	ge
1	emerge			
2	large			
3	fudge			
4	page			
5	edge			
6	stage			
7	budge			
8	judge			

Word ending challenge

You now know that English words do not end in the letter 'j'. But did you know that English words also do not end in q or v?

Your challenge is to find words that end in the letters of the alphabet. Complete the table with two words for each letter.

9 a	10 b	11 c	12 d	13 e
14 f	15 g	16 h	17 k	18 l
19 m	20 n	21 o	22 p	23 r
24 s	25 t	26 w	27 x	28 y
29 z				

Score 2 points for each correct answer! SCORE /58

TERM 3

AC9E5LY04, AC9E5LY05, AC9E5LE04, AC9HS5K04

Imaginative text – Poetry

Sonnets and Place

Sonnets are a form of poem that have been around for over 700 years. Some poems, such as haikus and limericks, which are more well-known, have rules, and sonnets also have rules. In poetry, you do not need to follow rules to write your own poems; however, it can be fun to try and write different forms of poetry while following the rules.

The rules for a sonnet are:

- 14 lines
- you write about a big feeling or issue
- there is a rhyming scheme ABAB CDCD EFEF GG
- 10 syllables on each line.

These two sonnets are about 'place'. Place is sometimes hard to understand. It can be where you live and belong – it has importance. Place influences how you live, and how you live influences and impacts the place. The first poem is about a place very close to home while the second poem hints at the different types of places that exist in Australia.

TERM 3

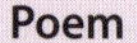

Poem 1

What or where on Earth is this thing called place?
I instantly thought of home, my backyard.
Some of our dogs are buried in a space,
Out the back where the soil isn't hard.

The old iron fence rises from the dirt,
It creaks, groans and snarls against any wind.
Once climbing, shook me off and ripped my shirt,
I fell in a bruised heap on the green bin.

I lie and stare up at clouds scudding by,
As ants march determinedly up shins.
Followed by a wild slap dance as they die,
My backyard battles I will always win.

So maybe home, the backyard, is my place,
I connect, it's important, it's my space.

Poem 2

Dressing in a coat of shimmering heat,
The sun climbs higher in its sky-blue dome.
Corrugated roads bounce you in your seat,
laugh and speech, as rippled as the road home.

Foamed tongue of a tireless dog of sea,
Waves lick the sand, dribbling on your ankles.
Azure and calm or tangled jaws you flee,
It retreats but leaves the sand with wrinkles.

Flat, undulating or smothered in trees,
Multi shades of green skin, crawling with life.
Grasslands, forests, farms, water is the key,
It breathes and grows, part of Australian life.

It's place, significant to you and me,
Different but still connected go and see.

TARGETING ENGLISH HOMEWORK YEAR 5 © PASCAL PRESS ISBN 978 1 925726 62 6

Reading & Comprehension

Write the answer or shade the bubble next to the correct answer.

The answers to these questions are in the text.

1. How many years have **sonnets** been around?

____

2. Write the **rules** for a sonnet.

____
____
____
____

3. All poems have rules.

◯ True ◯ False

4. Where is 'place' in **poem one**?

____

Think about these questions and search for the answers in the text.

5. In poem two, what type of environment or place is the **first paragraph** describing?

____

6. In poem two, what type of environment or place is the **second paragraph** describing?

____

7. There is a line in poem one that says, **followed by a wild slap dance as they die**. What does it mean?

____
____

8. What is this text telling you about **place**?

◯ The place where you live influences you, and you influence it.
◯ Places cannot be changed; they stay the same.
◯ Places are nothing special as they are all around us.

Use inferencing skills to answer this question. The answer is not in the text. Think about what you know and what the author says.

9. Place influences how you live. Imagine your family has been relocated to the South Pole. How does this influence how you live? Complete the table.

Clothes needed	Type of house needed	How to travel around

Use your experience and opinions to answer this question. The answer is not in the text.

10. What place is important to you or your family? Write one sentence to describe the place. Write another sentence to explain why it is important to you or your family.

____
____
____
____

TERM 3

Comprehension Reflections

Look at the top of the opposite page. This text is an I__________ text – P__________.

Write one thing you learned or found interesting:

____

Write one question you have or something you want to find more information about:

____
____

Rating   

Score 2 points for each correct answer! SCORE /20   

Grammar & Punctuation

AC9E5LE04

Descriptive language – Imagery

The two poems in the text use descriptive language such as imagery or specific words to create a picture.

Examples: Use **'march determinedly'** instead of 'walk'. (poem 1)

Use **'azure'** instead of 'blue'. (poem 2)

Find the precise vocabulary used in poem one to mean the phrases in the table below.

Example:	Ants ran up my legs.	... ants march determinedly up shins.
1	I quickly get the ants off my legs.	
2	I dropped down and hurt myself.	
3	I saw the wind blowing the clouds.	
4	I feel powerful in the backyard.	

Personification

Another way to add description is to use personification. This is where non-human objects are given human characteristics, actions or emotions.

Examples: The **fence** seems alive as it creaks and groans, doing actions that a human would do. (poem 1)

The **sun** takes on human actions like being dressed in a coat and climbing. (poem 2)

Match the personifications to the meanings. Underline the exact words that make the actions sound like a human is doing them.

Example:	The old fence is standing in the dirt.	The old iron fence rises from the dirt.
5	The fence is noisy when the wind blows.	
6	I fell off the fence once and tore my shirt.	
7	The sun is hot.	
8	The sun rises.	

Metaphors

Metaphors are another way of using descriptive language when writing. A metaphor compares two things by saying one thing takes on the qualities of another.

Example: Poem two compares the **sea** to a **dog**.

Match the metaphor with its meaning by drawing a line to join them.

	Metaphor	Meaning
9	*Foamed tongue of a tireless dog of sea*	When you wade into the water, waves wash over your feet like a dog dribbling on you.
10	*Waves lick the sand*	Waves never stop the in-and-out movement at the shore like a dog's tongue in and out of its mouth.
11	*dribbling on your ankles*	When it gets rough, you leave the beach like a dog becoming angry, showing its teeth.
12	*tangled jaws you flee*	Waves wet the sand like a dog licking you.

Score 2 points for each correct answer!

TERM 3

TARGETING ENGLISH HOMEWORK YEAR 5 © PASCAL PRESS ISBN 978 1 925726 62 6

AC9E5LY09

Borrowed French words with 'gue'

Many English words that end in 'gue' are borrowed from the French language. *Examples:* vogue, dialogue

In these 'gue' words, the 'g' makes a hard /g/ sound. *Example:* wagon

Usually, when 'g' is followed by 'e', 'i', or 'y', it makes the soft /j/ sound as in cage. If 'g' is followed by any other letter, it makes the hard /g/ sound as in lagoon.

Find your inner French knowledge and choose the correct meaning of each 'gue' word in the text below.

1. I visited France but was very **vague** about its history.
   unhappy / unclear / uninterested
2. I started to read about it, but I needed to do star jumps to fight off the **fatigue** as the book was so big.
   insects / high-fat food / tiredness
3. I decided to ring a **colleague** for help.
   college professor / classmate / helpline
4. After some **dialogue**, it was evident that they knew less than me.
   discussion / time / food
5. I ended up wearing a beret as it was in **vogue**.
   fashion / the shops / bright colours

Borrowed French words with 'que'

Words ending in 'que' are usually French in origin and make a /k/ sound.
Examples: anti**que** (pronounced 'an-teek'), brus**que** (pronounced 'brusk')

Circle the correct meanings for each 'que' word.

6	antique	very old an insect a type of aunt
7	boutique	a place to buy boots a small shop usually selling clothes a type of wood
8	brusque	abrupt or impolite energetic and active polite or courteous
9	grotesque	enormous or huge hideous or horrible attractive or beautiful
10	opaque	pay for something something you cannot see through a type of stone or jewel
11	picturesque	using a camera ugly attractive
12	technique	an expert computers method of doing something
13	unique	only one of something or something special a bicycle with one wheel something common and found anywhere

Speak French! Unjumble the French-derived words in this passage. All the words are listed somewhere on this page.

I visited a little **uteubioq** (14) ______________ and bought some **ieuuqn** (15) ______________ shoes. Once I got home, I tried them on. They were **steeqorgu** (16) ______________! What was I thinking? I sold them to a **leegclaou** (17) ______________ who wasn't so fussy.

Score 2 points for each correct answer!

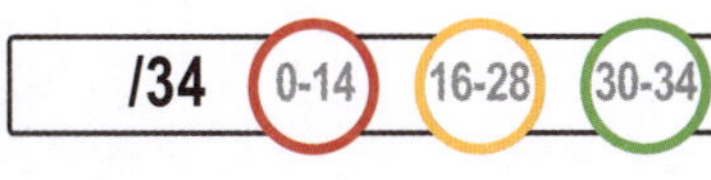

TERM 3

AC9E5LY04, AC9E5LY05, AC9HS5K04, AC9HS5K05

Informative text – Explanation

Managing the Environment

Places influence how we live. For example, living in a natural environment, such as a desert, would be very different from living in a tropical or coastal location, in the mountains or even living in a built-up environment such as a city. Climate influences where people live in Australia, with greater concentrations of people around the coast than in the interior. Therefore, the environment we live in influences how we live.

At the same time, we also influence the environment by the way we manage and organise the spaces that we live in, so people and environments influence each other. Over time, there have been changes to the environment due to the way the land has been managed. This has created issues, such as increased floods and bushfires.

Bushfires and floods are natural disasters that threaten human life and property. We cannot control them, but we can develop better ways of managing their effects and reducing their damage. Councils and governments have put laws in place that affect the type of buildings allowed in areas prone to fire and flood. Planning by governments has involved research and development of better water management and laws to determine zoning or how the land is used. Early warning systems help people to prepare and take action to reduce the effects of fire or floods. Controlled burning, which is not a new idea, is another way to help prevent a destructive bushfire.

First Nations Australian communities deliberately used fire to keep the country more open, clearing out thick bushy areas to protect the plants used for food. Over time, their use of fire changed the Australian landscape. As a result, large, intense bushfires, such as those that occur today, were uncommon.

The environment is significant in our lives, and there is an important interrelationship between humans and the environment. We influence each other, so of course it is in our interest to look after and manage the places that we live.

TARGETING ENGLISH HOMEWORK YEAR 5 © PASCAL PRESS ISBN 978 1 925726 62 6

Reading & Comprehension

Write the answer or shade the bubble next to the correct answer.

The answers to these questions are in the text.

① Over time, changes to the environment due to the way the land has been managed have created issues. Name the **issues**.

② We can control bushfires and floods.

○ True ○ False

③ What **laws** have councils and governments put in place to manage the effects and damage of bushfires and floods?

④ What **planning** have governments put in place to manage the effects and damage of bushfires and floods?

○ research and development of better water management
○ laws to determine zoning or how the land is used
○ early warning systems to help people prepare
○ controlled burning
○ all of the above

Think about these questions and search for the answers in the text.

⑤ What **environments** are mentioned in the text?

⑥ How did First Nations Australian communities prevent the **large, intense bushfires** that we experience today?

Use inferencing skills to answer the following questions. The answers are not in the text. Think about what you know and what the author says.

⑦ All places are affected by their weather and climate. Why are there greater concentrations of people around the **coast** than in the interior of Australia?

⑧ Why is it in our interests to look after and manage the places in which we live?

Use your experience and opinions to answer these questions. The answers are not in the text.

Think of the environment where you live. All places are affected by their climate and weather. Weather includes phenomena such as rain, wind, sunshine, heat, cold, frost, fog, clouds, thunderstorms, lightning, snow etc.

⑨ What elements of the climate and weather where you live make life **pleasant**?

⑩ What elements of the climate and weather where you live can be **dangerous or at times make life difficult**?

Comprehension Reflections

Look at the top of the opposite page. This text is an I__________ text – E__________.

Write one thing you learned or found interesting:

Write one question you have or something you want to find more information about:

Rating   

Score 2 points for each correct answer! SCORE  /20   

TERM 3

Grammar & Punctuation

AC9E5LA09

Commas

Punctuation helps the reader make sense of a text. In this unit's text, commas separate groups of words to help readers understand the ideas expressed. Beware! If you write without punctuation, you may say something you do not mean.

Example:
The student, said the teacher, is a delight.
OR The student said the teacher is a delight.
Who is a delight? The commas make a difference to the meaning.

In the table, draw the meaning of each sentence in the space provided. The first one has been done for you.

Example:	Look at that huge hot dog!	Look at that huge, hot dog!
①	Let's eat, Grandma!	Let's eat Grandma!
②	Sam loves cooking, her dog and her family.	Sam loves cooking her dog and her family.

TERM 3

③ **There was a lady carrying a dog wearing pink pyjamas. Circle the true statement.**

The lady was wearing pink pyjamas.

The dog was wearing pink pyjamas.

④ **Rewrite the sentence so the other statement is true. Where will you put the comma?**

____

____

⑤ **Despite being told time and time again, Sam, said the teacher, is in a lot of trouble. Circle the true statement.**

Sam is in a lot of trouble.

Sam's teacher is in a lot of trouble.

⑥ **Rewrite the sentence so the other statement is true. Where will you put the comma?**

____

____

____

⑦ **Insert a comma in this sentence to make it clear that only Chris and Pat went to the football.**

After they left Sam Chris and Pat went to the football.

⑧ **Insert commas into this sentence to make it clear that all three went to the football.**

After they left Sam Chris and Pat went to the football.

Score 2 points for each correct answer!

TARGETING ENGLISH HOMEWORK YEAR 5 © PASCAL PRESS ISBN 978 1 925726 62 6

Phonic & Word Knowledge

AC9E5LY09

Pronouncing the letter 'c'

When you see the letter 'c' in a word, how do you know if it makes a soft /s/ sound or a hard /k/ sound? And why does it make that sound?

Here is a spelling generalisation to help: 'C' says /s/ before 'e', 'i' and 'y'! C says /k/ before all the rest, that's why!

Examples from the text with the /s/ sound: council, concentration, reducing, influence, place

Examples with the /k/ sound: count, clap, crack, calf, curse

Read each word and tick if the 'c' makes a soft /s/ sound or a hard /k/ sound. Write why this is the case.

		Soft /s/ sound	Hard /k/ sound	Why?
Example:	cyber	✓		The 'c' comes before 'y'.
1	cobra			
2	curse			
3	cereal			
4	bounce			
5	cider			

Silent 'c'

Sometimes when the letter 'c' follows the letter 's', the letter 'c' is silent. We do not pronounce it. Together, the letters 'sc' spell the 's' sound. *Example:* scent

Some of these words should have a silent 'c'. Write the word correctly if it is misspelt, inserting the silent 'c' if it is omitted. Tick the words if they are already correct. Be careful! Not all words need a silent 'c'

6 sience ____________

7 sene ____________

8 desend ____________

9 scissors ____________

10 seen ____________

11 paste ____________

In each of these words, the letter 's' is followed by the letter 'c'. But the letter 'c' is not silent in all the words. When the letter 'c' is the first letter of a syllable, it has the soft 'c' or 's' sound.

Draw a line to separate the syllables in words with two or more syllables. Circle the words that have a silent 'c'.
Example: **mus / cle ('c' has soft 's' sound)**

12 scent

13 descent

14 crescent

15 fascinated

16 ascent

Complete the text with words from the previous activity.

I started my 17 ________________ up the hill to see my place from a height. I knew the 18 ________________ would be a lot easier as the hill is quite steep. The 19 ________________ of the flowers was overpowering, and I was 20 ________________ by the colours of the land before me. My place is special to me, especially when I see the moon as a 21 ________________ above the hills.

The C challenge

Complete the 'C' challenge by writing two words for each question that start with 'c'. The words cannot be plural (adding 's'). Write words with the correct number of letters.

Example: 5 letters cable cobra	22 6 letters	23 7 letters
24 8 letters	25 9 letters	26 10 letters

Score 2 points for each correct answer! SCORE /52 0-24  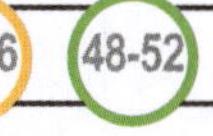

Reading & Comprehension

AC9E5LY04, AC9E5LY05, AC9E5LE04, AC9E5LE05

Imaginative text – Poetry

Poetry and Figurative Language

Poetry is a type of literature where the author or poet uses special or figurative language to bring out our emotions or stir our imaginations. Poems can follow rules or be freeform and follow no formal structure. Each line in a poem starts with a capital letter. Sentence structure is not adhered to, so poetry is where you can play with words.

Figurative language is used for effect in poetry. For example:

- Simile – A simile uses the words 'like' or 'as' to compare two things, for example, *as quiet as a mouse.*
- Metaphor – A metaphor compares two things but does not use 'like' or 'as', for example, *the sea is a hungry beast.* This compares the sea to a beast.
- Personification – This gives human characteristics to non-human things, for example, *the old car coughed and spat and wheezed before deciding to give up.* A car is not human and so cannot cough or make decisions.
- Alliteration – This is a sound device where a series of words repeats the same letter sound, for example, ***s**melly, **s**oggy **s**ock**s**.*

Poems with rules

These are examples of a cinquain which is a poem that has five lines.

Flooding
Murky, muddy, *(alliteration)*
Inundates, swamps, engulfs,
Building levees to hold it back,
Deluge.

Bushfire
Hungry, greedy, *(personification)*
Consumes all in its path,
Armies battle the giant's roar, *(personification)*
Ablaze.

The rules are:
Line 1: 2 syllables, a noun
Line 2: 4 syllables, adjectives to describe the noun
Line 3: 6 syllables, action verbs that describe what the noun does
Line 4: 8 syllables, how you feel about the noun or subject of the poem
Line 5: 2 syllables, another word for the subject of the poem

Limericks are usually a verse with 3 long and 2 short rhyming lines. They are short, rhyming, funny and have a bouncy rhythm.

I invited my friend to my place,
Smelly sneaker stench hit their face,
(alliteration)
As pungent as a wet bog, *(simile)*
So I blamed the poor dog,
And we left for the mall posthaste.

The rules are:
The rhyme scheme is AABBA.
The first two lines are longer, and they rhyme.
The next two lines are shorter, and they rhyme.
The last line is longer, and it rhymes with the first two lines.

Now try some of your own poems. You can follow the rules or just write freeform – no rules.

TERM 3

TARGETING ENGLISH HOMEWORK YEAR 5 © PASCAL PRESS ISBN 978 1 925726 62 6

Reading & Comprehension

Write the answer or shade the bubble next to the correct answer.

The answers to these questions are in the text.

1. What must each line in a poem start with?

___

2. List the four types of **figurative language**.

___

___

3. Poetry has strict sentence structure.

○ True ○ False

4. Out of the five lines, which lines **rhyme** in a limerick?

___

___

5. How many **syllables** should a cinquain poem have altogether?

___

Think about these questions and search for the answers in the text.

6. There are two **alliterations** in the poetry on the previous page. Write them below.

___

___

7. What is the difference between a **simile** and a **metaphor**?

___

___

8. How are limericks and cinquains **the same**?

___

___

___

9. How are limericks and cinquains **different**?

___

___

___

10. The cinquains about bushfires and floods:

○ show how wonderful and powerful bushfires and floods can be.

○ show respect and admiration for bushfires and floods.

○ show the destruction caused by bushfires and floods.

Use inferencing skills to answer this question. The answer is not in the text. Think about what you know and what the author says.

11. The word **pungent** is used in the limerick. The sentences around it (context clues) give you an idea of its meaning. Which word has a similar meaning?

○ fresh ○ fruity

○ bland ○ foul

Use your experience and opinions to answer this question. The answer is not in the text.

12. Write a **limerick** of your own, following all the rules.

___

___

___

___

___

Comprehension Reflections

Look at the top of the opposite page. This text is an I__________ text – P__________.

Write one thing you learned or found interesting:

___

Write one question you have or something you want to find more information about:

___

___

Rating   

Score 2 points for each correct answer!

SCORE /24   

TERM 3

Grammar & Punctuation

AC9E5LE04, AC9E5LE05

Figurative language – Similes

Similes compare two things using the words like or as.

Example: The teacher was **as** angry **as** a lion.

The two things being compared are a teacher and a lion. The teacher resembles a lion perhaps in the way they pace the room, snarl, are dangerous and scary, look for prey or weaknesses or are large and intimidating.

Example: The students were **like** squeaky chairs.

The two things being compared are students and squeaky chairs. The students resemble squeaky chairs perhaps in the way they make a constant irritating noise – no matter what you try, the noise continues.

Using the previous examples of similes, complete these sentences.

1. The Year One student was **as** cute **as** a puppy. The two things being compared are ____________ and ____________. The student resembles a puppy perhaps in the way they ______________________________.
2. The middle school students were buzzing **like** a beehive. The two things being compared are ____________ and ____________. The students resemble a beehive perhaps in the way they ______________________________.

Devise your own similes.

3. The teacher looked at me **like** ____________ ______________________________.
4. Chris looked at the test with a stare **as** blank **as** ______________________________.
5. The student approached her hamburger **like** ______________________________.

Metaphors

A metaphor is a way to imagine how one thing is the same as another thing because they have the same characteristics. You do not use 'like' or 'as'; instead, you directly say something is or was something else.

Example: After two hours in the sun, he **was** a lobster. He is compared to a lobster. This means he looks red just like a lobster.

Example: Sam **is** a shining star. Sam is compared to a shining star. This is flattering and implies or suggests that Sam is bright and a standout.

Example: In contrast, Sam's bedroom **is** a black hole. This is less positive as it implies or suggests a vast collection of objects in one small space.

Write your own metaphors. Explain what your choice of comparison implies.

6. My bedroom is ______________________________ ______________________________.
   This implies or suggests ______________________________ ______________________________.
7. My hair is ______________________________ ______________________________.
   This implies or suggests ______________________________ ______________________________.
8. My toenails are ______________________________ ______________________________.
   This implies or suggests ______________________________ ______________________________.
9. My thoughts are ______________________________ ______________________________.
   This implies or suggests ______________________________ ______________________________.

Hyperbole

Pronounced hi-per-buh-lee, this is an exaggeration that is not meant to be believed.

Example: I could eat a horse.

This means I am very hungry and not that I would literally eat a horse. Hyperbole is often used in writing to strongly emphasise certain sentiments, emotions or situations.

Finish each statement using exaggeration to make it a hyperbole.

10. My bed is so comfortable I could ______________________________ ______________________________.
11. I am so happy I could ______________________________ ______________________________.
12. I'm so hungry I ______________________________ ______________________________.
13. I am so talented I ______________________________ ______________________________.

Score 2 points for each correct answer! SCORE /26

TERM 3

TARGETING ENGLISH HOMEWORK YEAR 5 © PASCAL PRESS ISBN 978 1 925726 62 6

AC9E5LY09

French base words 'cinq' and 'cinque'

The text has some difficult words which have been borrowed from other languages. Cinquain, which is a type of poem with five lines, has been borrowed from the French language. The words cinq and cinque are French words meaning five.

Here are some other difficult words and their origins and meanings.

French	Latin	Old English	Meaning
	pungent		strong smell or taste
engulf	deluge inundates		drowns and overwhelms
	consumes		eats up
		posthaste	as quickly as possible
		stench	stink

One way to learn to spell and use new words (like the 7 bold words in the paragraph below) is by dictation. Learn the paragraph, and then have someone read it back to you several words at a time while you write it. Of course, you will cover the dictation paragraph first!

① – ⑦

One of the students left the tap running in the wet area. Unfortunately, the sink was blocked, so the wet area was **inundated** with water. It **engulfed** the entire floor. The student ran to the teacher **posthaste**, who used a mop that **consumed** the water like a giant sponge and stopped the **deluge**. However, several days later, the area had a **pungent** smell. The **stench** reached the classrooms. The students and teachers were not happy.

Rhyming words

In some forms of poetry, rhyming words are necessary, but it is not always easy to think of words that rhyme.

Find two rhyming words for each of these words.

	Example: stench	drench	bench
⑧	pungent		
⑨	consumes		
⑩	posthaste		
⑪	inundate		

Vocabulary for good and bad smells

Stench means stink, which is when something smells really bad. English has many words meaning some type of smell. Sort these 13 'smell' words into good and bad smells.

⑫ – ㉔

Smell words	Good smells	Bad smells
aroma		
odorous		
perfumed		
rancid		
acrid		
fragrant		
putrid		
bouquet		
reek		
malodorous		
aromatic		
scented		
fetid		

Score 2 points for each correct answer! SCORE

TERM 3

AC9E5LY04, AC9E5LY05, AC9HS5K01

Imaginative text – Recount

Memoir

As my eyes are fading and I find it more difficult to write these days, I realise I need to start writing my memoir or my own history. It will be a way for my children and grandchildren to know what life was like when I was a young child growing up in 18th-century Britain.

I grew up in the country. My father worked the land for Lord Wilson while my mother worked in the kitchens at the Great House, owned by Lord Wilson. The Great House was very grand. It looked like a magical kingdom stocked with food and beautiful furniture, and it was richly decorated. However, we lived in a three-room house on the Lord's land – my parents and five children. A charity school opened in the village and all five children started school, but we also worked the land to help our father. Life was simple and hard, but we managed.

Then something called the Industrial Revolution happened. All I know is that my father's job was replaced by a machine, and we lost our little house. It was time to move to London. My father believed we could all find work there as new factories had opened.

In London, we lived in a terrible one-room place near the river. It was cold and damp and stank of rotting fish and sweaty bodies. Everyone had to work to make enough money to eat as food was expensive, and there were no schools for the poor. I worked 12 to 14 hours a day in a noisy and very crowded cotton spinning mill with other children – many younger than me. Most nights, I slept in the factory on a wooden floor that was cold, hard and filthy. The owner was supposed to provide us with food and clothing, but I received no clothing and very little food. I was starving and my belly often ached with hunger.

I remember it so clearly. I had been thinking of food when a waft of air caught my attention – the sweet smell of freshly baked bread. My mouth watered as I was drawn to the delicious aroma. I had no control. Before I knew it, I had grabbed a loaf of bread off the shop counter and run for my life, but not fast enough. Rough hands grabbed me, and I was hauled off to prison. Because things were so terrible at that time and the rules so strict, many people were jailed for stealing, even if they were starving.

The prisons were crowded, filthy cells full of desperate people. Many prisoners were going to be transported on ships to a new colony called Australia to start a new settlement. To my horror, the judge also sentenced me to transportation to Australia for seven years.

I will never forget the feeling when I stepped onto the small, three-mast sailing ship, knowing I would never see my family again. I was one of 14 children on the First Fleet. I was only 15 years of age at the time. It was the end of one life but the beginning of another.

TERM 3

TARGETING ENGLISH HOMEWORK YEAR 5 © PASCAL PRESS ISBN 978 1 925726 62 6

Reading & Comprehension

Write the answer or shade the bubble next to the correct answer.

The answers to these questions are in the text.

1. What is a **memoir**?

2. How did the **Industrial Revolution** change the author's life?

3. Children did not go to prison in the 18th century.
   - ◯ True
   - ◯ False

4. What was one of the **factories** in London?

5. Why did the author steal the bread?

Think about these questions and search for the answers in the text.

6. How did the author's life change after moving to London?

7. Why were the **prisons** so crowded?

8. If you were zapped into the 18th century, taking the author's place on the streets of London, how would your life be different? Name three differences.

9. The author was sentenced to **transportation**. What does that mean?

10. The author noticed the **aroma** of the bread. This means it:
    - ◯ stank.
    - ◯ smelt nice.
    - ◯ was a strong smell.

Use inferencing skills to answer this question. The answer is not in the text. Think about what you know and what the author says.

11. What do you think the author means by **'it was the end of one life and the beginning of another'**?

Use your experience and opinions to answer this question. The answer is not in the text.

12. Is it okay to steal food if you are starving? Write **one point for** stealing food for survival and **one point against**.

For

Against

Comprehension Reflections

Look at the top of the opposite page. This text is an I__________ text – R__________.

Write one thing you learned or found interesting:

Write one question you have or something you want to find more information about:

Rating

Score 2 points for each correct answer! SCORE /24 0-10 12-18 20-24

TERM 3

Simple past and past continuous

Recounts are usually written in past tense. This is a memoir, which tells about the past, so it is written in past tense. There are four past tense forms: simple past, past continuous, past perfect and past perfect continuous.

Simple past	Past continuous
Actions were completed in the past.	Actions that were taking place in the past.
Add 'ed' to the end of regular verbs *e.g.* wash – wash**ed**. Was/were can be a verb on their own.	Use was/were AND add 'ing' on the end of verbs *e.g.* **was** clean**ing**, **were** work**ing**.
Change the spelling of irregular verbs *e.g.* sing – sang.	
Examples: I **sang** first. I **watched** TV.	*Example:* The kids **were playing**.
Examples from the text: grew, worked, lived, opened, believed, it **was** cold, food **was** expensive	*Examples from the text:* was working, was starving, were starving, were going

Read these sentences and note the verbs in bold. Circle if the verbs are simple past or past continuous tense.

① I **sailed** on the next available convict ship.
simple past / past continuous

② I know that I **was looking** forward to the end of the journey.
simple past / past continuous

③ During storms, we **were freezing**, wet from seawater and sewage.
simple past / past continuous

④ In the calm, hot weather, I **was suffocating** with the heat below deck.
simple past / past continuous

Write your own sentences using the following simple past and past continuous verbs.

⑤ believed: ______________________________

⑥ was starving: ______________________________

⑦ were going: ______________________________

Past perfect and past perfect continuous

Past perfect	Past perfect continuous
A past action took place before another action.	An action began in the past and continued for some time in the past.
Use had AND add 'ed' to the end of regular verbs *e.g.* **had** clean**ed**, **had** wash**ed**.	Use had been AND use 'ing' on the end of verbs *e.g.* **had been** work**ing**.
Example: Pat **had visited** me many times.	*Example:* They **had been working**.
Examples from the text: had slept (irregular), had opened	*Example from the text:* had been thinking

Read these sentences and note the verbs in bold. Circle if the verbs are past perfect or past perfect continuous tense.

⑧ One day, I **had eaten** all my rations for breakfast.
past perfect / past perfect continuous

⑨ I **had been starving** for so long.
past perfect / past perfect continuous

⑩ Others **had warned** me.
past perfect / past perfect continuous

⑪ But I **had been sulking** and didn't listen.
past perfect / past perfect continuous

Underline the verbs in this text.

⑫ –⑰

One day, I was playing below deck when I heard a shout from above, "Land Ho!" I had been hoping that we would land soon. I had arrived – my new future was waiting for me.

Score 2 points for each correct answer!

SCORE /34 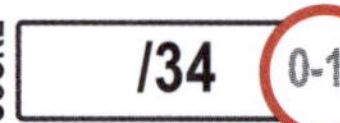 0-14  16-28  30-34

TERM 3

AC9E5LY09

Word building with 'transport'

The word transport was used in the text to explain that convicts were put on ships and moved to Australia. 'Trans' is a Latin prefix meaning across, beyond, or on the other side of. The Latin root word 'port' means to carry. Therefore, the convicts were carried to the other side of the world.

Words used in the crossword

report	transmit	transact
support	reporter	transitory
export	portfolio	deport
transcend	portly	portable
transparent	transition	translation
porter	important	transit
import	transformation	

Complete this crossword with Latin trans and port words. Use the clues below and the list of 'trans' and 'port' words above.

Down

1. to carry out of a country, sell to another
2. to carry away from, get rid of
3. brief and lasting a very short time
5. to carry in from another country
7. to exceed or go beyond
10. clear or see-through
11. someone who does the carrying
13. when someone carries too much body weight
15. a folder or collection of work
16. to move across, pass through the airport
17. to carry or hold the weight of something
18. to do business or perform

Across

4. a makeover or change
6. vital and essential
8. an interpretation from another language
9. to communicate and send a broadcast
12. someone who carries back the information
13. when something is easily carried
14. a collection of writing that carries information
16. to change over or move from one to another

Score 2 points for each correct answer! SCORE 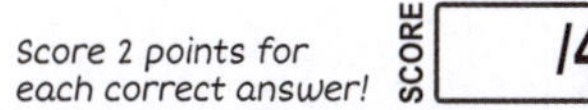 /40  0-18 20-34 36-40

AC9E5LY04, AC9E5LY05, AC9HS5K01

Persuasive text – Argument

Official London Report

Dated 13th April 1787

From Royal Magistrate Barnaby Ferguson

It has been noted that crime has increased over the last few months. I have no sympathy for the poor as we all know that they are to blame for their situation. The poor have to help themselves. However, the population of London has increased dramatically, leading to housing shortages and an increase in prices for food.

We have taken a very firm stand against crime as shown by the large numbers in our prisons. However, we need to do something to reduce the number of convicts in our cells. We have in the past sent our convicts to the colony in America. Unfortunately, since the revolution, we are unable to continue doing so.

We have loaded many old sailing ships or hulks in the harbour with convicts. Some have been in the ships for many a year. These floating prisons are just one solution, but we need a more permanent one. A fellow called Joseph Banks suggested a place in the Great Southern Land called Botany Bay. He visited the bay when travelling with Cook, Captain James Cook. This might be one way to rid ourselves of many convicts as well as making sure other countries such as France, Holland and Spain do not claim this southern land for themselves. The convicts will become settlers of this new land.

I hereby recommend the sending of a fleet of ships to Botany Bay as quicky as possible, led by Captain Arthur Phillip.

Barnaby Ferguson

TARGETING ENGLISH HOMEWORK YEAR 5 © PASCAL PRESS ISBN 978 1 925726 62 6

Reading & Comprehension

Write the answer or shade the bubble next to the correct answer.

The answers to these questions are in the text.

1. Who wrote the report?

2. When was the report written?

3. Where have the convicts previously been sent?

4. Why can't they be sent there anymore?

5. Which **countries** does the author worry will take over the Great Southern Land?

Think about these questions and search for the answers in the text.

6. What does the author think of the **poor**?

7. What is the purpose of sending convicts to **Botany Bay**?

8. What is a **hulk** in this text? How were they used?

9. The author does not want other countries settling the Great Southern Land. This means:
   - ◯ Britain wanted it for themselves.
   - ◯ Britain wanted to protect the original inhabitants.
   - ◯ Britain thought it wasn't worth possessing.

Use inferencing skills to answer this question. The answer is not in the text. Think about what you know and what the author says.

10. Is the **author** rich or poor? How do you know?

Use your experience and opinions to answer these questions. The answers are not in the text.

11. The First Fleet set sail in May 1787 but arrived in Botany Bay in January 1788. Why would it have taken so long?

12. What if this report was rejected and no First Fleet was sent? Write two possible **consequences** if this had happened.

Comprehension Reflections

Look at the top of the opposite page. This text is a P__________ text – A__________.

Write one thing you learned or found interesting:

Write one question you have or something you want to find more information about:

Rating   

Score 2 points for each correct answer!

SCORE 

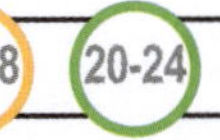

TERM 3

Grammar & Punctuation

AC9E5LA05

Complex sentences

Remember! A complex sentence has a main clause that can stand on its own and a subordinate clause that cannot. These clauses can be joined by a conjunction.

Example:
Children stole food **because** they were starving.

subordinate clause — main clause — conjunction

These sentences are complex sentences. Rewrite each sentence with the conjunction (in bold) first. Don't forget to put the comma after the subordinate clause.

Example:

We have taken a very firm stand against crime **as** our overcrowded prisons show.

As our overcrowded prisons show, we have taken a very firm stand against crime.

1. I hereby recommend sending a fleet of ships to Botany Bay immediately **because** the hulks are overcrowded.

2. Joseph Banks visited Botany Bay **when** he was travelling with Captain James Cook.

3. I have no sympathy for them **since** we all know that the poor are to blame for their situation.

4. The convicts will become settlers **after** they arrive at Botany Bay.

TERM 3

Conditional conjunctions

Conditionals are sentences that say what will happen, depending on another thing. *Examples:* **If** I won the lottery, I would buy a new house. (Buying a new house depends on winning the lottery.)

Unless you practise, you won't improve your playing skills. (Improving your skills depends on practising.)

Conditional conjunctions include if, as long as, until and unless. There are different types of conditional sentences which use different verb tenses. Conditional sentences can give an example, be persuasive, make your audience think and provide more information.

This is a 'second conditional' sentence which expresses a hypothetical or unrealistic situation.

simple past tense verb — past tense modal verb — verb in base form

Example: If I **had** my own car, I **would drive** myself to school. (This is unrealistic because you're not old enough to have a car and drive.)

Rewrite this second conditional sentence by putting the conjunction in the middle of the sentence. Don't forget to leave out the comma as the first clause is independent.

Example: **If** I were a convict, I would try very hard to escape.

I would try very hard to escape **if** I were a convict.

5. **If** I were transported to Australia, I would never see my family again.

Finish these second conditional sentences. Rewrite them with the conjunction in the middle of the sentence.

6. **If** I were a convict, I ...

7. **If** I were starving, I ...

Score 2 points for each correct answer!

SCORE /14

TARGETING ENGLISH HOMEWORK YEAR 5 © PASCAL PRESS ISBN 978 1 925726 62 6

Phonic & Word Knowledge

AC9E5LY09

Homophones

In the text, the Royal Magistrate, Barnaby Ferguson, wrote an official report which would need to be written without any mistakes. However, Barnaby had difficulty with spelling homophones. These are words that sound the same or similar but may have a different spelling and meaning.

Example: effect (usually used as a noun, meaning result or consequence)

affect (a verb, meaning to produce change)

The **effect** or consequence of poor spelling would **affect** Barnaby's career.

Help Barnaby by circling the correct homophone in these sentences.

1. The convicts were in their **cells / sells** onboard floating hulks or ships.
2. They never **new / knew** when they **would / wood** be transported to Australia.
3. Nothing would **effect /affect** Barnaby's decision to send convicts to Australia.
4. One **effect /affect** of being in cramped conditions on the hulks was that diseases spread quickly.
5. Barnaby thought the **one / won** solution to the problem was transportation.
6. The **poor / pour** convicts would have **their / there / they're** lives changed forever with the signing of the report to send them to Australia.

Past or passed?

Pass, when used as a verb, is often used to express physical motion or movement. The past tense of 'pass' is passed. *Example:* The car **passed** the truck.

Past is never used as a verb. It can mean 'gone by in time'. *Examples:* It is **past** my bedtime. (used here as a preposition)

In **past** years, my family lived with my grandparents. (used here as an adjective)

Past can also mean 'belonging to an earlier time'. *Example:* In the **past**, I actually loved eating vegetables! (used here as a noun)

And past can mean 'going beyond a point or one side to another'. *Example:* I ran **past** the teacher. (used here as an adverb)

Help Barnaby by circling the correct homophones in these sentences.

7. The convicts' **past / passed** lives were to be forgotten as they set sail for Australia.
8. As they **past / passed** the last harbour walls, **their / there / they're** adventure started.
9. The **past / passed** voyages of Captain Cook led to the First Fleet sailing to Australia, or as it was known then, the Great Southern Land.
10. Australia was **affected / effected** by the landing of the First Fleet. Changes to its people and land would follow.

Draw the front cover of these homophone book titles.

They won one!
11

Beware! Bytes bite!
12

Score 2 points for each correct answer! SCORE /24

TERM 3

Imaginative text – Recount

On the First Fleet

The First Fleet set sail in May 1787, carrying approximately 1400 people. Of these, 775 were convicts and the rest were crew, soldiers and marines, and family members. The eleven ships – six carrying convicts, two Royal Navy vessels and three supply ships – took over eight months to arrive at Botany Bay. So, what was life like on board?

Mary: *I was 15 when I was sentenced to seven years' transportation for stealing. Fine men's silk handkerchiefs were my specialty. I could pick a pocket and they would not know, except for that one time.*

We set sail in the ship Lady Penrhyn. *This ship had the most women convicts of all the six ships carrying convicts. At first, convicts were shackled or handcuffed, but Captain Arthur Phillip stopped this after two weeks. You didn't want to misbehave, or you would be back in them before you knew it.*

It was cramped in the cabins below deck and could be suffocatingly hot. We used buckets as toilets and had to scrub these out every day. We got rations twice a day and slept on thin mattresses as bedding which we took up to the deck to air as often as we were permitted.

We were allowed on deck in good weather to wash with sea water and soap, but in bad weather we had to stay below, lying on our sleeping racks. There was no natural light, and lanterns and candles were forbidden because of the risk of fire. So it was often dark, smelly, hot and very cramped.

We had to clean the cabins regularly as some held twelve women and some less, but they needed cleaning out, especially after a violent storm when sea water and sewage could wash through the hatches. During rough weather, many of us would get violently seasick and quite a few women were injured, tossed around the cabins with the violence of the waves. It was terrifying.

Diseases spread quickly. I heard some had cholera and pneumonia. We were not given any new clothes, so we had to live in what we walked onto the ship with for eight months until the Captain, that Arthur Phillip, gave out some clothing they'd packed to take to this Botany place. Wasn't much good though. It fell to pieces, so we had to make clothes out of the bags they stored rice in – so scratchy and uncomfortable – or use any material bought at the stops along the way.

Mary survived the 24 000 km journey which took 259 days. Sixty-two of those days they were anchored at stops along the way to reload the supply ships. Some children were born along the way, and approximately 48 people died, which is an amazing accomplishment considering the conditions. However, arriving was just the first step in a long and difficult road for the new settlement and for the original inhabitants of Australia.

TARGETING ENGLISH HOMEWORK YEAR 5 © PASCAL PRESS ISBN 978 1 925726 62 6

Reading & Comprehension

Write your answers on the lines provided.

1. What was Mary's **crime**?

2. How many ships **did not** carry convicts?

3. What was used as a **toilet**?

4. How were **women** injured during storms?

5. What would happen to you if you misbehaved along the way?

It is said conditions were hard. What is so hard about lying in bed all day? Give three reasons why conditions were hard.

6.

7.

8.

9. How did the convicts get new **clothing**?

10. Why wouldn't all ships carry convicts? Think of two reasons why the other ships came along with the convict ships.

11. Why would the cabins get hot if they started the journey in winter in Britain? Think of two reasons.

12. Why would it be important for the convicts to clean out the cabins and air their mattresses?

13. If stuck below deck in cramped conditions for long periods of time, what could the convicts have done to help pass the time?

TERM 3

Score 2 points for each correct answer!

SCORE /26   

Grammar & Punctuation

Conversation

Punctuate the following conversation. You may need to use the punctuation marks in brackets (“_” , . ? ! ’). And don’t forget the capital letters!

1. Captain Phillip Sir the Lieutenant said the convicts are asking for more clothing
2. Captain Phillip thought deeply can we get to the clothing saved for Botany Bay
3. Do you mean on the supply ships questioned the Lieutenant it will be difficult but I can try
4. Thank you Lieutenant answered the Captain please make your way to one of the supply ships
5. Yes Sir the Lieutenant answered loudly and with that he headed off to search for the supplies

Second conditional poem and tenses

Conditional sentences say what will happen depending on whether another thing happens. This poem uses ‘if’ (conditional conjunction) to start each hypothetical sentence.

If I <u>had</u> a billion dollars, I **would buy** a pet monkey.

If I <u>bought</u> a pet monkey, I **would join** a circus.

If I <u>joined</u> a circus, I **would become** famous.

If I <u>became</u> famous, I **could own** my own jet.

If I <u>owned</u> my own jet, I **might see** UFOs.

If I <u>saw</u> UFOs, I **might join** them.

If I <u>joined</u> them, I ...

Remember! One side of a second conditional sentence has a <u>past simple verb</u> (underlined). The other side has modal verbs **would, could** and **might** with the **base form of the main verb** (in bold).

6 – 12 **Write your own second conditional poem using at least seven conditionals. Be careful of the change in tense!**

____

____

____

____

____

____

____

____

____

____

____

____

____

Nominalisation generalisations

Nominalisation is where verbs (actions or events) or adjectives (describing words) are changed into nouns (things or ideas). This can be done by adding certain suffixes or changing the spelling. *Examples:* accomplish (verb) – accomplishment (noun)

transport (verb) – transportation (noun)

Read these sentences and change the verb in brackets to a noun by adding a suffix.

13. The (disappear) ________________ of a billion dollars is being investigated.
14. The police made an (announce) ________________ that a monkey was in custody.
15. They expected a quick (resolve) ________________ to the case.
16. The monkey made a full (confess) ________________ and begged for (forgive) ________________.
17. However, a famous jet pilot questioned the police on their lack of (prove) ________________.

Score 2 points for each correct answer! SCORE /34  0-14  16-28  30-34 

TARGETING ENGLISH HOMEWORK YEAR 5 © PASCAL PRESS ISBN 978 1 925726 62 6

Phonic & Word Knowledge

Hard and soft sounds

Circle all the soft sounds in red (c says /s/ and g says /j/). Circle all the hard sounds in blue (c says /k/ and g says /g/).

C says /s/ before 'e', 'i' and 'y'!
C says /k/ before all the rest, that's why!
When g is in front of 'i', 'y' or 'e', it is soft and says /j/.
When g is in front of any other letter, it is hard and says /g/.

Example: circumference	(4) pencil	(8) circuit	(12) again	(16) ginger	(20) gentle	(24) react
(1) rancid	(5) lucid	(9) cinnamon	(13) ghost	(17) gym	(21) giant	(25) recite
(2) icicle	(6) excite	(10) circus	(14) guess	(18) genius	(22) client	(26) escape
(3) cinder	(7) civil	(11) career	(15) green	(19) giraffe	(23) gobble	

(27) – (53)

Find all the words (27) from the previous activity in the Word Find. Words can go forwards and backwards in a horizontal and vertical direction.

a	a	s	d	f	g	h	j	g	k	l	p	o	i	n	o	m	a	n	n	i	c	u	y	t	r
z	l	q		z	q	s	d	i	h	j	b							e	a	l	t	x	e		h
x	i	w		x	d	f	g	n	l	m	n	e	b	g	w	x	l	i	z	l	m	h	r		g
c	c	e		c	i	h	j	g	i	e	g	t	f	y	q	p	u	l	j	e	r	s	s		o
v	n	r		v	c	k	l	e	c	i	r	c	u	m	f	e	r	e	n	c	e	y	s		b
b	e	t		b	u	a	s	r	i	a	e		e	z	e	y	t	f	s		p	i	e		b
n	p	y	o	n	l	d	f	g	n	y	e		g	e		q	v	f	e		r	k	u		l
s		u	p	m	h	j	k	l	d	e	n		j	x		a	e	a	b		e	h	g		e
u		d	l						e	e	i		k	c		v	u	r	t		c	z	v		b
c		i	c	i	c	l	e	u	r	e	j		a	i		f	x	i	k		i	s	b		i
r		c	k	q	z	x	c							t		i	r	g	e	n	t	l	e		j
i		n	j	a	v	b	c	i	v	i	l	m	b	e		t	q	j	i	y	e	h	e	l	r
c		a	g	a	i	n			g		e	a	h	k		t						u	p	m	e
m		r	h	z	s	d	f	g	i		p	b	w	t		c	k	p	t	i	u	c	r	i	c
l		i	g	x					a		a	w	z	r	l	a	s	b	u	b	v	p	k	x	a
k	s	u	i	n	e	g	q	w	n		c	j	c	a	r	e	e	r							
j	h	g	f	d	d	s	a	q	t		s	x	b	h	a	r	i	l	m	j	b	h	k	m	e
g	h	o	s	t	e	r	t	y	u	i	e	d	f	g	h	j	k	l	p	t	n	e	i	l	c

French 'gue' and 'que' words

Unscramble the words in bold in this paragraph. (Hint: You will find the words in the box.)

vague, colleague, dialogue, meringue, fatigue, antique, boutique, brusque, grotesque, opaque, technique, unique

I asked a French schoolmate or **eeoauclgl** (54) __________________ how to make a **eeginumr** (55) __________________. His manner was **qsebuur** (56) __________________ when he suggested I could buy the recipe off him for $30. I laughed and went instead to a **ieuuotqb** (57) __________________ shop that only sells French desserts. I'm still not sure how to make them. I haven't got the right **eeiuthqnc** (58) __________________ as they come out very flat and chewy.

Score 2 points for each correct answer! SCORE /116 0-56 58-110 112-116

AC9E5LY04, AC9E5LY05, AC9E5LE03, AC9HS5K02, AC9HS5K03

Informative text – Explanation

Hit the Reverse Button on Colonisation

A third-person point of view

History is written from different points of view and may not be written at the point in time that it describes. This is what makes history both a little bit tricky and very interesting. That's why you always need to ask: Whose viewpoint of history are we seeing and whose is missing?

Let's delve into history in an imaginative way. What if colonisation by the British had not taken place in Australia from 1788 onwards? This means the eleven First Fleet ships carrying 1500 people would not have landed at Sydney Cove. How would things be different and for whom?

First Nations people belong to many different groups, each with its own language, laws, beliefs and customs. European contact brought a sudden change to this traditional way of life and to the land. What if we hit the reverse button?

This means that the thick, woody, natural bushland and plants growing along the streams would not have disappeared. If plants and trees are removed from the banks of a stream, the banks can become unstable and collapse into the water. This would not have happened. There would be no run-off from surrounding land flowing into the stream damaging the ecosystems in and around the water. You would then take away the introduced animals like cows, horses, sheep and pigs. These animals drink the water, their hard hooves trample the soil, and their waste goes into the water. Take them away and there would be no destruction of waterways and land.

The First Nations people's knowledge about bush medicine is great; however, they were unable to treat an introduced virus like smallpox. This disease, brought by the Europeans on the First Fleet, spread rapidly, killing 50–80% of the First Nations population. If colonisation had not happened, then no-one would have died of smallpox.

Early relations between the First Nations people and the Europeans were friendly, but as the colony grew and spread inland from the coast, competition for land and resources led to conflict. First Nations people fought hard to preserve their way of life and culture, and resistance leaders such as Pemulwuy led the fight against the Europeans as part of what many people now call the Frontier Wars. If colonisation had not happened, then a traditional way of life would have continued for First Nations people.

So, look out the window and ask yourself ... what if?

TARGETING ENGLISH HOMEWORK YEAR 5 © PASCAL PRESS ISBN 978 1 925726 62 6

Reading & Comprehension

Write the answer or shade the bubble next to the correct answer.

The answers to these questions are in the text.

1. What makes history a bit **tricky**?

2. First Nations people belong to many different groups. What does each different group have?

3. What happens if plants and trees are **removed** from the banks of a stream?

4. What **effects** do cows, horses, sheep and pigs have on the environment?

5. What **disease** caused a significant loss of life for First Nations people?

6. What **effect** did this disease have on First Nations people?

Think about these questions and search for the answers in the text.

7. What **point of view** is this text based on?
   - ◯ convicts and the environment
   - ◯ First Nations people and the environment
   - ◯ the environment

8. If colonisation **had not happened**, name three things that would not have occurred according to the text.

Use inferencing skills to answer these questions. The answers are not in the text. Think about what you know and what the author says.

9. After reading the text, what do you think **third-person point of view** means?

10. One of the resistance leaders was a First Nations man, Pemulwuy. What were the First Nations people **resisting**?

Use your experience and opinions to answer this question. The answer is not in the text.

11. If colonisation had not happened, how would your view be different? Look outside of a window near you.

Comprehension Reflections

Look at the top of the opposite page. This text is an I__________ text – E__________.

Write one thing you learned or found interesting:

Write one question you have or something you want to find more information about:

Rating   

Score 2 points for each correct answer! SCORE /22 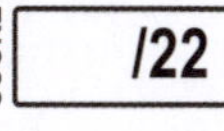 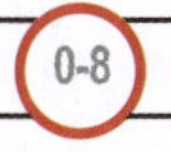 
0-8 10-16 18-22

Grammar & Punctuation

AC9E5LA09

Apostrophes of possession – Single nouns

In the text, this sentence contains an apostrophe of possession: The First Nations **people's** knowledge about bush medicine is great. It shows that the 'knowledge' belongs to the First Nations people. Let's recap and extend our knowledge of apostrophes of possession.

For single nouns, just add an apostrophe and an 's'.
Example: the **ship's** mast (The mast belongs to the ship.)

Put apostrophes in these phrases.

1. the convicts shoe
   (The shoe belongs to the convict.)
2. the streams banks
   (The banks belong to the stream.)
3. the captains crew
   (The crew belongs to the captain.)

Plural nouns

For plural nouns, if the word already ends in 's', add only an apostrophe after the 's'.
Example: the **convicts'** shoes (The shoes belong to more than one convict.)

Put apostrophes in these phrases.

4. the captains crews
   (The crews belong to more than one captain.)
5. the trees roots
   (The roots belong to more than one tree.)
6. the cows hooves
   (The hooves belong to more than one cow.)

Tricky plural nouns

For tricky plurals, add an apostrophe and an 's'. The word 'children' is a plural noun, but it does not end in 's'. *Example:* the **children's** books

Put apostrophes in these phrases.

7. the mens shirts
   (The shirts belong to the men.)
8. the womens shoes
   (The shoes belong to the women.)
9. the childrens toys
   (The toys belong to the children.)

Apostrophes with collective nouns

When there is more than one owner, the apostrophe is used for the last owner in the list. *Example:* the cat and **kitten's** bowls (The bowls belong to the cat and the kitten.)

Put apostrophes in these sentences.

10. It was John and Pats idea to escape the colony. No more convict life for us!
11. The escape tunnel and trapdoors design was foolproof.
12. If only I had Grandma and Grandpas shovel to help dig the tunnel.
13. Mum and Dads song came into my head. I used to sing it when I was scared.

If each individual owns something, then there is an apostrophe on each subject.
Example: It was John**'s** and Pat**'s ideas** that helped us to escape. (John and Pat each had ideas. Notice that 'idea' is now plural.)

Put apostrophes in these sentences.

14. My mums and dads faces appeared in my memory as I crawled through the tunnel.
15. Johns and Pats hands helped me out of the trapdoor.
16. Then I saw the two soldiers. The corporals and sergeants guns were aimed towards me.

Now try a mix of all you have practised. Put apostrophes in this paragraph.

17 – 20 The mens guns were held close to my belly. The sergeants and corporals fingers were ready on the triggers. My bellys rumbling showed my nervousness. I started to sing.

Score 2 points for each correct answer! SCORE /40   

TERM 4

TARGETING ENGLISH HOMEWORK YEAR 5 © PASCAL PRESS ISBN 978 1 925726 62 6

AC9E5LY08, AC9E5LY09, AC9E5LY10

Nominalisation

Nominalisation is when we transform actions (verbs) or descriptions of nouns (adjectives) into things or people (nouns). Your writing will be more creative and interesting if you use nominalisations.

One way to do this is to use the suffix 'tion'. The suffix 'tion' sounds like 'shun' and is far more common than the suffix 'sion'.

If the root word ends in 't', add the suffix 'ion' which forms 'tion'. *Example:* op**t** + ion = op**tion**

Complete these sentences by adding 'ion' to the verbs in brackets.

1. The (direct) ____________ of the escape tunnel led straight to the soldiers' quarters.
2. I had no (opt) ____________ but to surrender.
3. My (act) ____________ earnt me hard labour on a farm.
4. My attempted escape was even printed in the first (edit) ____________ of the colony's newsletter. I thought I was famous!

For words ending in 'te', drop the 'e' to add 'ion'. *Example:* celebra**te** + ion = celebra**tion**

Complete these sentences by adding 'ion' to the verbs in brackets.

5. Working on the farm felt like a (vacate) ____________ after being on the ship.
6. The (locate) ____________ was very remote and I saw many First Australians who were not happy to be moved off their land. I wouldn't like it either.
7. I did not have any (educate) ____________, so I couldn't read or write.
8. However, I wasn't happy with the (create) ____________ of a school for convict kids.

Complete the text by filling in the correct words from the list. These base words contain a long 'o' vowel sound.

lotion	devotion
emotion	promotion

I was a good student though, and I received a (9) ____________ to head student in the little school. My (10) ____________ to my studies even surprised me. I was actually proud of myself, an (11) ____________ I had never had before. Unfortunately, I caught smallpox and the farmer's wife applied a smelly (12) ____________ which relieved the pain.

The text at the start of this unit contains 'tion' words where the verb or adjective has been changed into a noun – nominalisation.

Unscramble the words from the text below. The beginning letter is in brackets to help you for the first four.

13. stnnoai (n)____________
14. nooppiault (p)____________
15. oooiiannslct (c)____________
16. mttiiooenpc (c)____________
17. tealsroni ____________
18. criedstunot ____________

Common 'ie' letter patterns with different pronunciations

The word 'view' is important in the text at the start of this unit. It follows the spelling generalisation 'i' before 'e' except after 'c'; however, there are exceptions. Here are words that follow this generalisation but the 'ie' has different pronunciations.

(19) – (29)
Circle the words red or blue depending on their pronunciation (see the example words).

Examples: th**ie**f (bee sound) p**ie** (eye sound)

tried	relief	achieve	lie	belief
died	believe	chief	shield	priest
yield				

Score 2 points for each correct answer!

TERM 4

AC9E5LY04, AC9E5LY05, AC9E5LE03, AC9HS5K02

Imaginative text – Narrative

A New Life

I was one of 14 children on the First Fleet, and I was only 15 years of age at the time. It was the end of one life but the beginning of another. I will tell you how my life began again in this strange land, with strange animals and the First Australians whose land we took and moulded to our way of life.

When we finally landed, we were given new clothing. It was all adult-sized, so belts and braces were needed to make the clothes fit. Not what I wanted, but better than the rags I had been wearing on the ship. We initially lived in tents and then built two-roomed huts to sleep in. The local clay was mixed with things like straw, and it was called 'wattle and daub'. At least 12 years later, proper barracks and buildings of stone were built to accommodate us convicts, but things were tough to begin with.

If that wasn't bad enough, there was not enough food for everyone. I heard a rumour that the food was supposed to last two years, but the Governor knew we were in trouble two months after landing. The crops that we planted didn't grow in many places, so the Governor cut our rations. We were weak with hunger, and many diseases such as tuberculosis, influenza, measles and smallpox were common in the colony.

Kids were treated no differently to adults. We had to find where to sleep and we were expected to work like the adults because work was part of our punishment for our crimes, or so I was told. My new life was very tough. Things improved for children 20 years after the colony started, with some education and training in trades, only for the boys of course. The boys would work in the colony, constructing buildings and working for the Governor in the town, or they would work on farms. Girls like me were servants or worked at spinning, weaving and laundry at a female factory. There were many more boy convicts than girl convicts, and overall, there were more men than women in the colony at the beginning.

I served my seven years in the colony and knew I would not go back to Britain because I did have a new life. I am married now. My husband and I bought land and have a small farm that we will leave to our eight surviving children. To think it all started with the theft of a silk handkerchief and has ended with a family in a land thousands of miles away. This is now my home and my life.

TARGETING ENGLISH HOMEWORK YEAR 5 © PASCAL PRESS ISBN 978 1 925726 62 6

Reading & Comprehension

Write the answer or shade the bubble next to the correct answer.

The answers to these questions are in the text.

1. What was **wattle and daub**?

2. How long was the food brought on the First Fleet **supposed to last**?

3. How long after landing did the Governor know the colony was running out of food?

4. Why did **child** convicts have to work?

5. In the beginning of the colony, there were the **same number** of female and male convicts.
   - ◯ True ◯ False

6. **Child convicts** were treated differently to adult convicts.
   - ◯ True ◯ False

7. What **work** did girl or female convicts do?

Think about these questions and search for the answers in the text.

8. The author says, **'My new life was tough'.** Write three things that made her life tough.

9. How old was the author **after serving her sentence** working in the colony?

10. Why did the author not go back to Britain?

Use inferencing skills to answer these questions. The answers are not in the text. Think about what you know and what the author says.

11. What does **rations** mean in this text?

12. What happened as a result of **cutting** everyone's rations?

13. What do you think the author is telling us by the phrase, **our eight surviving children**?

Use your experience and opinions to answer this question. The answer is not in the text.

14. If children and adults were treated the same today, how would your life be different? List three differences.

Comprehension Reflections

Look at the top of the opposite page. This text is an I__________ text – N__________.

Write one thing you learned or found interesting:

Write one question you have or something you want to find more information about:

Rating   

Score 2 points for each correct answer! SCORE 

TERM 4

Grammar & Punctuation

AC9E5LA09, AC9E5LA05

Commas after prepositional phrases

Commas are very important as they help the reader to make sense of a text. However, they are often misunderstood or not used at all!

Prepositions link parts of sentences together. They can describe location, position, direction, time or manner. Some prepositions can also act as conjunctions. *Examples of common prepositions:* in, on, to, at, before, after, during, with, under, between, above, below, with, beside

A comma is used after a prepositional phrase at the start of a sentence. *Example:* **During** a heavy thunderstorm, I hide under the blankets.

No comma is needed if the prepositional phrase comes at the end of a sentence. *Example:* I hide under the blankets **during** a heavy thunderstorm.

Add commas to these sentences. The preposition is in bold.

1. **At** exactly six o'clock I must go home.
2. **In** five minutes my friends will be picking me up.
3. **Before** I leave home I will check I have a phone or watch.
4. **On** many occasions I have forgotten about the time.
5. **Between** the four of us someone will remind me.

In these sentences, some prepositional phrases are at the start and some at the end of the sentence. Add commas where they are needed.

6. I left the house **in** a hurry.
7. **After** a quick bike ride I arrived at my friend's house.
8. **With** my backpack on my back I looked like a turtle.
9. My friends were waiting for me **by** the front gate.

Commas after dependent clauses

A complex sentence has an independent and dependent clause. A comma is used if the sentence starts with a dependent clause. *Example:* **As the evening wore on,** I forgot about the time.

The first part of the sentence does not make sense on its own so it is called a dependent clause.

No comma is needed when the dependent clause is at the end of the sentence. *Example:* I forgot about the time **as the evening wore on.**

Add commas where they are needed. For the first three sentences, the dependent clause is in bold.

10. **When I finally looked at the time** I was horrified to find it past six o'clock.
11. I tried to think of a really good excuse **before I got home.**
12. **After I talked to my friends** I felt much better.
13. I thought it was a great idea as I believe in aliens and UFOs.
14. After my family finished laughing I was told off for being late.

Score 2 points for each correct answer! SCORE /28  0-12  14-22  24-28 

TERM 4

TARGETING ENGLISH HOMEWORK YEAR 5 © PASCAL PRESS ISBN 978 1 925726 62 6

Phonic & Word Knowledge

AC9E5LY08, AC9E5LY09

Stressed syllables

Some syllables in a word are said louder and stronger. These are accented or stressed.

The meaning of some words changes if you stress a different syllable.

Say both of these example sentences with stress placed on the syllable that is in bold and in capitals.

Examples: What is that **OB**-ject over there? (thing)

Would anyone ob-**JECT** if I opened a window? (complain)

Different stress = different meaning

Circle the correct stressed syllable for these sentences.

1. Please don't _____ my cooking. (say something bad)
IN-sult / in-**SULT**
2. They threw my food in the bin. What an _____! (did something bad)
IN-sult / in-**SULT**
3. My cake was in the _____ bin, ready to be collected on Thursday. (rubbish)
REF-use / re-**FUSE**
4. I _____ to cook anymore! (say no)
REF-use / re-**FUSE**
5. My family tried to _____ me. (make me feel better)
CON-sole / con-**SOLE**
6. They then went to the computer _____ and ordered an UBER meal. (screen and controls)
CON-sole / con-**SOLE**

Lazy vowel sound 'schwa'

The most common vowel sound in the English language is 'schwa'. It is the easiest sound to make as your mouth does not have to open very much. It is a lazy sound.

In this exercise, we will be looking at the 'schwa' sound in the unaccented syllable at the end of a word.

'Schwa' makes spelling tricky because the final 'schwa' sound in many words is the same, but there are different spelling choices. *Examples:* doct**or**, sist**er**, doll**ar**

These words have an 'uh' sound at the end but different spellings.

There is no one way to be certain about which spelling to use for the 'schwa' sound, but here are some tips:

- The most common way of spelling 'schwa' is 'er', then 'or' and then 'ar'.
- If the word is an adjective, meaning more, use 'er'. *Examples:* bigger, faster
- The 'er' also means one who. *Example:* builder
- The 'or' can usually follow ct, it, at, rr or ess. *Examples:* actor, visitor, dictator, terror
- The 'ar' often follows l. *Examples:* collar, regular, similar

7 – 26

Sort these words into the table by the same ending.

sharper, elevator, baker, dancer, polar, operator, doctor, butcher, wider, indicator, regular, tidier, inspector, similar, instructor, senator, runner, hotter, collector, muscular

-er = 'more'	-er = 'one who'	-ctor words

-ator words	-lar words

Think of one more word for each column and write it below. Make sure the ending is right!

27. ____________________
28. ____________________
29. ____________________
30. ____________________
31. ____________________

Score 2 points for each correct answer! SCORE /62 0-28 30-56 58-62

TERM 4

AC9E5LY04, AC9E5LY05, AC9HS5K03

Informative text – Report

Chat Room: Pearls & Buttons

Hey, Sam! I need help with the homework assignment. I don't know what the teacher means by 'significant groups' in Australia's history. What does it mean and what on Earth is the clue, 'pearls and buttons?' Is it some old band the teacher once listened to?

LOL, they want us to look at groups of people who supported the development of Australia in things such as sport, arts, science, education and the economy or budget. The clue about pearls is for us to look at a particular migrant group like the Japanese pearl divers in Broome, Western Australia. That's the pearl clue, but I have no idea about buttons. It's kind of like – so what? What did this group do for Australia?

Here's what I found out. Pearls come from oysters. The pearl industry started in Western Australia in 1861. People had to dive into the shark-infested water and gather as many oyster shells as they could before they had to come up for air. In the beginning, First Nations people were the divers, then the government stopped that. People from Malaysia and many people from Japan were willing to take the risks because they were skilled at diving in their own country. It was a very dangerous job as they dived to great depths, and the death rate was high. It says they used heavy diving suits after 1870. They look very uncomfortable.

Well? What did they do?

I just looked it up. It was a booming business in Broome, WA, and the divers really helped the colony's economy. You're right, lots of divers died in the process. It seems the shiny inside of the oyster shells was also valuable and known as mother of pearl. The shiny inside of the shell was used to make buttons. Buttons? That's the clue!!!

Yeah, I saw that. Who would have thought there was a big business in buttons? I found out that the pearling industry almost closed because of several things. Plastic was being used for buttons, and people found out how to make cultured pearls, like a shortcut way of getting pearls. Also, World War 2 in 1939 meant trouble for the Japanese divers because we were not on the same side in the war. This meant many Japanese were put into camps as the government wanted to keep an eye on them. Hope this helps.

TARGETING ENGLISH HOMEWORK YEAR 5 © PASCAL PRESS ISBN 978 1 925726 62 6

Write the answer or shade the bubble next to the correct answer.

The answers to these questions are in the text.

1. What is meant by **significant groups**?

2. What did the **pearl** clue mean? What group did it link to?

3. What **animal** do pearls come from?

4. **When** and **where** did the pearl industry start in Australia?

Think about these questions and search for the answers in the text.

5. The **manufacture** of buttons was important to the pearl industry because:
   - ◯ buttons were made from pearls.
   - ◯ part of the shell of oysters was used to make buttons.
   - ◯ plastic was made from oyster shells.

6. The **Japanese pearl divers** were a significant group in Australia's history. What did they do for Australia?

7. Why was diving for pearls a dangerous job?

8. What country did the divers come from and why were they willing to take the risks?

Use inferencing skills to answer these questions. The answers are not in the text. Think about what you know and what the author says.

9. Why would **plastic buttons** make a difference to the pearl industry?

10. Why would **World War 2** affect the Japanese pearl divers?

Use your experience and opinions to answer these questions. The answers are not in the text.

After 1870, many divers wore a diving suit. Before that, divers held their breath and dived wearing only goggles.

11. Think of one reason why wearing the suit would be an **advantage** when diving for pearls.

12. Think of one reason why **diving without the suit**, the original method, would be better.

Comprehension Reflections

Look at the top of the opposite page. This text is an I__________ text – R__________.

Write one thing you learned or found interesting:

Write one question you have or something you want to find more information about:

Rating   

Score 2 points for each correct answer!

SCORE /24 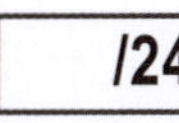   

TERM 4

TARGETING ENGLISH HOMEWORK YEAR 5 © PASCAL PRESS ISBN 978 1 925726 62 6

Grammar & Punctuation

AC9E5LA06, AC9E5LA09, AC9E5LY06

Apostrophes of possession

Apostrophes of possession have been used in the text. *Examples:* Australia**'s** history, the colony**'s** economy

For names that don't end with 's', we add an apostrophe and then 's' after.
Example: **Sam's** diving suit was on the floor.

But what about adding apostrophes to words ending in 's'?

If a name ends in 's', it is preferred in Australia to add an apostrophe and an 's'.
Example: **James's** diving suit was hanging on the ladder.

However, it is also acceptable to use just the apostrophe.
Example: **James'** boots

Circle the sentence with the correct use of apostrophes and 's'.

1. Sam and James's plan was to go diving for pearls.
   Sam and Jame's plan was to go diving for pearls.
2. Sam's and James suit's were ready to put on.
   Sam's and James's suits were ready to put on.
3. James's friend Paris' was going with them.
   James's friend Paris was going with them.
4. Paris's suit was already on the boat.
   Pari's suits was already on the boat.
5. The three friend's fear of sharks unsettled them.
   The three friends' fear of sharks unsettled them.
6. However, the boats' captain was certain no shark's were in the area.
   However, the boat's captain was certain no sharks were in the area.

Expanding noun groups

Using description and adding detail in a noun group gives the reader a much clearer picture of what you are writing about. Noun groups can consist of a single word or can be expanded by adding words before the noun and/or after the noun.

Example: A shark (shark is the noun)

A menacing shark (adjective added)

A huge, menacing shark (another adjective added)

A huge, menacing shark with jagged teeth circled the boat. (prepositional phrase added)

Prepositional phrases could start with on, in, at, from, above, with, of, under, opposite, under, in front of, behind, between.

Build your own noun group and complete a sentence.

7. A shark

   A ______________ shark

   A ______________ ______________ shark

   A ______________ ______________ shark with ______________________.

8. A pearl

   A ______________________________

   A ______________________________

   A ______________________________

9. A button

   A ______________________________

   A ______________________________

   A ______________________________

Score 2 points for each correct answer! SCORE /18  0-6  8-14  16-18

TARGETING ENGLISH HOMEWORK YEAR 5 © PASCAL PRESS ISBN 978 1 925726 62 6

Phonic & Word Knowledge

AC9E5LY08, AC9E5LY09

Spelling generalisations for the 'oi' sound

The text at the start of this unit is about pearls and oysters, and the pearling industry. The word 'oyster' has the 'oi' sound.

There are two spellings for the 'oi' sound: oi as in boil and oy as in boy.

Which one to use?

A generalisation for this sound is: oi is usually in the middle of the word and oy is usually at the end of the word. Be careful if a suffix is added.

Examples of oi words:

boil, coil, coin, devoid, foil, hoist, humanoid, join, joint, moist, noise, oil, point, poise, soil, spoil, subsoil, tinfoil, toil, toilet, turmoil, uncoil, void

Examples of oy words:

alloy, annoy, boy, boycott, convoy, coy, decoy, deploy, destroy, employ, enjoy, foyer, joy, overjoy, oyster, ploy, soy, toy

Using the words in the 'oi' and 'oy' lists, match the words with their meanings in this table.

	'oi' Words	Meaning
1		empty
2		confusion and unrest
3		lift and raise, winch
4		emptiness
5		grace and dignity
6		soggy, damp
	'oy' Words	**Meaning**
7		hallway
8		defeat and crush
9		shy and timid
10		a trick or a plan
11		hire or use
12		a mixture of metals
13		irritate

Learn this dictation text.

Roy made a **choice** about being a diver. He was **poised** above the water when he heard a **noise**. It was a **voice** calling him to stop. The **coil** of air hose had been cut to **spoil** any chance of him getting **oysters** from the seabed. The **ploy** was to **spoil Roy's joy**.

14 – 25 Have the dictation read back to you and write it below. Score points for all the 'oi' sounding words.

____

____

____

____

____

____

____

____

Generalisations for adding the suffix 'y'

The suffix 'y' usually changes nouns into adjectives, so shine into shiny. *Example from the text:* The **shiny** inside of the shell was used to make buttons.

Here are some spelling generalisations for adding the suffix 'y':

- If the noun is a CVC word, double the last letter and add 'y'. *Example:* fog = fo**ggy**
- If the noun ends in a consonant then 'e', drop the 'e' and add 'y'. *Example:* shine = shin**y**
- If the noun does not end in an 'e', or is not a CVC word, just add the 'y'. *Example:* cloud = cloud**y**

Add 'y' to these words.

26 cheese ______________________

27 yum ______________________

28 noise ______________________

29 run ______________________

30 wind ______________________

31 bag ______________________

Score 2 points for each correct answer! SCORE /62   

TERM 4

AC9E5LY04, AC9E5LY05, AC9HS5K04

Imaginative text – Narrative

The Tree

It struggled against the hard soil until it erupted into a world of sun and wind. Then it slept. Years passed and it grew strong and tall along the river, the cream-coloured trunk covered in slabs of bark. It was proud of its usefulness and its role in the rhythm of life.

Many animals sheltered from the heat under its branches, and birds and smaller animals made homes in its hollows while insects lived out their lives under its bark. The First Australians used the wood to make bowls to carry food and water, and they used the resin and bark to heal and soothe. They managed the land and knew its importance. They knew the tree provided food, shelter and life for many. Then it slept.

When it woke, the land had changed. Different animals grazed under its branches and the First Australians were gone. Different people managed the land. The banks of the river had crumbled as the land had been cleared, and the rich soil washed into the river, leaving bare patches on the ground. The large trees were gone. It stood lonely in its isolation, the last one left standing. The water changed colour and strangled the fish and animals that lived within it. Fences crisscrossed the land like stitches in a blanket. The wetlands around it were dry. The land was dry. Then it slept.

The heat seared its trunk and burnt the canopy of leaves that reached for the sky. Fierce flames licked the life from its branches and turned the land black. Life within and life outside of it died along with the flames once they passed.

It struggled against the hard soil until it erupted into a world of sun and wind. It had been born from seeds that fell after the flames had passed. There was a difference to the land. The grazing animals had gone, and more seedlings grew along the banks of the river. The water had returned, and life with it. There were new guardians of the land, guardians who managed the land and knew its importance.

TARGETING ENGLISH HOMEWORK YEAR 5 © PASCAL PRESS ISBN 978 1 925726 62 6

Reading & Comprehension

Write the answer or shade the bubble next to the correct answer.

The answers to these questions are in the text.

1. Where did **smaller animals** make their homes?

2. The First Australians knew the tree **provided** things. What did the tree provide?

3. What caused the **bare patches on the ground**?

Think about these questions and search for the answers in the text.

4. The third paragraph lists lots of **changes to the land**. List three of them.

5. What evidence in the last paragraph shows that the **new guardians** were managing the land successfully?

Use inferencing skills to answer these questions. The answers are not in the text. Think about what you know and what the author says.

6. In the first paragraph, **'It struggled against the hard soil …'**. What was **'it'**?

7. In the third paragraph, what could the **different animals** be that grazed under its branches?

8. Find **isolation** in the third paragraph. The sentences around it give you an idea of its meaning. Which word has a similar meaning?
   - ◯ icy cold
   - ◯ separation
   - ◯ position

9. Locate the **simile** (comparison using 'like' or 'as') in the third paragraph. What two things are being compared?

   ______ & ______

10. How are they **alike**?

11. What event happened in the fourth paragraph?

12. What happened to the tree after this event?

13. How many different guardians did the land have according to the text?

14. Who were the first **managers** of the land?

Use your experience and opinions to answer this question. The answer is not in the text.

15. If this text was described as a cycle, coming back to where it started, what would that mean?

Comprehension Reflections

Look at the top of the opposite page. This text is an I__________ text – N__________.

Write one thing you learned or found interesting:

Write one question you have or something you want to find more information about:

Rating   

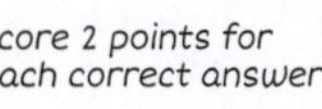
Score 2 points for each correct answer!

SCORE /30  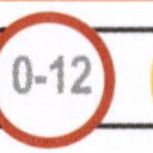 

TERM 4

Grammar & Punctuation

AC9E5LA04, AC9E5LA05, AC9E5LA09

Topic sentences

Usually, the sentence at the start of a paragraph is the topic sentence. In the text, each 'topic sentence' or first sentence of each paragraph lets you know what the rest of the paragraph will be about.
Example: When it woke, the land had changed.

This sentence lets you know the paragraph will be about the changes to the land.

Circle the correct topic sentence for each paragraph.

1. **Content of paragraph – Different types of bushfires**

   Investigators found out why my house caught on fire.

   Grassfires occur mainly on grazing, farming or remote scrub country.

   There are three main types of bushfires.

2. **Content of paragraph – How bushfires start**

   If you are in a bushfire area, you need to have a bushfire plan.

   Bushfires can be caused either naturally or by the actions of people.

   Embers and other hot materials get blown well ahead of the flames.

3. **Content of paragraph – Where and when bushfires occur**

   At any time of the year, some parts of Australia are prone to bushfires.

   Surface bushfires are the most common and happen frequently.

   Fires need fuel, heat and oxygen.

Different sentence starters

Do you find that your sentences often begin with the same words repeated over and over?

Using different sentence starters adds variety and interest to your writing.

Starting with participles

If you take a verb and add 'ing' or 'ed' to the end of it, it becomes a participle. You can start a sentence with a participle to make your writing more interesting. This forms a participial phrase, so a comma is needed. *Example:* Smil**ing** from ear to ear, Sam ate all the chocolate. (smile + ing = smiling and add the comma after the participial phrase)

Choose the correct participles from the list to add to these sentences. Add the comma where it is needed.

List of participles: holding, chased, **excited**, disappointed, panting, delayed

Example: **Excited** to be offered chocolate**,** Sam scoffed the lot.

4. ________________ heavily Sam slowly ran to catch the bus.
5. ________________ by a stray dog Sam increased his pace.
6. ________________ by the heavy traffic the bus made slow progress.
7. ________________ at being late Sam ate more chocolate.
8. ________________ onto the wrappers Sam counted how many chocolates he had eaten.

Starting with prepositional phrases

Prepositions link parts of sentences together and tell where, when and how. *Examples of prepositions:* in, at, on, from, under, between, before, above, below, with, beside, by

You can start a sentence with a prepositional phrase but remember to add a comma after it. *Example:* **Before** the accident, the bus was running on time.

Write sentences about Sam, starting with the prepositions given in the sentences. Insert a comma after the prepositional phrase.

9. **(How)** – With ____
   ____.
10. **(When)** – At ____
   ____.
11. **(Where)** – From ____
   ____.

Score 2 points for each correct answer! SCORE /22  0-8  10-16  18-22 

TARGETING ENGLISH HOMEWORK YEAR 5 © PASCAL PRESS ISBN 978 1 925726 62 6

Phonic & Word Knowledge

UNIT 28

AC9E5LY08, AC9E5LY09

An 'o' isn't always an 'o'

In the text, the word 'canopy' is used, meaning the covering of leaves on the tree. The 'o' in this word has the 'schwa' sound of 'uh' as it is an unstressed syllable. It's a lazy syllable, 'uh'.
Example: can-o-py pronounced kan-**uh**-pee

The English letter 'o' has more than one sound! The letter 'o' often represents three different sounds. Are you aware of pronouncing them correctly?

Long 'o': go, home, only

Short 'o': hot, copy, on

Short 'u' sound: money, done, love

Schwa 'uh' sound in unstressed syllables: bott**o**m, freed**o**m, carr**o**t

① – ⑯

Sort these 'o' words into their correct sound in the table.

melody, gone, low, coffee, know, oven, won, wrong, over, parrot, tongue, most, wagon, song, some, dinosaur

Long 'o' sound	Short 'o' sound	Short 'u' sound	Schwa 'uh' sound

Unpredictable 'ou'

The vowel pair 'ou' is quite unpredictable. There are at least 8 different ways it can be pronounced. Yes – 8! Here are a few:

Long 'o' (as in no): dough, though

Long 'u' (as in true): soup, group

Short 'u' (as in fun): country, young

Short 'oo' (as in good): could, would

'aw' / 'ow' sound: about, cloud

Schwa ('uh' sound for 'ous'): nervous, serious

⑰ – ㊵

Sort these 'ou' words into their correct sound in the table.

although, couple, famous, should, through, obvious, cousin, wouldn't, open, youth, amount, count, enough, cautious, mouse, routine, couldn't, various, you, toe, tough, thousand, shouldn't, dough

Long 'o' (as in no)	Long 'u' (as in true)	Short 'u' (as in fun)

Short 'oo' (as in good)	'aw' / 'ow' (as in about)	Schwa 'uh' (as in serious)

Score 2 points for each correct answer!

SCORE /80  0-38 40-74  76-80

TERM 4

Informative text – Explanation

A Chip off the Old Rock

Have you ever come into the classroom after playing outside and then discovered your hands are dirty? What is dirt? Is dirt the same as soil? Think of an answer before reading on.

The answer is no. Soil and dirt are not the same thing. We can't grow plants in dirt because it lacks minerals, organic or natural matter and living organisms. Believe it or not, there are more microorganisms in a handful of soil than there are people on Earth. Soil has dirt in it, but dirt is only one part of what makes up soil. It's the part that you track into the classroom and gets under your fingernails. Soil forms continuously, but slowly, from the gradual breakdown of rocks through weathering. What's weathering? Look at the flow chart below that explains weathering.

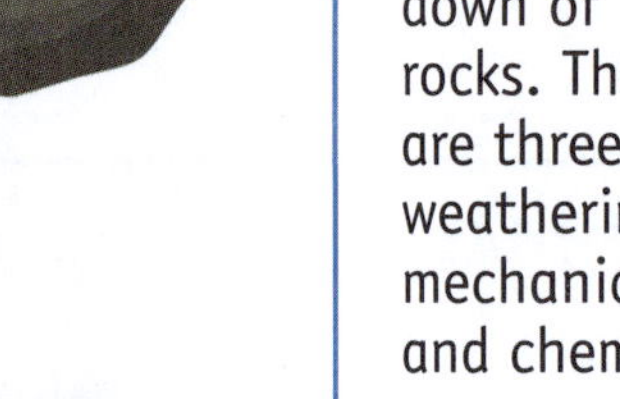

Weathering is the breaking down of rocks. There are three types of weathering: biological, mechanical (or physical) and chemical.

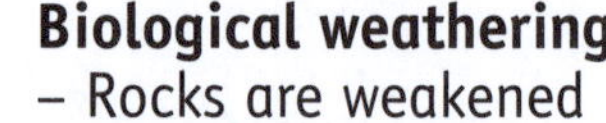

Biological weathering – Rocks are weakened and worn away by plants, animals and microbes. Plant roots can follow small cracks and eventually crack the rock.

Mechanical weathering – Rocks crumble because water can seep into a crack and then freeze. This widens the crack. If this is repeated, the rock breaks apart.

Chemical weathering – Rain can slowly eat away at rocks. Along the coastline, salt water can slowly eat away at rocks.

So, rocks are broken down by weathering, but this is not soil until organic or natural matter and living organisms are added. This can take hundreds to thousands of years to develop. Unfortunately, soil can be destroyed or blown away in minutes. Therefore, soil is a resource we need to take care of because we rely on it to grow our food, and we cannot easily get more if we need it. Think about that next time you wash the dirt off your hands.

TARGETING ENGLISH HOMEWORK YEAR 5 © PASCAL PRESS ISBN 978 1 925726 62 6

Reading & Comprehension

Write the answer or shade the bubble next to the correct answer.

The answers to these questions are in the text.

① **Dirt is the same as soil.**

◯ True ◯ False

② **You can't grow plants in dirt because it lacks what?**

____

____

③ **Soil forms ________________.**

◯ only at the coast

◯ only every thousand years

◯ continuously

④ **How does soil form?**

____

____

⑤ **What is weathering and how many types are there?**

____

____

Think about these questions and search for the answers in the text.

⑥ **Why is soil a resource that we need to take care of?**

____

____

⑦ **How does water help in the weathering process?**

____

____

Use inferencing skills to answer these questions. The answers are not in the text. Think about what you know and what the author says.

⑧ **Where do you think mechanical weathering could occur in Australia?**

____

____

⑨ **Soil contains living organisms/creatures. Ants are one example of a small organism. Name two more living organisms/creatures that live in soil.**

____

⑩ **Why would cliffs and rocks by the beach become weathered?**

____

____

____

Use your experience and opinions to answer these questions. The answers are not in the text.

⑪ **Soil is a resource that cannot easily be renewed. How can it be lost or destroyed?**

____

____

____

____

⑫ **What alternatives could there be to using soil to grow food?**

____

____

____

____

Comprehension Reflections

Look at the top of the opposite page. This text is an I__________ text – E__________.

Write one thing you learned or found interesting:

____

Write one question you have or something you want to find more information about:

____

____

Rating    

Score 2 points for each correct answer! SCORE /24 0-10 12-18 20-24

TERM 4

Grammar & Punctuation

AC9E5LA04

Sentence starters for non-fiction texts

It can sometimes be difficult to start a sentence to express your ideas. In the table below, are some sentence beginnings for an information text.

The first column shows sentence beginnings to introduce the topic, the next column to introduce an idea and the last column to summarise the information.

To start – What is the topic?	Introduce ideas	Summarise your thinking
Even though … Although … The issue is … In the past …	For example … I believe … In addition … Furthermore … More importantly …	In conclusion … Finally … Therefore … Overall … As a result …

Examples:

Even though soil seems to be everywhere, it takes thousands of years to develop.

More importantly, we cannot make soil as it occurs due to weathering.

In conclusion, we have to manage the soil we have with care.

Write your own three sentences about what you found out in the text about weathering. Use the sentence beginnings in the table to help you.

1. ______________________________

2. ______________________________

3. ______________________________

Write your own three sentences about a topic you have some knowledge about. Use the sentence beginnings below to help you.

4. The issue is ______________________________.

5. Furthermore ______________________________.

6. In conclusion ______________________________.

In *Charlie and the Chocolate Factory* by Roald Dahl, the Chocolate Room is a very large and beautiful garden-like room of candy where everything inside is edible, including the grass and dirt. What if the school had an oval of edible soil/dirt?

Write persuasive sentences with the starters provided. You decide whether to give points for or against the idea of edible dirt on your oval.

Introduction – The topic	Three reasons for or against	Summary
What if …	Firstly … Secondly … Thirdly …	In conclusion …

7. What if ______________________________.

8. Firstly ______________________________.

9. Secondly ______________________________.

10. Thirdly ______________________________.

11. In conclusion ______________________________.

Score 2 points for each correct answer! SCORE /22

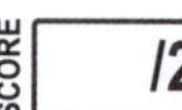

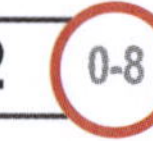

TERM 4

TARGETING ENGLISH HOMEWORK YEAR 5 © PASCAL PRESS ISBN 978 1 925726 62 6

AC9E5LY08, AC9E5LY09, AC9E5LA08

Greek prefixes 'micro' and 'macro'

According to the text, there are more microorganisms in a handful of soil than there are people on Earth. 'Micro' is a Greek prefix that goes in front of a word and means something is small. The opposite is a Greek prefix 'macro' meaning long or large.

A prefix is a group of letters that can be added to the beginning of a word to create a new word. Prefixes have different meanings, and they can be used to change the meanings of words.

'Micro' is a prefix that shows something is small (size). *Examples:* **micro**biologist, **micro**wave, **micro**organism, **micro**scope

Match the example words above to these meanings.

1. An instrument that makes small things large enough to see. ______________
2. A very small living creature you cannot see with just your eyes. ______________
3. A scientist who studies small living creatures. ______________
4. A machine that uses small radio waves. ______________

Prefixes that show size

Other prefixes that show size include:

Macro (big, often used for scientific words): **macro**scopic

Hyper (excess, exaggeration): **hyper**active, **hyper**sensitive

Hypo (less than normal, beneath, below): **hypo**thermia, **hypo**dermic

Match the example words above to these meanings.

5. A needle that goes **beneath** the skin ______________
6. Very energetic with **excess** energy ______________
7. **Large** enough to be visible with just your eyes ______________
8. Body temperature **below** normal ______________
9. Being **excessively** sensitive ______________

Number prefixes

Prefixes can also mean a quantity or number.
Example: Humans are **bipeds** (Latin). We go around on 'bi' = **two** 'ped'= **feet**.

You will use many of these prefixes in maths.
Examples: **hexa**gon, **penta**gon

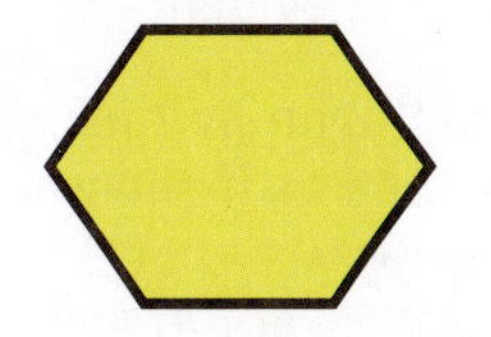

Draw lines from the Greek and Latin prefixes to the correct number.

10	uni / mono	many
11	hexa	three
12	poly / multi	two
13	tri	five
14	quad / tetra	one
15	nona	seven
16	bi / di	six
17	deca	nine
18	hepta	ten
19	octa	four
20	penta	eight

Score 2 points for each correct answer! SCORE /40

TERM 4

Persuasive text – Discussion

Your Honour, I'm the Victim!

The judge sat behind a large, dark bench. The case before her was Mr BB Wolf suing Ms LRR Hood for grievous bodily harm. The judge was to make a ruling whether Mr Wolf could claim damages from Ms Hood.

Mr Wolf was called to give evidence.

"Your Honour, I was set upon by this thug dressed up in her red cape as if she was sweet and innocent. However, that is definitely not the case. I'm sure there is a black belt for martial arts hidden under that cape. I was in the woods picking flowers for my wife when Ms Hood passed by. I greeted her and found out she was visiting her grandma, a mean woman who lives in the woods. Since I had the flowers in my hands, I thought I should at least be neighbourly and give them to Grandma, so the house would look nice for the visit by Ms Hood. At that time, Ms Hood seemed to be quite a nice person. Little did I know that she would turn out to be a dangerous and vicious ninja. I knew a shortcut so off I went.

"I arrived at the house and knocked at the door. An angry voice told me to go away, but I opened the door and saw the old woman in bed. I showed her the flowers and something like a smile hovered over her lips. As she got up to get a vase, I thought I would keep the bed warm for her, so I got in the bed. Just at that time, Ms Hood came in and thought I had done away with the old woman. Without even asking for an explanation, she beat me up within an inch of my life. If it wasn't for my friend the woodcutter arriving, she would have killed me."

Ms Hood was called to give evidence.

"Your Honour, imagine arriving at your grandma's house and seeing a wolf in her bed. What am I to think? I wasn't going to ask questions of a wolf. We all know their reputation, and I do not like wolves, never have. I did what any ninja-trained person would do. I set upon him with gusto. I would have finished him off and got rid of one more wolf if his friend hadn't shown up. I could have taken him on too, but I was nervous about the axe he held. I'm an innocent, cute, little girl who wears a red cape and loves her grandma."

In the printed stories about this event, the point of view you read influences how you think about the events and the characters themselves. But now that you have heard both points of view, what would your verdict be? Did their testimonies sway your opinion?

The judge prepared to make her ruling.

TARGETING ENGLISH HOMEWORK YEAR 5 © PASCAL PRESS ISBN 978 1 925726 62 6

Reading & Comprehension

Write the answer or shade the bubble next to the correct answer.

The answers to these questions are in the text.

① Mr Wolf is not **married**.

◯ True ◯ False

② What does Mr Wolf think about **Grandma**?

___

___

③ Ms Hood likes wolves.

◯ True ◯ False

Think about this question and search for the answer in the text.

④ Mr Wolf is suing Ms Hood for **grievous bodily harm**. After reading the text, what do you think that phrase means?

___

___

Use inferencing skills to answer this question. The answer is not in the text. Think about what you know and what the author says.

⑤ In the text is the phrase, **something like a smile hovered over her lips**. What does this phrase mean and what clue does that give about Grandma's personality?

___

___

Use your experience and opinions to answer these questions. The answers are not in the text.

In the text is the sentence, **As she got up to get a vase, I thought I would keep the bed warm for her, so I got in the bed.**

⑥ If you were **Mr Wolf's lawyer**, write one point why this would be considered a normal and quite considerate thing to do, not deserving Ms Hood's reaction.

___

___

⑦ If you were **Ms Hood's lawyer**, write one point why this would be considered an act that deserved Ms Hood's reaction.

___

___

⑧ Is Ms Hood **... an innocent, cute, little girl who wears a red cape and loves her grandma**? Or is she **... a dangerous and vicious ninja**? After hearing both points of view, does your view of Ms Hood change as you read the text?

◯ Yes ◯ No

⑨ Explain the thinking behind your answer.

___

___

⑩ If you were the judge, what would your ruling be? Can Mr Wolf sue Ms Hood for **grievous bodily harm**?

◯ Yes ◯ No

⑪ Explain the thinking behind your answer.

___

___

⑫ Who is at fault in this story? Would you circle more than one?

◯ Ms Hood ◯ the woodcutter
◯ Mr Wolf ◯ everyone
◯ Grandma ◯ no-one

⑬ Explain the thinking behind your answer.

___

___

Comprehension Reflections

Look at the top of the opposite page. This text is a P__________ text – D__________.

Write one thing you learned or found interesting:

___

Write one question you have or something you want to find more information about:

___

___

Rating

Score 2 points for each correct answer! SCORE /26 0-10 12-20 22-26

TERM 4

AC9E5LA03, AC9E5LA05

Complex sentences – Conjunctions and their effects

Complex sentences have an independent clause and a dependent, or subordinate, clause. They are joined by a conjunction. A comma is used if the first part of the sentence is a dependent clause.

Complex sentences can be used for different effects depending on the conjunctions used (see in the table). Notice where the commas are in the examples in the last column.

Effects	Conjunctions	Examples from the text
gives a reason	that, because, since, as so that, to, in order that	**Since** I had the flowers in my hands, I thought I should at least be neighbourly.
makes a condition	if, in that case, provided that, unless	I would have finished him off and got rid of one more wolf **if** his friend hadn't shown up.
concession	although, even though, however, despite	Mr Wolf brought flowers to Grandma **even though** he did not like her.
shows time	while, after, before, next, once, whenever, when	I was in the woods picking flowers for my wife **when** Ms Hood passed by.

Read these sentences and work out what effect they use. Write the words: reason, condition, concession or time in the spaces.

1. After Grandma got out of bed, she went to collect a vase. ________________
2. Once she left the room, Mr Wolf quickly got into her bed. ________________
3. Ms Hood entered the house while Mr Wolf was occupying the bed. ________________
4. Ms Hood says she attacked the wolf because she was defending her grandma. ________________
5. If that was the case, is it okay that she did not wait for an explanation? ________________
6. Ms Hood attacked Mr Wolf even though he had not hurt Grandma. ________________
7. Even though Mr Wolf explained in great detail, his behaviour may not have been appropriate. ________________
8. If the judge thinks both Mr Wolf and Ms Hood are guilty of some misdoing, the two of them may be fined or sent to prison. ________________

Choose an effect and its conjunction from the table and write them in the spaces provided. Next, write a sentence from Mr Wolf's point of view using that conjunction. Don't forget the comma if the conjunction is used at the start of the sentence.

9. The effect is ________________.
   The conjunction is ________________.
   ____
   ____

Now choose a different effect and conjunction and write a point of view from Ms Hood.

10. The effect is ________________.
    The conjunction is ________________.
    ____
    ____

Now choose a different effect and conjunction and write a point of view from Grandma.

11. The effect is ________________.
    The conjunction is ________________.
    ____
    ____

Score 2 points for each correct answer! SCORE /22   0-8  10-16  18-22

TERM 4

TARGETING ENGLISH HOMEWORK YEAR 5 © PASCAL PRESS ISBN 978 1 925726 62 6

AC9E5LY09

Spelling generalisations with 'ie' and 'ei'

The text has some 'ie' and 'ei' words. Grievous is spelt with 'ie', but neighbourly is spelt 'ei'. How do you know which one to use?

A good way to remember the 'ie' generalisation is to say, 'i before e except after c'. This is mainly true if the sound they make is an 'ee' sound.

	Spelt with 'ie'	Spelt with 'c', write 'ei'
Examples: 'ee' sounding words	achieve believe chief piece	receive deceive ceiling receipt

Read these sentences and fill in the missing words with 'ie' or 'ei' words from the table.

The police ① ____________ was called into the case. She did not know who to ② ____________ as both Mr Wolf and Ms Hood thought they were right. To ③ ____________ the best results and make certain the right character would ④ ____________ what they deserved, she interviewed them all. Was one of them trying to ⑤ ____________ her?

The generalisation explains the 'ie' in grievous, but what about neighbourly? Sometimes words that make the 'ay' sound and a long 'i' sound are spelt 'ei'.

	Spelt with 'ei'
Examples: 'ay' sounding words	beige neighbour weight eight
Examples: long 'i' sounding words	height either (eye-thuh) neither (n-eye-thuh)

Exceptions to these generalisations are foreign, caffeine, leisure, weird and seize.

Read these sentences and fill in the missing words with 'ei' words from the table.

Would ⑥ ____________ Ms Hood or Mr Wolf be found innocent, or would ⑦ ____________ of them be innocent? The woodcutter was Grandma's ⑧ ____________ and was asked what he saw. After ⑨ ____________ hours on the case, a decision was made. The guilty character was arrested, their ⑩ h____________ and ⑪ w____________ was recorded with their fingerprints, and a mug shot was taken.

The 'ie' and 'ei' words from this page have been coded using this table. Decode the words and write them correctly. For example, 2-8, 0-8, 1-5, 3-8, 0-8 = seize

0	A	B	C	D	E	F	G
1	H	I	J	K	L	M	N
2	O	P	Q	R	S	T	U
3	V	W	X	Y	Z		
	4	5	6	7	8	9	10

⑫ 0-6, 0-8, 1-5, 1-8, 1-5, 1-10, 0-10

____

⑬ 3-5, 0-8, 1-5, 0-10, 1-4, 2-9

____

⑭ 2-7, 0-8, 0-6, 0-8, 1-5, 2-5, 2-9

____

⑮ 1-4, 0-8, 1-5, 0-10, 1-4, 2-9

____

⑯ 0-6, 0-4, 0-9, 0-9, 0-8, 1-5, 1-10, 0-8

____

⑰ 0-4, 0-6, 1-4, 1-5, 0-8, 3-4, 0-8

____

Score 2 points for each correct answer! SCORE /34    

TERM 4

AC9E5LY01, AC9E5LY04, AC9E5LY05, AC9E5LE03, AC9HP6P03

Informative text – Explanation

The Changing Face of Fairytales

In many popular and well-known fairytales we read today, the girls are supposed to be beautiful, good and helpless while the boys are supposed to be handsome, active and brave. But there are thousands of folktales where both girls and boys are strong and resourceful. So why don't we know these stories?

Folktales are oral stories that have no one author. They were not originally written down but were spread by travellers passing through the country and told to audiences that included adults and children. Original folktales were stories about how people dealt with the difficult conditions in which they lived and often had a lesson or moral to learn. They could be quite violent and brutal and showed girls and boys as tough and resourceful in dealing with the issues of those times. The term 'fairytale' grew out of folktales once they were written down.

Many of the fairytales we know today were collected and written 100–200 years ago. The stories reflect a time when girls were supposed to be meek and mild. These tales were printed over and over again while many of the other tales were forgotten. One example is the story of Little Red Riding Hood (LRRH). This story has had many retellings, and depending at what time the story is set, LRRH behaves in different ways.

In one of the earliest versions of LRRH, which is around 1000 years old, instead of needing to be rescued, LRRH realises the danger she is in and tricks the wolf into letting her escape. In the story that the Grimm brothers collected 200 years ago, both the Grandma and LRRH are rescued by a man working in the woods. In many modern retellings of the story, LRRH often rescues herself. So over time, LRRH's behaviour changes depending on how girls and boys are expected to behave at that point in time.

Think of the stories you have been told or have read and think how the characters behaved. Were the children strong and independent, or were they waiting to be rescued and if so, by whom?

TARGETING ENGLISH HOMEWORK YEAR 5 © PASCAL PRESS ISBN 978 1 925726 62 6

Reading & Comprehension

Write the answer or shade the bubble next to the correct answer.

The answers to these questions are in the text.

1. **In many popular and well-known fairytales of today, the girls are supposed to be:**

____

2. **What are folktales?**

____

____

3. **How were folktales spread?**

____

____

4. **Originally, folktales were stories about what?**

____

____

5. **How were boys and girls shown in original folktales?**

____

____

6. **When were many of the fairytales we know today written down?**

____

Think about this question and search for the answers in the text.

7. **What are the differences and similarities between folktales and today's fairytales? Fill in the table.**

Folktales – Differences	Similarities – How are they the same?	Today's fairytales – Differences

Use inferencing skills to answer these questions. The answers are not in the text. Think about what you know and what the author says.

8. **The way girls and boys behave in stories depends on how girls and boys are expected to behave at the time the story is written. How would you want a boy and girl character to behave in a fairytale you had to write today?**

____

____

____

9. **Why would you want them to behave that way?**

____

____

____

Use your experience and opinions to answer these questions. The answers are not in the text.

10. **If you were asked to read stories to a younger year level, would you read them a fairytale?**

◯ Yes ◯ No

11. **Explain why.**

____

____

____

Comprehension Reflections

Look at the top of the opposite page. This text is an I__________ text – E__________.

Write one thing you learned or found interesting:

____

Write one question you have or something you want to find more information about:

____

____

Rating   

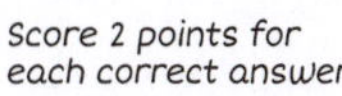

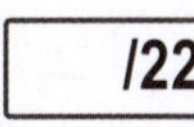

TERM 4

AC9E5LA06, AC9E5LA08, AC9E5LY06

Verb groups – Auxiliary and modal verbs

Remember! A verb is an action or doing word. In writing, verb groups have various jobs in a sentence:

- Verb groups say what is happening. The main verb can be on its own, or it can have a helper or auxiliary verb. *Examples:* The wolf **picked** some flowers. (main verb on its own) The wolf **is picking** some flowers. (auxiliary verb + main verb)
- Verb groups create tense. *Examples:* The wolf **walks** to Grandma's house. (present) The wolf **walked** to Grandma's house. (past) The wolf **will walk** to Grandma's house. (future)
- Verbs can also have helper/auxiliary verbs called modal verbs. Modality verbs show how likely or possible the action or verb is. *Example:* Little Red Riding Hood **must walk** to Grandma's house!

Circle the verb group in these sentences and write what type of modal verb it is. Use the table to help you with the modality.

High modality	Medium modality	Low modality
must	will	may
will	should	should
ought to	can	could
shall	need to	might
have to		would

Example: The wolf (can be) very tricky. medium

1. Boys and girls could be the hero. ______________
2. The wolf may eat Grandma in the story. ______________
3. The girl must wear a red cloak. ______________
4. Fairytales ought to have boys and girls as heroes. ______________
5. Students might believe what they read. ______________

Write your own sentences using the verb group in brackets. Write what type of modal verb was used.

6. (must sing) ______________
Type of modal verb ______________
7. (ought to complete) ______________
Type of modal verb ______________
8. (have to go) ______________
Type of modal verb ______________
9. (will watch) ______________
Type of modal verb ______________

Underline the verb groups that show tense. Circle the auxiliary verb if there is one.

Example: The wolf (had) eaten Grandma.

10. Red Riding Hood was waiting for the wolf.
11. She did not move when the wolf appeared.
12. She threw a bag over his head.
13. The wolf had eaten his last grandma.
14. Now Red is wearing a lovely fur coat.
15. She has told everyone her story.
16. She will be known as 'Big Red' in future.

Score 2 points for each correct answer! SCORE /32

TERM 4

TARGETING ENGLISH HOMEWORK YEAR 5 © PASCAL PRESS ISBN 978 1 925726 62 6

AC9E5LY09

Australian and American spelling differences

The text uses the word 'realise' spelt with an 's'.

A common question students ask is, "When do I use 'z' or 's' to spell words?"

Australian English follows British spelling very closely, but many common words are spelt differently in American English. Despite being spelt differently, the meaning of the word is the same.

British/Australian spelling	American spelling
analyse apologise organise	analyze apologize organize
Both Americans and Australians spell these words the same: exercise, surprise, enterprise.	
British and Australian English words with 'our' in them are spelt with 'or' in American English.	
colour favourite	color favorite
Words that end in '-re' in Australian and British English are spelt with '-er' in American English.	
centre litre	center liter

Use this list of letters to make four Australian spelt words. You can use the letters as often as needed.

L N U C S E R A T Y O I

① ______________________

② ______________________

③ ______________________

④ ______________________

Spelling Australian words with double 'l'

Australian/British English uses a double 'l', in words such as in travelling, travelled and traveller. However, American English uses a single 'l': traveling, traveled and traveler.

Insert travelling, travelled and traveller where they belong in these sentences.

I have ⑤ ______________ a long way to see Big Red. I believe she is ⑥ ______________ in a caravan with a large wolf painted on the side. Not many ⑦ ______________s will have this form of transport.

Use any of the Australian-spelt words on this page to insert in these sentences.

⑧ Big Red does not ______________ for her behaviour towards the wolf.

⑨ The police wish to ______________ the coat to see if it is Mr Wolf.

⑩ Although Big Red loves being the ______________ of attention, she has let it be known that the coat is fake fur.

⑪ So where is Mr Wolf? The police will ______________ a search party.

⑫ It is believed Mr Wolf ______________ out of the country in fear of his life.

⑬ The case is ongoing. Meanwhile, Big Red will continue to wear the ______________ red as a warning to any other wolves who mean to eat grandmothers.

Score 2 points for each correct answer! SCORE /26   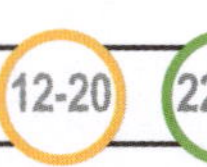 

TERM 4

AC9E5LY04, AC9E5LY05, AC9HP6P01

Persuasive text – Argument

KIDS BLOG

Be Kind

Kindness is like a gift that we can all afford to give. My blog today is about acts of kindness. As a blogger, I can influence those who read my blog, which gives me a form of power as an influencer. I want to use this power to create a kinder world.

Kindness is more than just being nice; it is being friendly, generous and considerate. It is something you do on purpose without being asked. Being kind helps others as well as yourself. Being kind can lower your blood pressure and stress levels, so people who are kind tend to be healthier and live longer. When we receive kindness, we feel better about ourselves and others. Kindness contributes to a positive view of the world.

A simple way to develop and share your kindness skills is to do something small on a daily basis. Kind Notes are a quick and easy way to practise kindness. Write a note to a friend, family member, or anyone in the school or wider community who you want to show your appreciation to, thank or encourage. Write general Kind Notes, for example, 'You are wonderful', 'Thank you for ...', 'I appreciate it when ...', 'Have a great day ...' You can pass them out or put them where the person will find them, such as in a lunchbox, in a drawer, on a desk or in a book or bag. You can even write a Kind Note to yourself, recognising something you like or a quality that makes you a kind person.

The great thing is that it isn't difficult to be kind. Everyone wants to be in a place where they feel safe and feel like they belong. When you choose to be kind you can make a positive difference to that person and their wellbeing and help them create a more positive self-identity.

So, what are you waiting for? Get writing and spread kindness.

Stay tuned for my next blog about becoming addicted to your devices.

TARGETING ENGLISH HOMEWORK YEAR 5 © PASCAL PRESS ISBN 978 1 925726 62 6

Reading & Comprehension

Write your answers on the lines provided.

The answers to these questions are in the text.

1. What kind of world does this influencer want to make?
2. What is kindness?
3. What is a simple way to **develop and share** your kindness skills?
4. Who can you write **Kind Notes** to?

Think about these questions and search for the answers in the text.

5. Name two good things that can happen when people show or accept kindness.
6. Where could you **hide or put** Kind Notes?

Use inferencing skills to answer these questions. The answers are not in the text. Think about what you know and what the author says.

7. The great thing is that it isn't difficult to be kind. Why is it not difficult?
8. When you choose to be kind, you can help a person create a more **positive self-identity**. What do you think that means?
9. If you wrote a Kind Note to yourself, recognising something you like or a quality that makes you a kind person, what would you write?

Use your experience and opinions to answer these questions. The answers are not in the text.

10. The author states, **'As a blogger, I can influence those who read my blog'**. Write a sentence on one way a blogger or influencer could **positively** influence students.
11. Write a sentence on one way a blogger or influencer could **negatively** influence students.
12. On the internet, there are many **kid influencers** – influencers who are kids. What could be one **positive point** for being a kid influencer?
13. What could be one **negative point** for being a kid influencer?

Comprehension Reflections

Look at the top of the opposite page. This text is a P__________ text – A__________.

Write one thing you learned or found interesting:

Write one question you have or something you want to find more information about:

Rating   

Score 2 points for each correct answer!

SCORE /26  0-10  12-20  22-26 

TERM 4

AC9E5LA06

Noun–verb agreement

Noun–verb agreement in a sentence means that if the subject of the sentence is singular, it must have a singular verb. If the subject of the sentence is plural, it must have a plural verb.

This is tricky because nouns ending with –s are often plural; however, verbs ending in –s are always singular.

Singular noun = singular verb	Plural noun = plural verb
The bird flies.	The birds fly.
The Kind Note flutters.	The Kind Notes flutter.
My blog today is about acts of kindness.	My blogs today are about acts of kindness.
My brother is getting a note.	My brother and father (2 people) are getting a note.
My brother was very happy.	My brother and father were very happy.

Using the information in the table, choose the correct verbs in these sentences.

1. Kindness and politeness __________ behaviours we should practise. is / are
2. I __________ delighted to eat chocolate for lunch. were / was
3. We __________ delighted to eat chocolate for lunch. were / was
4. Sam __________ the ball. kicks / kick
5. Sam and Pat __________ the ball. kicks / kick
6. The girls __________ on the oval every lunchtime. plays / play
7. The boy __________ on the oval every recess. plays / play
8. Sam and Pat __________ always polite. are / is
9. Pat __________ always polite. are / is

Collective nouns

Collective nouns (group, class, family, team etc.) refer to more than one person, but they are considered singular and use singular verbs.

Example: The class has the hall after lunch.

10 – 22

Read this news report. Circle the verb mistakes and write the correction above the mistake.

Kind Notes is popping up everywhere. They appears on the sides of buses and buildings. No-one know where they will pop up next. I are standing on the street right now. All around me people is pointing at all the latest notes. I personally can't wait to receive one. After all, I is a very well-known and popular reporter. My mother were very happy to get one from me. My boss and I waits for Kind Notes from our work team, but have none so far. The team are not cooperating. I will writes a note to myself saying how wonderful I am. After all, I are a very kind person. I deserves many notes. I think I will go and writes one now.

Score 2 points for each correct answer! SCORE /44  0-20  22-38  40-44 

TARGETING ENGLISH HOMEWORK YEAR 5 © PASCAL PRESS ISBN 978 1 925726 62 6

Phonic & Word Knowledge

UNIT 32

AC9E5LY09

Stressed English

Try to say the sentence, The internet is slow! in a 'robot voice'.

That means saying it without your voice changing at all. English is not spoken in a robot voice. If you say the sentence normally, you will find that you put stress on certain words, The INTERNET is SLOW! English uses stress for words, and stress for syllables in words.

Unstressed short vowel sounds often make the lazy vowel sound 'schwa'. It sounds like 'uh', and we hardly open our mouths to say it.

Examples: Lemon sounds like lem-**uh**n. (The 'o' is a 'schwa' sound.)

Camera sounds like cam-r**uh**.

The 'schwa' sound is the most common vowel sound in English and makes spelling tricky. The 'schwa' sound can be made by any short vowels and some letter combinations like or, ar, re, our and ou.

Become a detective to locate the tricky 'schwa' sounds!

Circle the letters that make the 'schwa' sound in these words. The first one in each row has been done for you.

1. about panda appreciate addicted comma
2. builder dollar doctor blogger figure
3. acre centre ogre
4. humour colour neighbour thorough flavour
5. anxious cautious famous jealous nervous

The letter 'y'

Vowels are an important part of spelling. Most words have at least one vowel. The vowels are a, e, i, o and u. But did you know that 'y' is often used as a vowel? When 'y' occurs at the beginning of a word like **y**ard and **y**es, it is a consonant. When it occurs in the middle of a word like c**y**cle, or at the end of a word like fl**y** or bo**y**, it is a vowel.

In these words, the letter 'y' is used as a vowel. Match them to their meanings.

sly	crypt	rhythm	cyst
pygmy	spry	myth	

6. A strong repeated pattern of movement and sound. ______________
7. Cunning and clever but also could be dishonest. ______________
8. Agile and moves quickly and easily. ______________
9. An underground room often used as a burial place. ______________
10. A person or animal that is small or miniature. ______________
11. A legend or fairy story often told over time. ______________
12. A lump or swelling that can grow on the body and is often filled with fluid. ______________

Score 2 points for each correct answer! SCORE /24  0-10  12-18  20-24 

TERM 4

AC9E5LY04, AC9E5LY05

Imaginative text – Narrative

The Dusty Old Box

The papers smelt musty with a layer of dust which covered them like a skin. I didn't really want to clean out the old shed at my grandparents' farm, but the promise of a burger and chips if I helped persuaded me. I lifted the papers out of the old metal box I had found in the back of the shed and shook off the skin of dust. I wasn't really interested in them as they were covered in cursive writing that I couldn't read. Then I noticed the date on top of the first page, 1788. That's when I took them to my grandparents and parents who immediately stopped what they were doing and unfolded the papers.

It seems that we had a relative who came over on the First Fleet as a convict. The rest of the family were delighted to have a relative on the First Fleet, but I'm not sure if being related to a convict is cool or not. We read the papers which were a collection of memoirs from her life. It seems that she stole silk handkerchiefs and, as a consequence, was sentenced to seven years' transportation. The journey over to Australia sounded very difficult and I can't imagine what she thought when she first stepped off the ship.

She started the farm once she had served her seven years and lived on the property with her husband and eight children. Of course, the house has been rebuilt and the farm added to and extended, but the farm dates back to colonial times. It was then that my grandfather remembered the old headstones under a large tree in one of the paddocks.

As we trudged over the paddocks, I wondered if one of the headstones belonged to the author of the memoirs. We stopped at the graves and could just make out the writing on the stones. There was her name on one of the stones and several of her children were buried under the tree as well. I found myself wishing I had met her, to see who this very strong and resilient person was. Would I have survived the same harsh conditions? I didn't know.

That night, we stayed at the farm and I had the bed in the attic. As I closed my eyes, my dreams were full of ocean waves and the feeling of suffocating in hot cabins below deck. I wandered dreamlike on the shores of Port Phillip Bay and saw none of the modern buildings that are there today. Then I had an overwhelming feeling of peace as my dreams led me to the farm. Although the farm looked very different, I knew it was my grandparents' farm. And at the end of my dream, I came face to face with the author of the memoirs. She was me. I looked into her eyes, and I knew her.

Reading & Comprehension

Write your answers on the lines provided.

1. Where was the old metal box found?

2. Why was the author of the memoirs sentenced to **transportation**?

3. How many children had lived on the farm in colonial times?

4. Where were the **headstones**?

5. The author of the text says, **"I found myself wishing I had met her ..."** Who are they referring to and why did they want to meet her?

6. When did the author have an **overwhelming feeling of peace** in their dreams?

7. In the text, the author could just make out the writing on the headstones. Why could they not read the writing clearly?

8. At the conclusion of the text, the author's dreams were memories. Whose memories were they?

9. In the text the author says, **"I'm not sure if being related to a convict is cool or not"**. Write one point why being related to a First Fleet convict would be cool.

10. Write one point why being related to a First Fleet convict would not be cool.

11. What do you think the author means when they say, **"I came face to face with the author of the memoirs. She was me. I looked into her eyes and knew her"**. Write one sentence to explain your thinking.

Score 2 points for each correct answer!

SCORE	/22	0-8	10-16	18-22

TERM 4

Grammar & Punctuation

Apostrophes

①–⑨

You are now the teacher. Using a different colour, correct the mistakes and add the missing apostrophes. At the end, give this student a score out of nine for their work.

Dream's are what a person sees and hears in their mind when they are sleeping. All people and many animal's dream when they are asleep. A persons dreams can seem very real. Sams and Pats dreams are often about what happened during the day. I have one dog and two cat's and they dream. My dogs dreams are of chasing cats. My cats dreams are of catching birds. James dreams are of eating chocolate.

Score /9

Commas

⑩–⑭

You are now the teacher. Using a different colour, add the missing commas. There are complex sentences and prepositional phrases. At the end, give this student a score out of five for their work.

While I was sleeping I had the strangest dream. Under the table in the kitchen I dreamt there was a large box of chocolates. When I walked into the kitchen the next morning I looked under the table to check for chocolates. My brother came in as I crawled under the table.

With great acting skills I made out I was sleepwalking. As I was leaving the kitchen I noticed chocolate smudges all around my brother's mouth.

Score /5

Building noun groups

Add more detail and description to your sentences. *Look at this example:* I want a puppy.

Add adjectives to describe the noun and a prepositional phrase to provide more information. *Example:* I want a cute, fluffy puppy with a great personality.

Add adjectives and a prepositional phrase to these sentences.

⑮ I love ________________, ________________ ice-cream with ________________________.

⑯ In my dreams, I saw a ________________, ________________ box under ________________________.

⑰ **Write a sentence about the noun 'chocolate'. Use at least two adjectives and add a prepositional phrase at the end. This can start with one of these words: under, with, below, beside, at, down, on, by, for.**

____

____

____

____

⑱ **Write a sentence about 'cake'. You need to add adjectives and a prepositional phrase.**

____

____

____

____

Score 2 points for each correct answer! SCORE /36

TARGETING ENGLISH HOMEWORK YEAR 5 © PASCAL PRESS ISBN 978 1 925726 62 6

'ie' or 'ei' patterns

Each coded letter stands for the letter which **follows it** in the alphabet.
For example, A = B, B = C, C = D, D = E, E = F, F = G ... Z = A
Therefore, C H I E F would be spelt B G H D E.

Using the code described, decode these words which have 'ie' or 'ei' patterns and write the word below the coded word.

① QDBDHUD	② MDHFGANTQ
③ ADKHDUD	④ VDHFGS

Australian and American spelling

⑤ – ⑫

Read the text and circle the correct Australian spelling.

After travelling/traveling for many a mile, Sam wanted to buy a liter/litre of chocolate milk, a favorite/favourite snack. Pat thought Sam should analyse/analyze his diet and make more appropriate choices. Sam saw no need to apologise/apologize for his love of chocolate milk and could not understand why Pat didn't make chocolate the center/centre of every meal. It would be easy to organise/organize. Sam often travelled/traveled to the shop to buy chocolate milk as well as to the dentist for the many fillings that were needed.

Stressed syllables

Circle the stressed syllable in each of these words.

Example: (fa)-ther

⑬ mem-ber
⑭ na-ture
⑮ cen-tre
⑯ sim-ple
⑰ an-nounce
⑱ a-mong
⑲ re-ceive

Unstressed syllables containing the lazy 'schwa' sound

The 'schwa' makes spelling tricky as the 'uh' sound can be represented by different letters and combinations.

Write the correct spelling of the words in the table. You have to work out what combination of letters equals the 'uh' or 'schwa' sound.
Example: lett**uh** = letter

'schwa'	Correct spelling
⑳ doctah	
㉑ buttah	
㉒ dolluh	
㉓ mirruh	
㉔ neighbah	
㉕ jaguuh	
㉖ centuh	
㉗ sailah	

Score 2 points for each correct answer! SCORE /54  0-24  26-48  50-54

TERM 4

MY READING LIST

Name: ______________________

____

	Title	Author	Rating	Date
1			☆☆☆☆☆	
2			☆☆☆☆☆	
3			☆☆☆☆☆	
4			☆☆☆☆☆	
5			☆☆☆☆☆	
6			☆☆☆☆☆	
7			☆☆☆☆☆	
8			☆☆☆☆☆	
9			☆☆☆☆☆	
10			☆☆☆☆☆	
11			☆☆☆☆☆	
12			☆☆☆☆☆	
13			☆☆☆☆☆	
14			☆☆☆☆☆	
15			☆☆☆☆☆	
16			☆☆☆☆☆	
17			☆☆☆☆☆	
18			☆☆☆☆☆	
19			☆☆☆☆☆	
20			☆☆☆☆☆	
21			☆☆☆☆☆	
22			☆☆☆☆☆	
23			☆☆☆☆☆	
24			☆☆☆☆☆	
25			☆☆☆☆☆	
26			☆☆☆☆☆	
27			☆☆☆☆☆	
28			☆☆☆☆☆	
29			☆☆☆☆☆	
30			☆☆☆☆☆	
31			☆☆☆☆☆	
32			☆☆☆☆☆	

TARGETING ENGLISH HOMEWORK YEAR 5 © PASCAL PRESS ISBN 978 1 925726 62 6

Answers

Term 1

Unit 1

Page 3 Reading & Comprehension

1 Whitby
2 They physically leaned away from Dracula.
3 long, pointed ears
4 curved or slightly bent
5 unease and fear, a feeling he was not entirely human, gasped in surprise, physically leaned away
6 inched further to the corner of the cafe, white teeth unnerved him, heart jumped into his throat and choked him with its pounding, he didn't move, didn't dare to breathe
7 pointed ears, a feeling he was not entirely human, something foreboding about his presence, cruel mouth, ruddy lips, protruding teeth, cold inhuman eyes of a predator seeking his next victim, eyes like search lights holding people captive, unable to move
8 causing their bodies to look as if they were caught in a giant gust of wind; They scanned the room like search lights
9 threatening
10 he was afraid, Dracula was looking for his next victim, the way Dracula scanned the room, the cold eyes of a predator
11 Answers may vary, but they need to explain a situation where they experienced fear.

Page 4 Grammar & Punctuation

1–4 Answers may vary as long as they fit in with the character of Dracula, a menacing figure. For example: His twisted hands, gnarled and veined.
5 chilled silence
6 prominent, aquiline nose
7 new and happier life
8 long, pointed ears (can also include 'that framed his face')
9–13 Answers may vary, for example: She swam like a mermaid.

Page 5 Phonic & Word Knowledge

1–2 caption, captain, capture, captor, captivity, captivate, captivating
3 apathetic
4 empathy
5 pathology
6 carried
7 business
8 beautiful
9 studious
10 played
11 buyer
12 laid
13 shyness
14 said
15 mislaid
16 presents
17 presence
18 presence

Unit 2

Page 7 Reading & Comprehension

1 False
2 reflected
3 absorbed or reflected
4 refraction and reflection
5 False
6 controlling light waves, changing the direction of light waves
7 both of the above
8 change course
9 Answers include: He cannot wrap over his eyes as he would not be able to see. The glasses replace the bandages.
10 Answers may relate to theft, spying, warfare or mischievous acts.

Page 8 Grammar & Punctuation

1 present
2 past
3 future
4 past
5 present
6 future
7 future
8 past
9 present
10 tried
11 invented
12 gave
13 kept
14 knew
15 left
16 had
17 saw
18 did

Page 9 Phonic & Word Knowledge

1	make		a
2	–ly		b
3	advancement		b
4	develop	–ment	
5	notable		a
6	changing		a
7	relies		c
8	imagination		a
9	heavy	–ly	c
10	use	–ing	a
11	playing		d
12	story	–s	c
13	invention		
14	direction		
15	refraction		
16	completion		
17	invention		
18	completion		
19	refraction, direction		

Unit 3

Page 11 Reading & Comprehension

1 True
2 plot
3 jet-black; polished
4 long, blue
5 soft, dangerous
6 confidently
7 around the room
8 down to the straw on the floor
9 marched
10 stared silently
11 laughed menacingly
12 The text seems to be set in the past. Clues: wearing a helmet, has long hair like Vikings, wears a cloak, straw floors, bare arms with rings of gold.

Page 12 Grammar & Punctuation

1 As the students sat quietly in the classroom, the powerful warrior appeared.
2 While his blue coat trailed the floor, the warrior strode around the room.
3 Until the doomed student stood up, the warrior's inhuman eyes continued to scan the room.
4 As a deep-throated laugh escaped from the warrior, the student gave a little gasp.
5 While the gold rings glinted in the fluorescent light, the strong arms remained folded.
6 Until the teacher intervened, the student continued to shake in fear.
7 Picking up her umbrella, the teacher approached the warrior.
8 Leaning towards the teacher, the warrior smiled a soft, dangerous smile.
9 Lifting the umbrella, the teacher struck the warrior across his folded arms.
10 Seeing the anger in the warrior's face, the teacher called for backup.
11 Picking up the student, the warrior stomped towards the door.
12 Blocking the warrior's path of escape, the teacher demanded the return of the student.

Answers

Page 13 Phonic & Word Knowledge

1 neat
2 straight
3 fascinating
4 graceful
5 composed
6–30 Amazed: aghast, astonished, flabbergasted, bewildered, awed, thunderstruck
Sneak: slink, skulk, steal, lurk, prowl, creep
Powerful: vigorous, robust, brawny, forceful, dynamic, potent
Dangerous: risky, threatening, perilous, formidable, treacherous, precarious, hazardous

Unit 4

Page 15 Reading & Comprehension

1 people's rule
2 Greek
3 1902
4 1962
5 We don't all attend Parliament but vote for the people we want to represent us; this is what happens at elections.
6 freedom, obeying the laws, treating people fairly, equally and with respect
7 In a non-democratic government, people have little to no power compared to a democratic government where people have a say in the decision-making process.
8 In Australia, you need to be 18 years of age to vote and stand for elections.
9 pass many rules about homework and perhaps about extending the summer holidays
10 Ms Wilson is P. Wilson's mother.
11 being able to express your ideas without being stopped
12 Answers may vary. The caveat is that they have the responsibility of doing the 'right thing' for the Year Five students/citizens. Answers must include reasons for their proposed change.

Page 16 Grammar & Punctuation

1 could
2 should
3 must
4 might not
5–9 Sentences can use the following verbs in any order, but only once: will, won't, must, must not, have to, can't, should, shouldn't
10 must
11 will
12 will
13 have to
14 have to
15 Answers may vary, but hopefully the answer is 'would'.

Page 17 Phonic & Word Knowledge

1 aristocracy: A group of people who have titles, such as Lord and Lady.
2 democracy: Government of the people, by the people.
3 plutocracy: A political system governed by wealthy people.
4 technocracy: A form of government in which scientists and technical experts are in control.
5 democrat: One who supports rule by the people.
6 demography: The study of populations, births, deaths, etc.
7 demophobia: The fear of crowds or masses of people.
8 antidemocratic: Someone against the idea of democracy.
9 democracy
10 technocracy
11 aristocrat
12 demography
13 antidemocratic
14 plutocracy
15 demophobia
16 democrat

Unit 5

Page 19 Reading & Comprehension

1 refraction
2 red, orange, yellow, green, blue, indigo, violet
3 White light is composed of all the different colours (red, orange, yellow, green, blue, indigo, violet) that the human eye can see.
4 Only the yellow wavelength of light is reflected from the lemon to you.
5 All wavelengths of light are absorbed and not reflected back to you.
6 infrared and ultraviolet
7 We don't see as many wavelengths of light reflected.
8 When you mix all the colours of paint together you get a muddy, brown colour. When paints are mixed, more and more wavelengths of light are absorbed and not reflected back to our eyes.
9 In reality, you can only see the full circle from a plane as the horizon stops you from seeing the whole circle. Answers may be creative and not necessarily accurate.

Page 20 Grammar & Punctuation

1 I like to look for rainbows.
2 The dog chased its tail.
3 You're going to be very happy.
4 Don't eat it, that's theirs.
5–13 It's, it's, there's, you're, Don't, can't, I'm, you'll, That's
14 biscuits
15 dog's
16 body's
17 brother's
18 toes
19 teachers'
20 Fives'
21 boys'
22 should've
23 didn't
24 brother's
25 tongue's
26 family's
27 cats'

Page 21 Phonic & Word Knowledge

1 rainbow
2 raindrops
3 wavelengths
4 folklore
5 Someone
6 therefore
7 -ion
8 -it
9 -er
10 -it
11 -ual
12 -itor
13 -eo
14 -ence
15 ultramicroscope
16 ultracold
17 ultrafast
18 ultrafine

Unit 6

Page 23 Reading & Comprehension

1 tries to run in different directions each time
2 cheese
3 running through a maze
4 a mouse
5 humans
6 scientist
7 an exercise wheel
8 drag
9 All options are chosen.
10 Answers may vary, for example, relies on memory, sense of direction, the number of turns and dead ends, time it takes, frustration it creates etc.

Page 24 Grammar & Punctuation

1 Incorporating the comma will be introduced further down; the focus is on direct speech. "I love cheese too. I could eat it all day," said her friend.
2 "Surely not all day," said the mouse.
3 "All day. Just you wait and see," said her friend.
4 The mouse said, "Be careful or you'll explode."

These are the most likely answers for 5–9; however, students may present a strong case for different words.

5 remarked
6 boasted
7 exclaimed
8 snapped
9 warned
10 ?
11 ?
12 !
13 .
14 "I dream of cheese," stated the mouse. The mouse stated, "I dream of cheese."
15 "Me too," agreed her friend. Her friend agreed, "Me too."

TARGETING ENGLISH HOMEWORK YEAR 5 © PASCAL PRESS ISBN 978 1 925726 62 6

Answers

Page 25 Phonic & Word Knowledge

1 snatched repelled
2 imprisoned released
3 careful foolish
4 purposely unintentionally
5 bodily mentally
6 easily laboriously
7 hopefully doubtfully
8 admit deny
9 adverse
10 admit
11 adopt
12 advise
13 advert
14 permit
15 submit
16 omit

Unit 7

Page 27 Reading & Comprehension

1 Citizens can have a say on matters that are important to them.
2 Year Five students
3 Year Five students feel invisible in their school.
4 have a remove common room just for Year Fives to use at lunchtimes
5 find a room or space to use in the school
6 talk to the teacher; talk to the principal; as a class, make flyers and give them to students, parents and staff; stand up at lunchtime and make speeches
7 decide on a problem, make a decision, research, activate and take action, vote
8 to have more useable sports equipment and avoid having flat balls
9 Answers may vary.

Page 28 Grammar & Punctuation

1 b
2 c
3 active
4 passive
5 active
6 passive
7 Action was taken by Year Fives.
8 Flyers were created by Year Fives.
9 Speeches were presented by Year Fives.

Page 29 Phonic & Word Knowledge

1–5 Can be performed in front of an adult if convenient.
6 B
7 A
8 A
9 B
10 A
11 A
12 A
13 Can be performed in front of an adult if convenient.
14–19 bear, buy, night, too, sale, buy

Unit 8

Page 31 Reading & Comprehension

1 joining words
2 as, after, when, because, if
3 main (independent) clause, dependent (subordinate) clause
4 dependent
5 The main clause is 'The chicken crossed the road'. The dependent clause is 'because the comedian paid it to do so'. The conjunction to join them together is 'because'.
6 No
7 The comedian was doing a deal with the chicken shop.
8 eagerly
9 Answers may vary. Encourage imaginative answers.

Page 32 Grammar & Punctuation

1 (The chicken became angry with the magician)
2 (The chicken would only work for the magician)
3 (the chicken agreed to help with magic tricks)
4 After
5 that
6 because
7 When
8 who
9 Magicians use rabbits because they are easy to handle and can fit into a hat.
10 After the duck crossed the road, it saw the comedian and the pet shop owner together.
11 The chicken and the duck came to a decision that the comedian and magician were not to be trusted.
12 When people laugh, I tell more jokes.
13 I feel embarrassed if people don't laugh.
14 If people don't laugh, I feel embarrassed.
15 I should be on TV because I am so good.
16 Because I am so good, I should be on TV.
17 I don't care if the chicken crossed the road.

Page 33 Phonic & Word Knowledge

1 Italian
2 historian
3 electrician
4 technician
5 musician
6 politician
7 urban: to do with cities
8 clinician: to do with health care
9 guardian: to do with protecting
10 pedestrian: to do with people and feet
11 equestrian: to do with horseriding
12 suburban: to do with suburbs
13 Whose
14 Who's
15 who
16 whose
17 Who's
18 whose
19 Who has
20 who is
21 Who has

Term 1 Review

Page 34–35 Reading & Comprehension

1 the swimming pool
2 swimming lessons
3 Wilson Primary School
4 climb the summit, fight a large beast
5 an active imagination
6 attention
7 frustrated
8 Answers could include blowing the whistle twice already; realising the child is not drowning as they are at the shallow end of the pool; waiting for the child to leave the pool; the child is seeking attention.
9 a bus
10 the steps in the pool to climb out of the pool and onto the decking
11 No. He was in the shallow end of the pool.
12 Answers may vary, but they show understanding of 'exasperated'.

Page 35–36 Grammar & Punctuation

1 b
2 a
3 a
4 c
5 child
6 surface
7 wall
8 surface
9 voice
10 arms
11 **before** he glided towards the steps in the pool
12 **before** he walked towards the bus
13 **that** was swallowing his classmates at a very fast rate
14 **If** he killed the large beast
15 **As** he climbed into the bus

Answers

Page 36–37 Phonic & Word Knowledge

1 gliding
2 imagination
3 behaviour
4 struggled
5 safety
6 excitable
7 congratulation
8 suggestion
9 request b
10 conquest g
11 requirement c
12 inquisitive a
13 questionnaire f
14 sequester d
15 their
16 They're
17 there
18 their
19 they're
20 their
21 there
22 their

Term 2

Unit 9

Page 39 Reading & Comprehension

1 A need is something that is required to live, such as food, water, shelter and clothing.
2 A want is defined as something we would like to have but is not necessary to stay alive, such as a bike, iPad or a new pet.
3 persuading readers that chocolate is a need and not a want
4 It was a drink only given to the priests and the nobility, or rich people.
5 Chocolate is a food Year Fives need to sustain them over a day's intense learning.
Chocolate is a special kind of food and has a rich history.
Chocolate has some beneficial health effects.
6 Answers may include: Chocolate is a want not a need as we do not need it to live. / It has unhealthy aspects such as high sugar content and can lead to obesity and other associated illnesses. / Teacher and/or parents will object. / Not all students like chocolate. / Too much sugar can lead to hyperactivity or poor behaviour. / The cost of supplying chocolate every day could be high.
7 Answers may vary; however, items listed must not be a need or an item required to live.
8 Answers may vary. Reasons for the answer need to be more than: I like/do not like chocolate. Encourage thinking at a deeper level. **Reasons against** can relate to health issues around the sugar content of chocolate, developing bad habits, costing involved. **Reasons for** can relate to the need of boosting flagging energy levels, the positive effect high sugar can have in boosting energy, a treat to encourage students to work in the afternoon.
9 Answers may vary. Encourage thinking at a deeper level. Reasons can be similar to question 8.

Page 40 Grammar & Punctuation

1 Rhetorical
2 Not rhetorical
3 Rhetorical
4 Not rhetorical
5 Rhetorical
6 Rhetorical
7 Not rhetorical
8 Rhetorical
9 Helps make the point.
10 Doesn't help make the point.
11 Helps make the point.
12 Helps make the point.
13 Doesn't help make the point.
14 Answers may include: Cats are cleaner. You don't need to pick up after them, less maintenance as you don't need to walk or bathe them, cheaper to feed. They are more self-sufficient and don't rely on you to make them happy, and they keep rats and mice away from the property.
15 Answers may include: Dogs are companions and can be part of your protection for the family. They are fun as you can play with them and walk them, can be trained, less destructive to the environment compared to cats. They keep cats, rats and mice away from the yard, and they are part of the family as they need human contact.
16–19 Answers may vary; however, the sentences must make sense and be high modality.

Page 41 Phonic & Word Knowledge

1 conservative
2 argumentative
3 cooperative
4 creative
5 talkative
6 glasses
7 boxes
8 lunches
9 wishes
10 topazes
11 classes
12 wolves
13 berries
14 puppies
15 toys
16 cities
17 calves
18 feet
19 women
20 sheep
21 mice
22 police
23 furniture
24 geese
25 teeth
26 scissors
27 At the day's end, we will all go home.
28 Six dogs came running to us.
29 These are two families' train tickets.

Unit 10

Page 43 Reading & Comprehension

1 dopamine
2 Makes us put on weight.
Leads to diseases and health issues such as diabetes and developing high blood pressure.
Can cause mood changes and depression.
3 Answers may vary.
4 Sugar has addictive properties.
It can become a hard habit to break.
It can be hard to change the way you think about chocolate.
It can be difficult to break the habit of when or how often you want to eat it.
5 Answers may vary; however, healthy in this text means food with less sugar content. This could lead to a lively class discussion on what they think is a healthy choice of food.
6 Answers may include going for a run or some physical activity to wake you up. Drink water because often we are thirsty, but we reach for a snack instead. If at home, move out of the room where the chocolate is or distract yourself by doing an activity. At school, play an afternoon game either outside or in the classroom to stay alert.
7 It comes from the cacao tree.
8 Remove chocolate milk from the school canteen and lunch orders. Educate students about consuming too much sugar.

Page 44 Grammar & Punctuation

1 is seen
2 interacts
3 could be
4 old habits
5 'sometimes' food
6 Answers may include: Chocolate **can lead** to **decayed teeth**. Sugar from chocolate and bacteria in your mouth form acid that **attacks** your teeth and **can lead** to **decayed teeth**. Sugar is not an **everyday food** as it is **addictive** and causes **health issues**.
7 Answers may include: I **enjoy** chocolate and its **sweet flavour**. There is **little evidence** that chocolate **is addictive**, so I just **enjoy** it. Chocolate **is addictive** and I want to make **better choices** in snacks.
8 Answers may include: Chocolate is an **everyday food** and there is **little evidence** that it **is addictive**. **Enjoy** chocolate as it triggers a **feel-good chemical** in the brain. Chocolate's **sweet flavour** will help you **enjoy** your day.
9 Swap a 'choccy' a day and keep the munchies at bay.
10 Answers may vary; however, encourage students to be creative. Examples: If munchies attack, fruit is my snack. Chocolate is my sometimes food, but fruit puts me in a better mood. A healthy snack is needed, so chocolate is superseded. If I eat a chocolate a day, my fat cells say hooray!

TARGETING ENGLISH HOMEWORK YEAR 5 © PASCAL PRESS ISBN 978 1 925726 62 6

Answers

Page 45 Phonic & Word Knowledge

1 d
2 e
3 a
4 h
5 g
6 b
7 c
8 f
9 favourite
10 requisite
11 infinite
12 granite
13 opposite
14 composite
15 definite
16 accurate, fortunate, desperate, appropriate, considerate
17 fortunate
18 desperate
19 accurate
20 stipulate

Unit 11

Page 47 Reading & Comprehension

1 lack of resources
2 natural, human, capital
3 No
4 There will be a scarcity of resources.
5 if there are enough resources at that point in time to produce what we want
6 No
7 natural
8 capital
9 human
10 natural
11 capital
12 Answers may include:
School needs – computers, desks, books, stationary, teachers, buildings, gym building, playing field, school bus
School wants – canteen, bigger oval, more support officers, more trees, new play equipment
13 Answers may include: computers, TVs, pens and pencils, school buildings and classrooms, school furniture, road that leads into the school, the power and water supplies to the school, the photocopiers, school bus
14 Natural resources could include: tomatoes, onions, mushrooms, olives, anchovies, garlic, peppers, salt, pepper, oregano, basil, water
Human resource could include: waiters, chef, kitchen hand, drivers
Capital resources could include: pots, spoons, knives, pizza pans, ovens, hats, aprons, graters, the restaurant building, tables, chairs, plates, glasses, silverware
15 Answers may include: **Positive points** – satisfaction, happiness, no more hunger or poverty, peace, equality. **Negative points** – greed, boredom, don't value anything, no surprises or excitement, scarcity of resources.

Page 48 Grammar & Punctuation

1 As each year level is catered for, it sounds ideal and fair.
2 If it indeed exists, it is also doubtful that Year Fives would have access to this technology.
3 If there are enough resources to produce them, we can satisfy our needs and wants.
4 If we all want things at the same time, there will be a scarcity of resources.
5 As soon as
6 When
7 after
8 Year Five students will print more PE teachers as soon as the new technology is invented.
9 There will be ovals for all year levels when more land becomes available.
10 After more PE teachers are printed, every Year Five student will be able to learn their chosen sport.

Page 49 Phonic & Word Knowledge

1 13 is very good: technician, technical, technique, technicolour, technically, technological, technology, nanotechnology, nano-technician, microtechnology, micro-technician, biotechnology, biotechnician
2 3
3 4
4 3
5 5
6 3
7 in-cludes
8 e-ver-more
9 state-ment
10 dur-ing
11 re-vealed
12 doubt-ful
13 un-kind-ly
14 les-son
15 sup-plies
16 fan-tas-tic
17 splen-did
18 an-swer
19 sur-vive
20 ac-cess
21 lev-el
22 lim-it
23 lim-it-ed
24 fin-ish
25 prac-tise
26 shel-ter
27 ex-am-ple
28 hu-man
29 e-nough
30 stu-dent
31 clo-thing
32 ca-ter
33 re-source
34 tea-cher

Unit 12

Page 51 Reading & Comprehension

1 Primary Times
2 liquid
3 a gas
4 gases
5 Answers include: in our rivers, lakes, oceans and streams. Also may include: with athletes, in 'junk foods' and other food products, with Year Five students.
6 athletes, Year Five students, those who eat 'junk food' or food products with Liquid X
7 It is linked to the erosion of natural landscapes and loss of people's houses in times of natural disasters. It has caused severe burns to people and is dangerous if you breathe it in.
8 water
9 You drown if you breathe in Liquid X as water fills your lungs.
10 floods
11 Answers may include: at the poles, glaciers, on mountains as snow or on the ground as snow, ice in your fridge, ice and snow, permafrost
12 As steam from different sources, in the atmosphere and in clouds.
13 Answers may vary. The answer can be considered correct if the reason provided supports it.
14 dams

Page 52 Grammar & Punctuation

1 Incorrect: In fact, I didn't buy **any** Liquid X.
2 Incorrect: No-one saw **anything**, so I am innocent!
3 Correct
4 Incorrect: I haven't yet received **an** answer to my request to enter.
5 Correct
6 Incorrect: Last time, I hardly **came** close to being a winner. / Last time, I **had not come** close to being a winner.
7 Incorrect: **Neither** of my contest results over the term were high enough to let me win.
8 Incorrect: If I can always break the record, it **is** scarcely a challenge. / If I can always break the record, it is **not a challenge.**
9 Incorrect: I **will never** break the chocolate-eating record for Year Five unless I use Liquid X to help wash it all down. / I **will not** break the chocolate-eating record for Year Five unless I use Liquid X to help wash it all down.

Page 53 Phonic & Word Knowledge

1 si**g**n
2 g**h**ost
3 s**c**ience
4 dou**b**t
5 of**t**en
6 colum**n**
7 mor**t**gage
8 **k**nife
9 i**s**land
10 Wednesday
11 column
12 doubt
13 often
14 mortgage
15 island
16 en-hance
17 ath-letes
18 lim-it
19 ex-hale
20 un-do
21 prop-er-ties
22 vol-ume
23 ex-plained
24 be-ing
25 whis-tle
26 tri-ckle
27 rid-dle
28 flu-id
29 me-di-a
30 bi-ol-o-gy
31 cas-tle
32 ment – dropped e
33 ure – dropped e
34 ous – dropped u
35 ation – dropped e
36 ition – dropped a
37 disastrous
38 properties
39 lion
40 consonant
41 administration
42 repetition

Answers

Unit 13

Page 55 Reading & Comprehension

1. 16
2. school drop-offs and pick-ups
3. Year Five students driving to school
4. You develop a lifelong skill. The earlier you become good at it, the more experienced and responsible a driver you will end up being.
5. No
6. second row
7. Driving to school gives the opportunity for students to get behind the wheel. If they want to drive, they have to attend school.
8. Answers may vary. Award points if the reason provided explains their answer.
9. Possible new points for 'should be allowed': cars easier to drive and can park themselves / cars have features to automatically stop if going to collide with anything / develops concentration / lessons from YouTube easily available
10. Possible new points for 'should not be allowed': too small to see over the steering wheel or reach pedals / cost of car insurance will rise / greater congestion on roads / may have increase in accidents / students may not go straight to or from school

Page 56 Grammar & Punctuation

1. After they learn to drive (both sentences)
2. when they are under pressure in traffic (both sentences)
3. if students were allowed to drive (both sentences)
4. freedom
5. happier
6. reckless
7. dangerous
8. powerful
9. responsible
10. vigilantly
11. an absorbed
12. a focused
13. navigated
14. relinquished

Page 57 Phonic & Word Knowledge

1. unsteadily
2. stingy
3. dramatic
4. energy
5. nervousness
6. ex-per-i-enced
7. man-age-ment
8. con-cen-tra-tion
9. dis-ad-van-tag-es
10. AL-bum
11. RAB-bit
12. in-SIST
13. un-LESS
14. SAD-ness
15. col-LECT

Unit 14

Page 59 Reading & Comprehension

1. 18 to 36 hours
2. Your lungs will explode.
3. lack of oxygen to the brain
4. take or give heat away
5. convection, conduction, radiation
6. radiation
7. Conduction: You are floating out in space and not touching anything as it is a vacuum.
   Convection: There is no air or water to allow heat to be taken away or transferred from you.
8. Freezing is a change of state from liquid to solid. Heat is taken (transferred) away from particles, so there's less energy and they stick together.
   Melting is a change of state from solid to liquid. Heat is given (transferred) to the particles, so there is more energy, and they move more rapidly, separating to a liquid.
9. They are given more energy and move more quickly.
10. Yes
11. You can take heat away (transfer) causing the molecules to lose energy and stick together to form a solid.
12. There is science involved that is complex for Year 5. What will happen is that any water in the chocolate will evaporate. Due to the lack of pressure, the boiling point of water increases. This heat transfer would decrease the temperature of the chocolate and it would freeze. However, students may surmise from the information given, that the chocolate will lose heat through radiation and eventually freeze.

Page 60 Grammar & Punctuation

1. Simple present
2. Present perfect continuous
3. Present perfect
4. Simple present
5. Present continuous
6. Present perfect
7. Present continuous
8. Present perfect
9. Present perfect
10. Present perfect continuous
11. Simple present
12. Present continuous
13. Your body will eventually freeze if you are without a spacesuit.
14. If you take a big breath and hold it, your lungs will explode.
15. As there is no matter in space, space is a vacuum.
16. A liquid turns into a solid because the liquid particles lose energy and move less.

Page 61 Phonic & Word Knowledge

1–6 Students need to complete the spelling task independently. They need to cover the list words when writing.

7. occurred
8. success
9. necessary
10. disappear
11. embarrass
12. possession

13–20 Students can try to pronounce the words independently. When ready, they pronounce it to an adult. The task is to practise sounding out unfamiliar words so the task needs to be completed.

Unit 15

Page 63 Reading & Comprehension

1. 5
2. $45
3. Freedom For Year Fives
4. A budget is a plan for saving and spending.

Relaxo	FFYF
5 $36.80	$40
6 $8.20	$5
7 this week	two weeks
8 5 weeks	does not say
9 no guarantees	money back guarantee if not satisfied
10 You will relax (in a beanbag listening to music) and have no worries if you use the machine.	The machine will make you cool and a groover.
11 Answers may vary.	Answers may vary.

12. Answers may vary; however, the sentence must explain their choice.
13. You are a loser.
14. The sentence needs to explain their choice.
15. Possible answers why it's a good idea include: It gives you more free time. / You'll have time to spend with the family. / You will get homework correct and get good grades. / You will be happier. / Parents and caregivers will be happier as they do not have to help you with homework or continually remind you to do it. / It means less stress at home.
16. Possible answers why it's not a good idea include: You will not learn or practise the work given so grades could suffer. / It is a form of cheating. / It defeats the purpose of homework. / It's unfair to those without a machine. / The machine may get it all wrong.

TARGETING ENGLISH HOMEWORK YEAR 5 © PASCAL PRESS ISBN 978 1 925726 62 6

Answers

Page 64 Grammar & Punctuation

1 Frisky
2 Fresh
3 Bright
4 Wildcats/Cougars
5 Hornets/Dragonflies
6 Falcons
7 Answers will vary; however, the sentence must explain their choice of name.
8 Answers will vary. Examples of possible alliterations: sensational slurping soda
9 dangerously delightful doughnuts
10 puffy potato pies
11 Answers will vary. Examples from the teacher: Take off your hat inside. / Get ready for your next lesson. / Eyes to the front of the room.
12 Examples from parents/caregivers: Do your homework. / No TV before breakfast. / Eat your dinner.
13 Examples from friends: Give me that ball. / Climb faster. / Get that new game.

Page 65 Phonic & Word Knowledge

1 incidental
2 coincide
3 homicide
4 pesticide
5 decide
6 herbicide
7 accident
8 concise
9 incisive
10 incision
11 decision
12 decision
13 coincide
14 accident
15 cleaner
16 fastest
17 noisier
18 noisiest
19 more
20 most

Unit 16

Page 67 Reading & Comprehension

1 3
2 below deck in a dark and damp cabin
3 summer
4 The sea had turned murderous. Crested waves tumbled to the shore, making it impossible to paddle back.
5 The air became as cold as a grave. / Their breath came out in little clouds of condensation. / Water that had been dripping from the cabin roof changed into icicles.
6 They lunged at the hatch until finally splintering the old wood and gaining freedom.
7 a crab
8 Answers may vary; however, the story infers that the three children joined the pirate crew.
9 The three coins relate to the story Chris had told at the start of the story. Each new crew member was paid a gold coin for joining the pirate ship.
10 If they had attempted to paddle to shore, they would have been killed by the waves; hence the idea that the sea could murder them. This could lead to a discussion of personification which is a descriptive technique.
11 fell
12 Answers may vary; however, the text alludes to sword fights and battles.
13 Various answers can be accepted as long as the supporting sentence explains the reason.

Page 68 Grammar & Punctuation

1 decaying, grey and battered ship
2 glorious summer day
3 quiet and peaceful sea
4 soft blue sky
5 scarred and bloodthirsty pirates
6 explosion of noise
7 sideways journey
8 Answers may vary. Example: loud and angry
9 Answers may vary. Example: red and fierce
10 Answers may vary. Example: wise and ancient
11 The air became as cold as a grave, and as quiet.
12 … icicles that hung like jagged arrows from above.
13 had decided
14 had slammed
15 had been exploring
16 was heard
17 was perched
18 was printed
19 desperately lunged
20 bobbing gently
21 finally splintered
22 slipped silently
23 was printed clearly
24 Examples: beautifully, woefully, sweetly, badly
25 awkwardly, poorly, loudly, softly, tunefully

Page 69 Phonic & Word Knowledge

1 trapped
2 dripped
3 bobbing
4 slipped
5 jagged
6 dripper
7 slipper
8 saddest
9 reddish
10 starry
11 sunny
12 snobbish
13 sadly
14 redness
15 shipment
16 capful
17 curious
18 enormous
19 courteous
20 furious
21 dangerous
22 outrageous
23 adventurous

Term 2 Review

Page 71 Reading & Comprehension

1 Classic class fun at Creek camp
2 You will be too busy having new experiences.
3 Abseiling is the opposite of climbing because you go down a rock face using a rope.
4 resilience and self-confidence
5 Most activities offered involve teamwork, communication and listening.
6 seven
7 Stated answers in the text are a natural water course, a cave system, trees as it is a wooded area, a valley. Some other possible answers: hills because there is a valley, cliffs for abseiling or rock climbing.
8 Answers may include: abseiling or rockclimbing due to a fear of heights and falling / water sports due to an inability to swim / exploring the caves due to fear of the dark or claustrophobia.
9 ability to bounce back after challenges and tough times
10 No. Instructors support you to 'have a go' and try all the activities offered.
11 Answers may include: actual address, contact details, a map of the camp, pictures of the venue, capacity or numbers catered for.
12 Answers may vary; however, the answer must be accompanied by a reasonable explanation. Answers such as: "Sounds good/Sounds interesting" do not provide details. Answers such as: "I have never abseiled before, and I would like to challenge myself" are more appropriate.

Page 72 Grammar & Punctuation

1 will coach and instruct – future
2 will be introduced – future
3 will study – future
4 have abseiled – present
5 are going – present
6 is not climbing – present
7 are planning – present
8 will ask – future
9 have packed – present
10 will be asking – future
11 has been waiting – present
12 am planning – present
13 will not leave – future
14 can breathe – present
15 grounds
16 valley
17 watercourse
18 activities
19 experiences
20 camp
21 bridges
22 Because you are going down a rock face, abseiling is the opposite of climbing.
23 As we are set in beautiful grounds in a small, green, wooded valley, you must come to the 4 Cs.

Answers

Page 73 Phonic & Word Knowledge

1 se-cret
2 rock-et
3 gath-er
4 bas-ket
5 cos-tume
6 Feb-ru-ar-y
7 syl-la-ble
8 cy – clone
9 un – **clear**
10 **thought** – ful
11 **help** – less
12 im-**pos**-si-ble
13 suc – **cess** – ful
14 re – **la** – tion
15 **PRE**-sent
16 **PRE**-sent
17 pre-**SENT**
18 **quea**sy
19 consc**ious**
20 **quie**tly
21 **see**ing
22 victor**ious**
23 sq**uea**l

Term 3

Unit 17

Page 75 Reading & Comprehension

1 5 syllables line 1; 7 syllables line 2; 5 syllables line 3
2 underground in caves
3 changes in body and behaviour to survive an environment
4 2240
5 behavioural, physiological, structural
6 False
7 ... colonists arrived many generations ago, we struggled to survive. Over many years, we have slowly adapted to the environment.
8 Similarities: caves, canyons, clouds, wind, dust storms, dry lake beds, danger and beauty
Differences: 1/3 of Earth's gravity, dark environment, less oxygen, dangerous UV rays, lower temperatures
9 Answers may include: Sam grew taller because his spine stretched due to less gravity. His spine will compact on Earth, and he may not be able to walk. He will be unused to his weight on Earth and may struggle to move. Being taller, he may not 'fit' into Earth-sized vehicles or houses. His eyes will find the Sun blinding. His skin will burn easily as he has lived in caves away from the sun. With his cooler blood, he will find it difficult to stay cool in Earth-like temperatures.
10 physiological
11 Answers may include:
- wanting to know about other planets helps us know about Earth
- having somewhere to go when Earth becomes unliveable
- might help answer whether life exists beyond Earth
- a small step (stepping stone) to interplanetary exploration

Page 76 Grammar & Punctuation

1 Sam's
2 Mars's
3 Martian's
4 men's
5 teachers'
6 drivers'
7 Sam and Jo's
8 Sam's and Jo's
9 All tyres new. Owner's manual included. Can drive on all Mars's moons.

Page 77 Phonic & Word Knowledge

1 face
2 body
3 treatment
4 doctors
5–14 Hard: **c**astle, **c**rystal, biologi**c**al / Soft: can**c**el, dan**c**e, **c**ircumference, re**c**ent, **c**ity, **c**ereal, **c**ircumspect
15–23 Hard: an**g**le, **g**irl, **g**et / Soft: **g**iraffe, an**g**el, brid**g**e, **g**yroscope, biolo**g**ical, **g**ym

Unit 18

Page 79 Reading & Comprehension

1 A food chain describes how different organisms eat each other, starting out with a plant and ending with an animal.
2 Plants and animals at the bottom or lower end of the food chain will have to protect themselves from being eaten.
3 Every living plant and animal must have energy to survive.
4 Animals have adapted camouflage to blend in with their surroundings and so avoid being hunted.
5 a beef burger and a bun or roll
6 A food chain starts with a plant, and plants rely on the soil, water and Sun for energy.
7 The tiger's stripes help it camouflage or blend into the shadows of the jungle so that it can sneak up on its prey.
8 The leafy stick insect has adapted camouflage to blend in with its surroundings and so avoid being hunted as it looks like a stick.
9 by animals high and low on the food chain
10 Sun, plants, insects, small birds, foxes
Sun, plants, insects, frogs, snakes, kookaburras
11 Answers may include: jungle – leopard; ocean – killer whales, great white shark, polar bears; Australia's inland – dingo
12 Answers may include: scavenger animals such as hyenas, Indian wild dogs, birds (e.g. vultures, crows and ravens), insects, worms

Page 80 Grammar & Punctuation

1 "What? You want me to tell you about food chains?" Cat asked.
2 Purple excitedly interrupted, "I know what they are, and I can even list the food chain for my burger."
3 Cat looked up briefly and stated very loudly, "It's the supermarket. Everyone knows that's where our food comes from!"
4 Purple looked up in alarm, "Oh Cat, don't you know that's not where food comes from originally?"
5 "Yeah, yeah, I suppose it involves a farm of some sort," said Cat.
6 Purple smiled, "Well it always starts with a plant at least, that's for sure."
7 anxiety
8 difference
9 depth
10 expectation
11 proof
12 adaptations, survival
13 assessment

Page 81 Phonic & Word Knowledge

1 natural
2 emotional
3 global
4 capital
5 national
6 accidental
7 seasonal
8 global
9 national
10 natural
11 seasonal
12 emotional
13–32 **France:** camouflage, ballet, beef, menu; **Germany:** kindergarten, pretzel, hamburger, poodle; **Italy:** broccoli, cartoon, spaghetti, cauliflower; **Japan:** ninja, tsunami, karate, origami; **India:** shampoo, pyjamas, jungle, veranda

Unit 19

Page 83 Reading & Comprehension

1 sunset
2 - sharp teeth to make small cuts into prey
- heat sensors on nose to locate prey
- strong hind legs and thumbs to help climb onto prey
3 True. They lap it up with their tongue.
4 anticoagulants in saliva so it can drink blood without it clotting

ANSWERS

TARGETING ENGLISH HOMEWORK YEAR 5 © PASCAL PRESS ISBN 978 1 925726 62 6

5 soft bones and very little muscle to survive in a high-pressure habitat
6 A fatty body helps them float as they do not have a swim bladder like other fish. Some students may include: They don't swim but drift with the movement of water.
7 On the surface, its jelly-like body does not hold its shape and so it collapses into a shapeless jelly blob.
8 These bats can fly, jump, run and walk, which aids them in finding their prey, then attaching to it for feeding. They have strong hind legs, and thumbs to help them climb onto prey.
9 a very light, small species of bat
10 Answers may include: the 'yuck' factor of having a bat or having one that drinks blood; difficulty obtaining blood to feed it every day; its association with evil and Dracula; they are nocturnal and so are not much company during the day; finding an appropriate cage
11 If it is brought to the surface, decompression or the lack of pressure can make it expand and cause its skin to relax, distorting its features. On the surface, its jelly-like body does not hold its shape and so it collapses into a shapeless jelly blob. It lives 1200 m below the surface and cannot survive in an aquarium.
12 mosquito, leech, tsetse fly, tick, flea and louse, mite, bed bug, horsefly, lamprey

Page 84 Grammar & Punctuation

1 "I have become an internet sensation," continued Blobfish, "and I am famous."
2 "You see!" shouted Vampire Bat. "You could have your own blog and fan club."
3 Blobfish smiled a jelly-like smile, "You really think so?" he wondered.
4 "You could," Vampire Bat said excitedly, "become a seafood expert or an influencer."
5 "Ah, my own recipe of crustacean pie," Blobfish replied. "I have always wanted to be a chef."
6 "Personally," said Vampire Bat, "I like something a little juicier."
7 Answers may include: commented, observed, replied, laughed.
8 Answers may include: questioned, observed.
9 Answers may include: announced, stated, replied.
10 Answers may include: shouted, screamed, observed.
11 Answers may include: pleaded, ordered.
12 Answers may vary.

Page 85 Phonic & Word Knowledge

Word	Has one syllable	Single short vowel	Which ending –'ge' or 'dge'?
change	yes	no	ge
emerge	no	no	ge
large	yes	no	ge
fudge	yes	yes	dge
page	yes	no	ge
edge	yes	yes	dge
stage	yes	no	ge
budge	yes	yes	dge
judge	yes	yes	dge

9–29 Answers may vary.

Unit 20

Page 87 Reading & Comprehension

1 700
2 14 lines; You write about a big feeling or issue. There is a rhyming scheme: ABAB CDCD EFEF GG. 10 syllables each line.
3 False
4 home and the backyard
5 the bush, outback
6 the beach or coastal environment
7 The line refers to killing the ants that are marching up and down the shins. It explains: My backyard battles I will always win.
8 The place where you live influences you, and you influence it.
9 Answers may vary. The emphasis is that where you live will influence how you live, the environment and climate will dictate the type of clothes, housing and ability to move freely around. It will dictate the work and jobs available. Students need to think how it will impact on the basics listed. Answers will depend on the depth of thinking shown by the students.
10 Answers will vary but students need to give thought as to why their 'place' is important.

Page 88 Grammar & Punctuation

1 a wild slap dance as they die
2 I fell in a bruised heap on the green bin.
3 I lie and stare up at clouds scudding by
4 My backyard battles I will always win
5 It <u>creaks, groans and snarls</u> against any wind.
6 Once climbing, <u>shook me off</u> and <u>ripped my shirt</u>
7 <u>Dressing in a coat</u> of shimmering heat
8 The sun <u>climbs</u> higher in <u>its sky-blue dome</u>
9 Waves never stop the in-and-out movement at the shore like a dog's tongue in and out of its mouth.
10 Waves wet the sand like a dog licking you.
11 When you wade into the water, waves wash over your feet like a dog dribbling on you.
12 When it gets rough, you leave the beach like a dog becoming angry, showing its teeth.

Page 89 Phonic & Word Knowledge

1 unclear
2 tiredness
3 classmate
4 discussion
5 fashion
6 very old
7 a small shop usually selling clothes
8 abrupt or impolite
9 hideous or horrible
10 something you cannot see through
11 attractive
12 method of doing something
13 only one of something or something special
14 boutique
15 unique
16 grotesque
17 colleague

Unit 21

Page 91 Reading & Comprehension

1 increased floods and bushfires
2 False
3 laws that affect the type of buildings to be built in areas prone to fire and flood
4 all of the above
5 desert, tropical, coastal, mountains and built-up environment such as a city
6 First Nations Australian communities deliberately used fire to keep the country more open, clearing out thick, bushy areas to protect the plants used for food. They changed the landscape which reduced fires. Today we have controlled burning but not to the same scale. We too have changed the landscape but not always in a positive way. Today, councils and governments work towards minimising the risks and effects of bushfires.
7 The environment and climate influence how we live. Over 80% of Australia's population lives in coastal regions. There are a number of reasons for this, the main one being that Australia's interior is too dry. The arid conditions make it difficult to live there in comparison to the east coast where the big rivers flow.

8 Answers may vary. Award points if the reason provided explains their answer. Place has significance to us, and it is important to respect and take care of natural and constructed environments. In the end it benefits us as we influence place but place influences us and how we live. To live well with clean air, water and surroundings, we need to take care of and manage where we live.
9 Answers may include: the features of weather such as rain, wind, sunshine, heat, cold, frost, fog, clouds, thunderstorms, lightning, snow.
10 Same as above.

Page 92 Grammar & Punctuation

1 The first picture has two people eating, Grandma with someone else. The second picture is Grandma being eaten.
2 The first picture is Sam showing their love of cooking, their dogs and their family. The second picture is Sam cooking their dog and family.
3 The dog was wearing pink pyjamas.
4 There was a lady carrying a dog, wearing pink pyjamas.
5 Sam is in a lot of trouble.
6 Despite being told time and time again, Sam said the teacher is in a lot of trouble.
7 After they left Sam, Chris and Pat went to the football.
8 After they left, Sam, Chris and Pat went to the football.

Page 93 Phonic & Word Knowledge

1 Hard – c does not come before e, i or y
2 Hard – c does not come before e, i or y
3 Soft – c comes before e
4 Soft – c comes before e
5 Soft – c comes before i
6 science
7 scene
8 descend
9 ✔
10 ✔
11 ✔
12 scent
13 des /cent
14 cres /cent
15 fas /cin / a / ted
16 as /cent
17 ascent
18 descent
19 scent
20 fascinated
21 crescent
22 Answers may include: carton, clever
23 Answers may include: cycling
24 Answers may include: calamari, cruising
25 Answers may include: customary, carefully
26 Answers may include: creatively, correction

Unit 22

Page 95 Reading & Comprehension

1 a capital letter
2 simile, metaphor, personification, alliteration
3 False
4 The first two lines rhyme; lines three and four rhyme; the last line rhymes with the first two. (AABBA)
5 22
6 murky, muddy / smelly sneaker stench
7 Similes use 'like' or 'as' to compare two things while metaphors do not.
8 Both have rules; have 5 lines; have short and long lines in the poem.
9 Limericks rhyme and have a bouncy rhythm and are often humorous while cinquains have a set number of syllables and do not have to rhyme or be humorous.
10 show the destruction caused by bushfires and floods
11 foul
12 Answers will vary, but students need to adhere to the rules for a limerick.

Page 96 Grammar & Punctuation

1 Year One student; a puppy. Resemble a puppy: bounce around the room, are young, look appealing, playful, cuddly
2 Middle school students; a beehive. Resemble a beehive: make constant noise, are dangerous, busy, always active, have no personal space, know what all the others are doing
3 Answers may vary but need to make sense and be original rather than over-used idioms. Possible answers: like melting chocolate, like a proud parent
4 Answers may vary. Possible answers: a cleaned whiteboard, a powered-down smartphone
5 Answers may vary. Possible answers: a circling shark, a lion approaching its prey, a hungry seagull after chips
6–9 Answers may vary but need to be original and the suggestions need to relate to the object named.
10 Answers may vary but again look for originality not worn-out phrases such as I could sleep forever. Possible answers: melt into the mattress; take it everywhere
11 Answers may vary. Possible answers: do all my homework smiling; sing to the teacher
12 Answers may vary. Possible answers: could devour my own hand; could inhale food
13 Answers may vary. Possible answers: would pay to see myself perform; should charge my parents board money

Page 97 Phonic & Word Knowledge

1–7 Dictation is a good tool for using spelling words in context. If possible, students are read the dictation by other students, by the teacher as a class or by adults at home. There are seven words, so it can be marked out of seven, or for more competent spellers, take a point off for every mistake and score out of ten.
8 Answers may include: detergent, diligent, agent, urgent, intelligent
9 Answers may include: blooms, costumes, perfumes, assumes
10 Answers may include: distaste, disgraced, embraced, replaced
11 Answers may include: activate, elevate, liquidate, intimidate
12–24 **Good smells:** aroma, perfumed, fragrant, bouquet, aromatic, scented. **Bad smells:** odorous, rancid, acrid, putrid, reek, malodorous, fetid.

Unit 23

Page 99 Reading & Comprehension

1 my history
2 father's job was replaced by a machine, family lost the little house, family moved to London to seek work
3 False
4 cotton spinning mill
5 They were starving.
6 The family slept and lived in one room by the river, so conditions worsened. The author worked in a factory, not in the fields and they did not go to school. They were starving and were arrested for stealing and consequently sentenced to transportation.
7 Conditions in London were so terrible at that time and the rules so strict, many people were jailed for stealing, even if they were starving.
8 Answers may include: no schooling, working in a factory for 12–14 hours, being hungry and living in poverty.
9 The author was transported on a ship to a new colony to start a new settlement in Australia. They were not allowed to return for seven years.
10 smelt nice
11 Answers may include: The author's life in London was over as they were being sent away from family and what they knew. It was the beginning of a totally new way of living in a totally new place, so a new life.
12 Answers may vary. There are no right or wrong answers; however, the points need to make sense and show a depth of thinking.

TARGETING ENGLISH HOMEWORK YEAR 5 © PASCAL PRESS ISBN 978 1 925726 62 6

Answers

Page 100 Grammar & Punctuation

1 simple past
2 past continuous
3 past continuous
4 past continuous
5–7 Sentences will vary but need to make sense and have sentence punctuation.
8 past perfect
9 past perfect continuous
10 past perfect
11 past perfect continuous
12–17 One day, I was playing below deck when I heard a shout from above, "Land Ho!" I had been hoping that we would land soon. I had arrived – my new future was waiting for me.

Page 101 Phonic & Word Knowledge

Down
1 export
2 deport
3 transitory
5 import
7 transcend
10 transparent
11 porter
13 portly
15 portfolio
16 transit
17 support
18 transact

Across
4 transformation
6 important
8 translation
9 transmit
12 reporter
13 portable
14 report
16 transition

Unit 24

Page 103 Reading & Comprehension

1 Royal Magistrate Barnaby Ferguson
2 13th April 1787
3 the colony in America
4 There was a revolution.
5 France, Holland and Spain
6 The poor are to blame for their situation and have to help themselves.
7 The reasons were: to produce a solution to rid the country of the many convicts that were in prisons; to settle the land to the south so that countries such as France, Holland and Spain did not claim this southern land for themselves; to use the convicts as settlers of the new land.
8 Hulks were old sailing ships. They were floating prisons as the prisons on land were full.
9 Britain wanted it for themselves.
10 Answers may include: The author is rich. They have a title and are educated. They have a negative view of the poor, so they are not one of them. They want to 'get rid' of the convicts, so they do not identify with them. They are powerful and can make important decisions, and they have special note paper and a seal.
11 The ships were sailing ships, so they had no motors, only sails. This meant they were at the mercy of the wind and weather. It is an incredibly long distance they had to travel. Some students may know that they had to take the long route as the Suez Canal had not been built.
12 Answers may include: One of the other countries i.e. France, Holland or Spain could have settled Australia so English would not be the main language spoken today. Australia would not have been a prison colony. The impact to First Nations Australians and the environment may have been different.

Page 104 Grammar & Punctuation

1 Because the hulks are overcrowded, I hereby recommend sending a fleet of ships to Botany Bay immediately.
2 When he was travelling with Captain James Cook, Joseph Banks visited Botany Bay.
3 Since we all know that the poor are to blame for their situation, I have no sympathy for them.
4 After they arrived at Botany Bay, convicts will become settlers.
5 I would never see my family again if I were transported to Australia.
6–7 Answers will vary.

Page 105 Phonic & Word Knowledge

1 cells
2 knew, would
3 affect (change)
4 effect (consequence)
5 one
6 poor, their
7 past
8 passed, their
9 past
10 affected
11 Drawings will differ but need to show understanding of the conjunctions.

Term 3 Review

Page 107 Reading & Comprehension

1 stealing, especially men's silk handkerchiefs
2 5
3 buckets
4 tossed around the cabins with the violence of the waves
5 shackled or handcuffed
6–8 Answers may include:
- It was cramped in the cabins below deck.
- It could be suffocatingly hot.
- They used buckets as toilets and had to scrub these out every day – lack of hygiene.
- They only ate twice a day.
- They were only allowed on deck in good weather.
- There was no natural light and no candles or lamps.
- The conditions were dark, smelly and hot.
- They slept on thin mattresses on racks, not beds.
- In a storm, sea water and sewage would wash into the cabin.
- People could be injured by the movement of the ship, especially in storms.
- Diseases spread quickly.
- There was a lack of clothing.
- It was boring with nothing to do.

9 There were three ways to get new clothing. Captain Arthur Phillip gave out some clothing they packed to take to Botany Bay. They made clothes out of the bags they stored rice in, and they used any material bought at the stops along the way.
10 Two Royal Navy ships with marines guarded the fleet from pirates and enemy ships. The three supply ships carried food and provisions for the trip and for the new settlement.
11 They sailed into tropical weather crossing the equator. There was no ventilation and there was overcrowding. Some students may suggest that the southern hemisphere will have summer while Britain has winter.
12 Diseases spread easily. This would be one way to help stop the spread. Fresh air would help kill bacteria. It would also give the convicts something to do.
13 Answers may include: Telling each other life stories, or stories of what might await them in Australia. If they could write and have access to paper, they may keep a journal. Played games, mended their clothes, prayed, sung, cleaned their cabins, possibly slept as they may be ill, hungry and/or hot.

Answers

Page 108 Grammar & Punctuation

1 "Captain Phillip, Sir," the Lieutenant said, "the convicts are asking for more clothing." OR "Captain Phillip, Sir," the Lieutenant said. "The convicts are asking for more clothing."
2 Captain Phillip thought deeply, "Can we get to the clothing saved for Botany Bay?"
3 "Do you mean on the supply ships?" questioned the Lieutenant. "It will be difficult, but I can try."
4 "Thank you, Lieutenant," answered the Captain, "please make your way to one of the supply ships." OR "Thank you, Lieutenant," answered the Captain. "Please make your way to one of the supply ships."
5 "Yes Sir!" the Lieutenant answered loudly, and with that he headed off to search for the supplies.
6-12 Answers will vary. Students need to use the correct tenses and follow the pattern demonstrated.
13 disappearance
14 announcement
15 resolution
16 confession, forgiveness
17 proof

Page 109 Phonic & Word Knowledge

1 rancid	14 guess
2 icicle	15 green
3 cinder	16 ginger
4 pencil	17 gym
5 lucid	18 genius
6 excite	19 giraffe
7 civil	20 gentle
8 circuit	21 giant
9 cinnamon	22 client
10 circus	23 gobble
11 career	24 react
12 again	25 recite
13 ghost	26 escape

27–53

								g						n	o	m	a	n	n	i	c				
	l							i																	
	i				d			n						g											g
	c				i			g			g			y									s		o
	n				c			e	c	i	r	c	u	m	f	e	r	e	n	c	e		s		b
	e				u			r	i		e							f					e		b
	p				l				n		e			e				f			r		u		l
s									d		n			x				a			e		g		e
u		d							e					c				r			c				
c		i	c	i	c	l	e		r					i				i			i				
r		c												t				g	e	n	t	l	e		
i		n					c	i	v	i	l			e							e				
c		a	g	a	i	n			g		e					t						u	p	m	e
		r							i		p					c			t	i	u	c	r	i	c
									a		a					a									
	s	u	i	n	e	g			n		c		c	a	r	e	e	r							
									t		s					r									
g	h	o	s	t							e									t	n	e	i	l	c

54 colleague
55 meringue
56 brusque
57 boutique
58 technique

Unit 25

Page 111 Reading & Comprehension

1 History is written from different points of view and may not be written at the point in time that it describes.
2 There are many different groups, each with its own language, laws, beliefs and customs.
3 The banks can become unstable and collapse into the water. Some students may add that run-off from surrounding land flowing into the stream damages the eco-systems in around the water.
4 They drink the water, their hard hooves trample the soil, and their waste goes into the water. Some students may add destroying waterways and land.
5 smallpox
6 It spread rapidly killing 50–80% of the First Nations' population.
7 First Nations people and the environment
8 Answers may include: eleven First Fleet ships carrying 1,500 people did not land at Sydney Cove; no sudden change to traditional way of life for First Nations people, no sudden change to the land; the thick, woody, natural bushland and plants growing along the streams did not disappear; no run-off from surrounding land flowing into the stream damaging the eco-systems in and around the water; no introduced animals like cows, horses, sheep and pigs so no destruction of waterways and land; no-one died of smallpox; no Frontier Wars.
9
- The author is not part of the story.
- The third person is being talked about and not to.
- The people (or land) in the story are not doing the talking but being talked about.

10 The colony grew and spread inland from the coast, so competition for land and resources led to conflict.
11 Answers may very but need to show evidence of thinking about the question. Possible answers: no built-up areas such as cities and roads; no traffic or pollution; natural landscape; First Nations people only seen; no introduced animals.

Page 112 Grammar & Punctuation

1 the convict's shoe
2 the stream's banks
3 the captain's crew
4 the captains' crews
5 the trees' roots
6 the cows' hooves
7 the men's shirts
8 the women's shoes
9 the children's toys

ANSWERS

TARGETING ENGLISH HOMEWORK YEAR 5 © PASCAL PRESS ISBN 978 1 925726 62 6

Answers

10 It was John and Pat's idea to escape the colony. No more convict life for us!
11 The escape tunnel and trapdoor's design was foolproof.
12 If only I had Grandma and Grandpa's shovel to help dig the tunnel.
13 Mum and Dad's song came into my head. I used to sing it when I was scared.
14 My mum's and dad's faces appeared in my memory as I crawled through the tunnel.
15 John's and Pat's hands helped me out of the trapdoor.
16 Then I saw the two soldiers. The corporal's and sergeant's guns were aimed towards me.
17–20 The **men's** guns were held close to my belly. The **sergeant's** and **corporal's** fingers were ready on the triggers. My **belly's** rumbling showed my nervousness. I started to sing.

Page 113 Phonic & Word Knowledge

1 direction
2 option
3 action
4 edition
5 vacation
6 location
7 education
8 creation
9 promotion
10 devotion
11 emotion
12 lotion
13 nations
14 population
15 colonisation
16 competition
17 relations
18 destruction

19–29 relief, achieve, belief, believe, chief, shield, priest, yield; tried, lie, died

Unit 26

Page 115 Reading & Comprehension

1 Local clay was mixed with things like straw to build houses.
2 2 years
3 2 months
4 Work was part of their punishment for their crimes.
5 False
6 False
7 Girls were servants or worked at spinning, weaving and laundry at a female factory.
8 New clothing was adult sized. They lived in tents and had to build their own huts. Convicts were weak with hunger because there wasn't enough food. Many diseases such as tuberculosis, influenza, measles and smallpox were common in the colony. Kids were treated no differently to adults. Work was part of the punishment for their crimes – girls as servants or in the female factory and boys on farms or working for the Governor in the colony. The surroundings were new and unfamiliar.
9 15 + 7 = 22 years old
10 She had a new life as she married, bought land and had a small farm and eight surviving children.
11 Rations = amount of food given to each person
12 Everyone was weak with hunger. Some students may make the connection that this led to many diseases such as tuberculosis, influenza, measles and smallpox being common in the colony.
13 It implies that more children were born but did not survive to become adults.
14 Answers will vary but there needs to be evidence of thinking about the question. Answers may include: children would be expected to behave like adults so no play but work instead.

Page 116 Grammar & Punctuation

A generalisation around the use of commas for prepositional phrases – whenever you have a prepositional phrase at the beginning of the sentence, the comma becomes obligatory if the phrase is longer than three words. If less, it is up to the writer's discretion. It is up to teachers whether to impart this piece of information to students.

1 At exactly six o'clock, I must go home.
2 In five minutes, my friends will be picking me up.
3 Before I leave home, I will check I have a phone or watch.
4 On many occasions, I have forgotten about the time.
5 Between the four of us, someone will remind me.
6 I left the house **in** a hurry.
7 **After** a quick bike ride, I arrived at my friend's house.
8 **With** my backpack on my back, I looked like a turtle.
9 My friends were waiting for me **by** the front gate.
10 **When I finally looked at the time,** I was horrified to find it past six o'clock.
11 I tried to think of a really good excuse **before I got home.**
12 **After talking to my friends,** I felt much better.
13 I thought it was a great idea as I believe in aliens and UFOs.
14 After my family finished laughing, I was told off for being late.

Page 117 Phonic & Word Knowledge

1 in-**SULT**
2 **IN**-sult
3 **REF**-use
4 re-**FUSE**
5 con-**SOLE**
6 **CON**-sole

7–26

-er meaning 'more'	-er meaning 'one who'	-ctor	-ator	-lar
sharper	baker	doctor	elevator	polar
wider	dancer	inspector	operator	regular
tidier	butcher	instructor	indicator	similar
hotter	runner	collector	senator	muscular

27–31 Answers will vary but need to follow the 'schwa' sound.

Unit 27

Page 119 Reading & Comprehension

1 groups of people who supported the development of Australia in things such as sport, arts, science, education and the economy or budget
2 Japanese pearl divers in Broome, Western Australia
3 oysters
4 1861, Broome, Western Australia
5 part of the shell of oysters was used to make buttons.
6 They helped the colony's economy.
7 The divers dived to great depths and the death rate was high. Some students may infer the danger of sharks, the bends, bad weather etc.
8 They came from Malaysia and Japan. They were skilled at diving in their own countries. Students may infer that there was more money to be made than in their home countries.
9 Plastic replaced mother of pearl shell in the making of buttons. Therefore, there was less demand for oyster shells.
10 The Japanese were Australia's enemy in WW2, so they were interned or put into camps. This meant a disruption to the pearling industry.
11 Answers may include: Divers stay down longer as air is pumped to the suit. The boots are heavy, so divers can walk on the seabed. Divers can go to greater depths. There is greater protection from sharks. Or any other reasonable idea students offer.
12 Answers may include: more freedom of movement, less uncomfortable, less need of other people to help you dive, or any other reasonable idea students offer.

Page 120 Grammar & Punctuation

1 Sam and James's plan was to go diving for pearls.
2 Sam's and James's suits were ready to put on.
3 James's friend Paris was going with them.
4 Paris's suit was already on the boat.
5 The three friends' fear of sharks unsettled them.
6 However, the boat's captain was certain no sharks were in the area.
7–9 Answers will vary; however, it is important that students are able to add adjectives and propositional phrases to build sentences.

Answers

Page 121 Phonic & Word Knowledge

1 devoid
2 turmoil
3 hoist
4 void
5 poise
6 moist
7 foyer
8 destroy
9 coy
10 ploy
11 employ
12 alloy
13 annoy

14-25 This can be done in class with classmates or at home with adults. The score can be out of 12 with marks taken for misspelt words from the lists, or points can be taken for any words misspelt.

26 cheesy
27 yummy
28 noisy
29 runny
30 windy
31 baggy

Unit 28

Page 123 Reading & Comprehension

1 Smaller animals made homes in its hollows.
2 They knew the tree provided food, shelter and life for many.
3 The banks of the river had crumbled as the land had been cleared, and the rich soil washed into the river, leaving bare patches on the ground.
4 Answers can include: Different animals grazed under its branches. First Australians were gone. Different people managed the land. The banks of the river had crumbled as the land had been cleared. Rich soil washed into the river, leaving bare patches on the ground. The water changed colour and strangled the fish and animals that lived within it. Fences crisscrossed the land. Wetlands around it were dry, and the land was dry.
5 There was a difference to the land. This may be expanded by students to include: Grazing animals had gone. More seedlings grew along the banks of the river. The water had returned. Life had returned to the river.
6 a seed of the tree
7 introduced animals such as cows, sheep, pigs etc.
8 separation
9 fences and stitches in a blanket
10 Answers may include: They both form a pattern. The fences look like the pattern the stitches form on a blanket. They both follow straight lines that cross. The pattern is repeated and uniform.
11 bushfire
12 The tree was burnt and died in the fire. Some students may add that its seed sprouted new life again after the fire.
13 three
14 First Nations Australians
15 Answers may vary but need to show thinking around the text. Answers may include: The start of the text is the seed coming to life which connects to the end of the text with new life of a seed sprouting. It's a cycle of life and death.

Page 124 Grammar & Punctuation

1 There are three main types of bushfires.
2 Bushfires can be caused either naturally or by the actions of people.
3 At any time of the year, some parts of Australia are prone to bushfires.
4 Panting heavily,
5 Chased by a stray dog,
6 Delayed by the heavy traffic,
7 Disappointed at being late,
8 Holding onto the wrappers,
9–11 Sentences need to be grammatically correct with commas and full stops. They also need correct spelling.

Page 125 Phonic & Word Knowledge

1–16

Long 'o' sound	Short 'o' sound	Short 'u' sound	Schwa 'uh' sound
low	gone	oven	melody
know	coffee	won	parrot
over	wrong	tongue	wagon
most	song	some	dinosaur

19–42

Long 'O' (as in no)	Long 'U' (as in true)	Short 'u' – (as in fun)
although	through	couple
open	youth	cousin
toe	routine	enough
dough	you	tough

Short 'oo' (as in good)	'aw' / 'ow' sound	Schwa – (uh sound)
should	amount	famous
wouldn't	count	obvious
couldn't	mouse	cautious
shouldn't	thousand	various

Unit 29

Page 127 Reading & Comprehension

1 False
2 It lacks minerals, organic or natural matter and living organisms.
3 continuously
4 Soil forms from the gradual breakdown of rocks through weathering.
5 Weathering is the breaking down of rocks.
There are three types of weathering: biological, mechanical (or physical) and chemical.
6
- We rely on soil to grow our food.
- Soil can take hundreds to thousands of years to develop but can be destroyed or blown away in minutes.
- It cannot be easily replaced.

7 Water is involved in chemical and mechanical weathering. Some students may provide further details: rain and salt water can eat away at rocks. Water can freeze and widen cracks within rocks.
8 Mechanical weathering needs water to freeze. The answer will include local knowledge and awareness of climate zones in Australia. This may include the locality of students and include mountainous areas, or Australian Highlands. It may include known cold areas of the state where the students are located.
9 Answers may include: rats, mice, spiders, worms, insects, bacteria.
10 Chemical weathering is when salt water eats away at rocks. This obviously occurs in coastal locations.
11 Soil can be blown away by wind or washed away by rains and floods. Soil can be washed away if vegetation is removed. Information from previous units explains how grazing animals can contribute to this process. Soils can be impacted by chemicals and pollution.
12 Students may not have knowledge of hydroponic farming, but answers need to show a depth of thinking around the question. Students may be creative in their replies, but there must be an answer provided.

Page 128 Grammar & Punctuation

1–11

Students have three sections where they provide proof that they are able to write sentences using the sentence starters provided. Sentences need to have correct spelling and punctuation.

TARGETING ENGLISH HOMEWORK YEAR 5 © PASCAL PRESS ISBN 978 1 925726 62 6

Answers

Page 129 Phonic & Word Knowledge

1	microscope	8	hypothermia	15	nine
2	microorganism	9	hypersensitive	16	two
3	microbiologist	10	one	17	ten
4	microwave	11	six	18	seven
5	hypodermic	12	many	19	eight
6	hyperactive	13	three	20	five
7	macroscopic	14	four		

Unit 30

Page 131 Reading & Comprehension

1 False
2 He found Grandma to be a mean woman.
3 False
4 Ms Hood beat Mr Wolf within an inch of his life. Answers refer to the physical harm caused by Ms Hood.
5 Grandma did not smile readily, and this reflects back on Mr Wolf's comment that she was a mean person. Answers can reflect that Grandma is not a particularly happy or nice person.
6 Answers may include: He was being neighbourly. Grandma is elderly and needs the bed to be warm. Any other creative answers that show thinking around the question.
7 Answers may include: Wolves are predators, so Ms Hood naturally thought he had eaten Grandma. It is impolite and not normal behaviour to hop into a bed and keep it warm. Any other creative answers that show thinking around the question.
8–13 Answers will vary. There are no right or wrong responses; however, answers need to show a depth of thinking before points can be awarded.

Page 132 Grammar & Punctuation

1	time	4	reason	7	concession
2	time	5	condition	8	condition
3	time	6	concession		

9–11 Sentences will vary; however, they need to: have correct spelling; make sense; have commas where needed; be complex sentences; provide the point of view asked. Example of answers: **Since** (reason) Ms Hood beat me up, I am suing her.
I wouldn't trust a wolf **unless (**condition) they were behind bars.
The wolf was going to eat me **despite** (concession) his story of keeping the bed warm.

Page 133 Phonic & Word Knowledge

1	chief	6	either	11	weight	16	CAFFEINE
2	believe	7	neither	12	CEILING	17	ACHIEVE
3	achieve	8	neighbour	13	WEIGHT		
4	receive	9	eight	14	RECEIPT		
5	deceive	10	height	15	HEIGHT		

Unit 31

Page 135 Reading & Comprehension

1 In many popular and well-known fairytales of today, the girls are supposed to be beautiful, good and helpless.
2 Folktales are oral stories that have no one author.
3 Folktales were spread by travellers passing through the country and told to audiences that included adults and children.
4 Original folktales were stories about how people dealt with the difficult conditions in which they lived and often had a lesson or moral to learn.
5 Original folktales showed girls and boys as tough and resourceful in dealing with the issues of those times.
6 100–200 years ago
7 **Folktales – Differences:** told not written; have more than one author; both girls and boys are strong, and resourceful; audience included adults and children; many folktales now forgotten
Similarities: behaviour of children changes depending on how girls and boys are expected to behave at that point in time
Today's fairytales – Differences: collected and written down; one author given credit; written at a time when girls were supposed to be meek and mild; stories printed over and over again.
8–11 Answers will vary. There are no right or wrong responses; however, answers need to show a depth of thinking before points can be awarded.

Page 136 Grammar & Punctuation

1 could be – low
2 may eat – low
3 must wear – high
4 ought to have – high
5 might believe – low
6 high – Answers will vary with the sentences the students write. They must have correct spelling and punctuation. For example: In stories, heroes must sing to show how brave they are.
7 high – For example: Students ought to complete their homework before watching TV.
8 high – For example: Students have to go to bed at a regular time each week night.
9 medium – For example: I will watch my favourite TV show tonight as it is Friday.
10 Red Riding Hood was waiting for the wolf.
11 She did not move when the wolf appeared.
12 She threw a bag over his head.
13 The wolf had eaten his last grandma.
14 Now Red is wearing a lovely fur coat.
15 She has told everyone her story.
16 She will be known as 'Big Red' in future.

Page 137 Phonic & Word Knowledge

1	analyse	6	travelling	11	organise
2	centre	7	travellers	12	travelled
3	colour	8	apologise	13	colour
4	litre	9	analyse		
5	travelled	10	centre		

Unit 32

Page 139 Reading & Comprehension

1 kinder world
2 Kindness is more than just being nice; it is being friendly, generous and considerate. It is something you do on purpose without being asked.
3 Do something small on a daily basis. Students may add or use the answer: Kind Notes are a quick and easy way to practise kindness.
4 Write a note to a friend, family member, or anyone in the school or wider community who you want to show your appreciation to thank or encourage.
5 Kindness lowers blood pressure; lowers stress levels; kind people are healthier and live longer; contributes to a positive view of the world; you can make a positive difference to a person and their wellbeing and help them create a more positive self-identity. When we receive kindness, we feel better about ourselves and others.
6 You can pass them out; put them in an easy spot to find as in a lunchbox, in a drawer, on a desk or in a book or bag.
7 It is not difficult as it can be as simple as leaving a note – a Kind Note. It is doing something small on a daily basis.
8 The answer can include: self-esteem, feeling good about themselves, knowing someone cares, not being so negative about themselves.
9 Answers will vary.
10 Positives: can give helpful advice; can answer questions from kid's perspective; can inspire; can make kids feel like they belong to a group; can reinforce positive behaviour and attitudes.
11 Negatives: could push specific products; too much attention to image and looks; push unrealistic body images; too much attention to food and nutrition.

Answers

12 money; fame; power; ability to inspire; the fun aspect of being in media and gaining many followers

13 Kid influencers can be an easy target for negative feedback on line; lack of privacy; danger when putting too much information about yourself online

Page 140 Grammar & Punctuation

1 are
2 was
3 were
4 kicks
5 kick
6 play
7 plays
8 are
9 is

10–22 Kind Notes ~~is~~ are popping up everywhere. They ~~appears~~ appear on the sides of buses and buildings.

No-one ~~know~~ knows where they will pop up next. I ~~are~~ am standing on the street right now.

All around me, people ~~is~~ are pointing at all the latest notes. I personally can't wait to receive one. After all, I ~~is~~ am a very well-known and popular reporter. My mother ~~were~~ was very happy to get one from me.

My boss and I ~~waits~~ wait for Kind Notes from our work team, but have none so far. The team ~~are~~ is not cooperating. I will ~~writes~~ write a note to myself saying how wonderful I am.

After all, I ~~are~~ am a very kind person. I ~~deserves~~ deserve many notes.

I think I will go and ~~writes~~ write one now.

Page 141 Phonic & Word Knowledge

1 The 'schwa' sound is in bold.
pand**a** **a**ppreciate **a**ddicted comm**a**
2 doll**ar** doct**or** blogg**er** fig**ure**
3 cent**re** og**re**
4 col**our** neighb**our** thor**ough** flav**our**
5 cauti**ous** fam**ous** jeal**ous** nerv**ous**
6 rhythm
7 sly
8 spry
9 crypt
10 pygmy
11 myth
12 cyst

Term 4 Review

Page 143 Reading & Comprehension

1 at the back of the shed at their grandparents' farm
2 stealing silk handkerchiefs
3 8
4 under a large tree in one of the paddocks
5 The person is the author of the memoirs. They wanted to see who this very strong and resilient person was.
6 The author felt peace as their dreams led to the farm.
7 Answers may include: Due to weathering and age, the writing had been worn off.; the quality of the stone and writing to begin with; limited technology of the time to create lasting work; They may have been hand done by the family, so poor quality.
8 The author of the memoirs.
9 Answers may include: being part of history; having such a long Australian family tree; being pleased at how far they have come when compared to their convict relative; pride at what their relative did after gaining their freedom or in surviving the hardships; fascination with what it would have been like for their ancestors at the time
10 Answers may include: ashamed of being related to convicts; people thinking you are as bad as your convict relative; being called a convict; being looked down upon
11 Answers may vary as long as there is evidence of thinking behind the answer. It could be they met their relative in the dream and they look alike. / They are them reborn into a different time.

Page 144 Grammar & Punctuation

1–9

~~Dream's~~ Dreams are what a person sees and hears in their mind when they are sleeping. All people and many ~~animal's~~ animals dream when they are asleep. A ~~persons~~ person's dreams can seem very real. ~~Sams~~ Sam's and ~~Pats~~ Pat's dreams are often about what happened during the day. I have one dog and two ~~cat's~~ cats and they dream. My ~~dogs~~ dog's dreams are of chasing cats. My ~~cats~~ cats' dreams are of catching birds. ~~James~~ James's dreams are of eating chocolate.

10–14

While I was sleeping, I had the strangest dream. Under the table in the kitchen, I dreamt there was a large box of chocolates. When I walked into the kitchen the next morning, I looked under the table to check for chocolates. My brother came in as I crawled under the table.

With great acting skills, I made out I was sleepwalking. As I was leaving the kitchen, I noticed chocolate smudges all around my brother's mouth.

15 Example: I love melted, vanilla ice-cream with caramel sauce on top.
16 Example: In my dreams, I saw a decorated cake box under the table.
17 Example: I dream of eating a family-sized, fruit and nut bar of chocolate by myself.
18 Example: I made a large, three-tier chocolate cake for my teacher.

Page 145 Phonic & Word Knowledge

1 RECEIVE
2 NEIGHBOUR
3 BELIEVE
4 WEIGHT
5 travelling
6 litre
7 favourite
8 analyse
9 apologise
10 centre
11 organise
12 travelled
13 **mem**-ber
14 **na**-ture
15 **cen**-tre
16 **sim**-ple
17 an-**nounce**
18 a-**mong**
19 re-**ceive**
20 doctor
21 butter
22 dollar
23 mirror
24 neighbour
25 jaguar
26 centre
27 sailor

TARGETING ENGLISH HOMEWORK YEAR 5 © PASCAL PRESS ISBN 978 1 925726 62 6